THE UTOPIAN
COMMUNIST

Weitling

THE UTOPIAN COMMUNIST

A BIOGRAPHY OF
WILHELM WEITLING
NINETEENTH-CENTURY
REFORMER

BY

CARL WITTKE

LOUISIANA STATE UNIVERSITY PRESS

BATON ROUGE

MADE IN THE UNITED STATES OF AMERICA

PREFACE

There were many varieties of radicals, reformers, and intellectuals among the German Forty-eighters who migrated to the United States in the middle of the last century. Some, like Carl Schurz, the best known of this group of German liberals, became completely adjusted to the American scene and rose to positions of eminence and trust in their adopted fatherland. Others, like Karl Heinzen, represented the militant, uncompromising radicals who remained the same irrepressible crusaders in America which they had been in Europe, were never completely at home in the United States, but nevertheless played an important role in many of the reforms of their time.

Wilhelm Weitling, also a Forty-eighter, belonged to the extreme left wing of the German immigration. A simple artisan, entirely self-educated, he had won fame in the radical movement of Europe long before he migrated to the United States. His books and his propaganda for a communist Utopia were known in western Europe before Karl Marx leaped into prominence with his Communist Manifesto and became the outstanding spokesman of proletarian revolution.

Weitling belonged to the working class. He was not a university man and he knew the sufferings of the poor from personal experience. He served a jail sentence in Switzerland because of his convictions. He was one of the most important figures in the history of pre-Marxian socialism. His philosophy of history and his brand of communism were very different from Marx's doctrines of economic determinism and the inevitability of the proletarian revolution, for Weitling, though an agnostic and a severe critic of all institutionalized religion, insisted on morality, ethics, and religion as a basis for social reform. The repudiation of this aspect of his "system" by the Marxians is not without significance for the present-day theory and practice of communism.

In the United States, Weitling tried once more to give practical application to the theories he had formulated and proclaimed in Europe. He deserves to be remembered, in spite of his failures and the unsound character of some of his proposals, because of the important place which he occupied in the early history of the American labor movement and its agitation for social security, social insurance, and co-operatives. His disastrous experiences with the colony at Communia, Iowa, constitute an interesting chapter in the history of the immigrant Utopias which were so numerous in the America of a hundred years ago. Finally defeated and disillusioned, he turned his eager, restless mind from social reform to the problems of astronomy, linguistics, and inventions.

Weitling's career might be summarily dismissed as simply another failure in a long line of failures by completely impractical and somewhat unbalanced dreamers. Yet this poor, self-educated, philosophical tailor had such a passion for social justice, such a fervent hope that public policy might be judged by the standards of ethics, such a craving and reverence for science and progress, and such a desire to make life more humane, that I believe he deserves to be rescued from among the forgotten men who, in every age, try to renew men's hopes for a better age than the one of which they are a part. If faith in the ultimate perfectibility of mankind should turn out to be only an illusion, it is at least a comforting illusion, and it has been a major force in the history of the human enterprise, for in all ages, men have had to walk part of their way by faith.

In acknowledging the help received in the preparation of this biography, I must express my thanks first of all to Terijon Weitling of Staten Island, New York, who so graciously made all the remaining papers of his father available to me and answered all my questions about those personal details which are so important in any biographical study.

I also have received aid and suggestions from my friends and colleagues, Dr. Ernst Feise of The Johns Hopkins University, Dr. Ferdinand Schevill of Chicago, and Dr. Traugott Böhme of Berlin. G. W. Hunt of Guttenberg, Iowa, and H. L. Meyer of Elkader, Iowa, have furnished data which helped me to unravel some of the confusion which surrounds the closing days of the Communia colony. I also am indebted to the library staffs of Western Reserve Historical Society, Western Reserve University, the Ohio Archaeological and Historical Society, the Wisconsin Historical Society, the Oberlin College Library and the library of Belleville, Illinois.

Some of the material contained in this volume has appeared earlier in the form of two articles, "Wilhelm Weitling's Literary Efforts," in *Monatshefte* (Madison, Wisconsin), XL (February, 1948), No. 2, pp. 63–68; and "Marx and Weitling," in *Essays in Political Theory, Presented to George H. Sabine* (Ithaca, 1948), 179–93.

CARL WITTKE

Cleveland, Ohio
March 1, 1949

CONTENTS

ILLUSTRATIONS

Chapter I

A CHILD OF WAR

THE old city of Magdeburg, on the banks of the Elbe, has been involved in many of the significant events that have shaped the history of the German people through the centuries. Developing from a little fishing village, it was officially founded in 940 A.D. by Otto the Great. It became a vital center of the Protestant Reformation and had to be almost entirely rebuilt after the ravages of Tilly's armies during the Thirty Years' War. The houses of its citizens stretched out along the one long street, known as the Breite Strasse, which was intersected by many cross streets. In the heart of the city was the famous Alte Markt.

Sandstone ornaments, arched doorways, and stately gables decorated many of the homes of the city burghers, and in the market place stood the statue of Otto the Great, where each year, on the morning of the first of May, the fisherfolk placed bouquets of flowers and glasses of liqueur, as though they were votive offerings to the city's patron saint. On the tenth of May, a panorama of Tilly's destruction of Magdeburg was regularly presented in the city's theater. On one of the several islands made of sand dunes in the Elbe, stood the citadel which dominated the town. In the center chapel of the cathedral, which was completed in 1363 and was the city's only real survival of the Middle Ages, was the sarcophagus of the English princess who had married Otto I. No less a person than Goethe visited the old cathedral in 1805 to study its graves and plastic monuments, walked around the walls of the ancient city, and viewed the bronze monuments of Magdeburg's three archbishops of the fifteenth century.

In 1806 the burghers of the city were once again living in crisis, for in that year the city capitulated, rather shamefully, to the armies of Napoleon which were thundering at the city gates. The town was raped and pillaged by the soldiers of Marshall Ney until sufficient tribute could be paid to save its citizens from further ravages. Thereupon Magdeburg became a part of Napoleon's puppet kingdom of Westphalia. For several years, the colorful uniforms of the French troops were visible everywhere; occasionally duels were fought in the quiet gardens of the burghers; and officers and men were billeted on the inhabitants throughout the city. French was heard so frequently on the streets of Magdeburg that many Germans learned enough of the language to carry on simple business transactions, while their children shouted "*vive l'Empereur*" on every appropriate occasion.

In 1812 and 1813, the fortunes of war no longer smiled on the great Napoleon, and the occupying forces in Magdeburg had to prepare for a countersiege by the Allied armies which were driving the Grand Army steadily back toward its own frontiers after the disastrous invasion of Russia. During the siege, the French destroyed some of the outlying sections of Magdeburg, used the churches as magazines for munitions, straw, and hay, and quartered cattle in the Katharinenkirche. After the Battle of the Nations at Leipzig, the Allies moved westward in pursuit of Napoleon, leaving Magdeburg and its French garrison under the siege of Prussian and Russian troops. Muskets rattled and cannon roared in and around the city as the beleaguered French made numerous sorties from the town, while the inhabitants lived in constant fear lest the French destroy the city or the Allies ravage it as Tilly's Catholic army had done in the Thirty Years' War.

In May, 1814, one month after Napoleon's abdication, the French in Magdeburg finally capitulated. As the French marched out to the strains of martial music through one of the gates of the city, the Don Cossacks rode in through another. Their brown uniforms, and black, silver-studded belts and pistols must have provided a picturesque setting for the triumphal entry of the Allies into Magdeburg, as these horsemen of the steppes rode wildly through the streets, singing their tribal songs to the accompaniment of the tambourine. They were followed by Russian infantry and by the less impressive soldiers of the King of Prussia. The Magdeburgers gathered in their old market place, heard an address delivered in behalf of His Prussian Majesty, and then solemnly raised their hands in a new oath of allegiance to their German king. Caricatures of Napoleon promptly appeared in the windows, bonfires were lighted on the surrounding hills, and the bells of the churches rang out in joyous celebration of the liberation of the city.

Fraternization between soldiers and citizens in an occupied area is a common experience whenever the conquerors are quartered on the conquered for any considerable period. Among the soldiers who were billeted in the homes of the Magdeburgers during the years of the French occupation was an attractive youth of twenty-two or three, a noncommissioned officer or perhaps even a captain in the French artillery, by the name of Guillaume Terijon. How or when he met Christine Weitling, a simple maidservant and a native of Gera in Thuringia, we do not know, nor how quickly their relations developed into a love affair. But on October 5, 1808, at 3:45 in the afternoon, the Thuringian girl gave birth, out of wedlock, to a son whose father was the gay young blade of the French artillery. The child was baptized, four days later, Wilhelm Christian Weitling. The baptismal record in St. John's Church of Magdeburg gives the full name of the mother as Christine Erdmuth Friedericke Weidlingen, and lists as witnesses to the ceremony Joachim Friedrich Kämpf and a journeyman stonemason named Johann Weidling, who probably was the girl's father and who was sometimes referred to in later years as Wilhelm Weitling's stepfather. Weitling, however, always gave that title to Christian Bern, a tailor who eventually married his mother.

Very little is known of Weitling's parents. The young French officer seems to have been a gay and dashing soldier of fortune, with a love for amateur theatricals. He often was seen striding through the streets of Magdeburg, arm in arm with a friend and singing at the top of his voice. Presently he became known as "jolly William." But in spite of his lightheartedness, he seems to have had a sense of obligation to the maid he had gotten with child and to their illegitimate son; for he gave the girl several gifts, tried to arrange a monthly allowance for her when he went off to the Russian campaign, and considered the possibility of having his son educated in France. Guillaume Terijon was part of the Grand Army which invaded Russia, and, like thousands of others who followed their emperor on that fateful march on Moscow in 1812, never was heard of again.

Very little is known of the family background of Christine Weitling. Her father was a stonemason. Her mother, nee Hahn, was the daughter of a clergyman who lived near Gera. Orphaned at an early age, this minister's daughter had been reared in the castle of the petty Princess of Reuss-Gratz-Löbenstein, and had become one of that lady's maidservants. When the girl married, she and her husband moved to Magdeburg, and here they had two sons and the daughter Christine, who became Weitling's mother.

Weitling's youth was one of such poverty and deprivation that he seldom referred to these early years in later life. He was reared in extreme poverty and never knew the protection and security which home and family can give. During the siege of Magdeburg, when he was a small child, his grandmother took the little boy out of the city and supported herself and her grandson by selling matches, lampwicks, tobacco, and chicory. As the boy grew old enough to have playmates, we may imagine him running through the streets of the old city, perhaps bathing in the Elbe in the summer and playing on the ice that covered the moat around the citadel in winter, but Weitling himself left few of the simple annals of the poor that would describe his boyhood days in Magdeburg. His mother worked out as a cook and housemaid, and the boy frequently was left in a pension in the care of others. Yet he always spoke affectionately and reverently of his mother, and even of the father whom he scarcely knew, and many years after, in the account of his life which he gave before a trial court in Zurich, he testified that he had never been abused or even punished by his parents.

The lad's formal schooling was limited to the elementary school of Magdeburg (*die mittlere Bürgerschule*). He read books from the local library, mostly novels and adventure tales which inspired the games of robber and "Robin Hood" he played with his young schoolmates. The boy seems always to have been quite sensitive, and it is reported that he was especially fond of dogs and could not bear to see them mistreated. Once he broke into a fury of tears when his schoolmaster accused him of petty dishonesty.

The young Weitling learned to write a beautiful Gothic script. As he grew older, he read much history and apparently absorbed an amazing amount and variety of information about the significant characters of the past, from antiquity, through the Thirty Years' War, to Napoleon. But most of what he learned was the result of unorganized, desultory reading. He never had the advantage of expert guidance in mastering any period of human history, nor the mental discipline that comes from exploring thoroughly some one field of knowledge. His religious training was rather systematic until he reached the age of twelve. It was strictly in the Catholic tradition and apparently made a deep and lasting impression which affected his views and influenced his conduct throughout his life. He read the Bible many times and knew it so thoroughly that few theologians could have matched his ability to quote from the Scriptures. For some reason, he was especially fond of reading the Books of the Maccabees.

Weitling never saw the inside of a German Gymnasium, much less a university, but he managed to absorb much information in many fields, as his writings clearly show. Perhaps because of his origin and environment, it was fairly easy for him to become bilingual in French and German, but he also learned to use English quite well and in due time mastered at least the rudiments of Latin and Italian. As a gifted, restless, eager, and romantic youth, Weitling was handicapped at every step in his development by grinding poverty. He knew most of the human miseries from firsthand experience, and they not only made him introspective, but probably were the most significant single cause for the role of rebel against the established order which he played throughout his later years.

At a tender age Weitling was apprenticed, after the fashion of the old guild system, to a tailor known as Master Schmidt, with whom he lived and from whom he learned his trade thoroughly. He became equally proficient in ladies' and men's tailoring. With legs crossed and back bent, the boy sat, often from early dawn to dark, on the tailor's bench. His food consisted of the black bread and sauerkraut that were important features of the diet of this part of Germany. Several times during his apprenticeship the lad suffered from severe illnesses, probably caused partly by malnutrition.

At eighteen, Weitling had achieved the goal of journeyman tailor and was ready to begin wandering from town to town as a *Handwerksbursche*, seeking employment and new experiences until he too would be ready to establish his shop as a master tailor. That goal Weitling never achieved. His restless spirit became absorbed in other things, and tailoring was merely the means of keeping body and soul together while his inquiring mind was engrossed in ambitious plans for the reconstruction of the social order.

Weitling left his native city almost immediately after he had completed his training. His career as a journeyman took him through a large part of western Europe. As he hiked from town to town, carrying his pack on his back like a snail his house, we may picture him pulling fruit from the trees along the public highways, sleeping in the shade of the roadside, begging for food at friendly homes, stopping at the various hostels maintained in order to provide cheap food and lodging for journeymen, talking and arguing with his fellow workers, or joining them in a song, a glass of wine, or a game of cards in the inns where they happened to meet, for this was the way of life of the old-fashioned European journeyman. Weitling always was regarded by his fellows as a thorough and conscientious craftsman and a quiet, harmless, and peaceful citizen. He early manifested a strange craving for "system" in everything, and he had a weakness for reading and book-learning; but he was no ascetic, and enjoyed to the full all the pleasures of genial intercourse with his comrades. There was something tender and sensitive and almost feminine about his character, and his hands were as soft as a woman's, yet he was very much of a man, and a good and jovial companion. On the pages of Weitling's *Wanderbuch*, which he received in Hamburg where he worked as a ladies' tailor for six months, the comments of each new employer were recorded, as he reported on the ability and the character traits of his employee, before Weitling moved on to work for another master in a new neighborhood. There is no evidence from these early years spent as a journeyman tailor that Weitling had any special interest in the political scene or in the still more complicated problems of economics.[1]

We can get some notion of what Weitling looked like when he was twenty years old from the report of the Hamburg police, recorded in his *Wanderbuch*. At that time, he was a young man about six feet tall, with medium-blond hair, a broad forehead, blue eyes, oval face, and a neatly trimmed blond beard. The record indicated that he still was using the middle name, Christian, but this he dropped soon thereafter. Fifteen years later, in the court record made in Zurich after his arrest and imprisonment, he was described as a "tailor and typesetter," thirty-five years of age, rather frail and with a haggard face. His hair and eyebrows had turned dark brown and his beard was black.[2]

For seven years, Weitling wandered through the little German

[1] Details are given in Weitling's "Note Book," a manuscript now in the possession of his son, Terijon Weitling; see also such general accounts as Franz Mehring's biographical introduction to Jubilee Edition of Weitling's *Garantieen der Harmonie und Freiheit* (Berlin, 1908); Wolfgang Joho, *Wilhelm Weitling: Der Ideengehalt seiner Schriften, entwickelt aus den geschichtlichen Zusammenhängen* (Heidelberg, 1932); F. Caille, *Wilhelm Weitling: Theoricien du Communisme, 1808–1870* (Paris, 1905).

[2] See Ernst Barnikol, *Weitling der Gefangene, und seine Gerechtigkeit* (Kiel, 1929), 195, 196.

states that constituted the disunited Germany of his day. In July, 1830, he arrived in Leipzig, where he remained until the fall of 1832 in the employ of Höpfner and Walsbach, ladies' tailors. Here he was well paid. He genuinely respected his employers and he had ample time for leisure and recreation. Indeed, he found conditions so satisfactory in this leisurely city of the easygoing Saxons that he later referred to this period of his activity as a tailor as the most satisfactory in his career. The work proved so pleasant that he considered it a joyous recreation. The comrade with whom he lived in Leipzig was August Schilling, who also became interested in socialism and communism, and the correspondence between these old friends continued until shortly before Weitling's death in New York.[3]

It was apparently in Leipzig that Weitling first tried his hand at writing. He sent satirical verses and several more serious articles on political and social questions to the *Leipziger Zeitung*, only to have them rejected, and he probably concluded at that early date that something was wrong with this business of freedom of the press. He may have played some minor part during the revolutionary upheaval of 1830 in Saxony, though in later years he expressed his disgust with its lack of a definite program, as he had seen this crisis develop in European affairs. According to some accounts, one of his satirical poems was used on a transparent sign and carried in a parade by Leipzig radicals.

By the fall of 1832, Weitling was in Dresden, and two years later he made his first appearance in Vienna. Here his first employer was Franz Bayerl, and he worked as an expert in ladies' tailoring at the unusually high wages of sixty to seventy gulden a week. After four months with Bayerl, he worked for two months for Christian Schwarz, and then for eight months for Johann Schmidt. At the end of April, 1835, he left the Austrian capital, presumably to return to Germany. Actually, he seems to have

[3] See Wilhelm Weitling to August Schilling, New York, July 22, 1869, in "Wilhelm Weitling und sein System der Harmonie und Freiheit," *Die Zukunft* (Berlin), I (1878), 585, 583–94, 606–15.

spent some time in Paris and then returned to Vienna for a second visit in January, 1836. This time he did not work for a master tailor, but made various trimmings, artificial flowers, and ribbons which he sold to ladies' tailors. He had a room at the home of a shoemaker's widow, and shared it with three rather stupid companions. During his sojourn in Vienna, he may have talked frequently about the conditions of the laboring class in Austria with Josef Schastag, a worker who was later tried for treason, but there is no evidence to show that Weitling himself was involved in any way in political activity. The severe penalties prescribed for communist agitators no doubt persuaded the young tailor that it would be wise to act circumspectly.

The Habsburg capital made a deep and lasting and, on the whole, very pleasing impression on the young journeyman. Years after, in his *Die Republik der Arbeiter*, the labor paper which he published in New York in the 1850's, he liked to recall that in all the months he spent in Vienna, he had never seen any but genial, friendly Viennese. In Vienna, visitors were not suspected of being potential thieves, and waiters did not stand by with open palms, demanding immediate payment for what their guests had ordered. The attitude of the Viennese toward each other and toward visitors from other areas was marked by "mutual trust."

Weitling reported that he had never seen a disastrous fire in Vienna; he remembered the marvelous baked goods which filled the tables in the taverns; he recalled the strange practice of faithful Catholics who brought food and drink to the churches on Easter to be blessed by the priests; and he had watched an elaborate parade in Vienna on the occasion when an old hat, supposedly worn by Francis I in his battles against Napoleon, was carried with pomp and ceremony to its final resting place in the city's museum.

Perhaps Vienna continued to evoke such pleasant memories primarily because it was there that Weitling had his first youthful adventure with a beautiful and romantic lady. His activity as a maker of artificial flowers and decorations for women's apparel brought him in contact with a young woman who also was the object of the attentions of a Habsburg prince. Various versions of this incident have been preserved in the literature about Weitling, but unfortunately none of them can be verified. Whatever the facts, we know that the tailor who had been so happy in old Vienna suddenly made a hurried exit from the city. It may be that the prince had discovered the relations between the deceitful lady of his attentions and the young journeyman, and that the latter sought safety in flight. Ever after, he denounced the caste system of the feudal court. But another less romantic tale relates that Weitling had returned to Vienna after his first brief sojourn in Paris to marry a tailoress of his acquaintance, only to find his prospective bride locked in jail on a charge of theft.[4]

Whatever the cause of the speedy departure from Austria, the event proved decisive for Weitling's whole career. Tramping through wind and rain, arrested at least once for begging on the public highways, the unhappy and disillusioned tailor made his way to Paris. In the French capital, the most important formative period of his life was about to begin.

[4] Ludwig Brügel, *Geschichte der österreichischen Sozialdemokratie* (Vienna, 1922), I, 22, 37; Sebastian Seiler, *Der Schriftsteller Wilhelm Weitling und der Kommunisten-lärm in Zürich* (Bern, 1843), 4–6.

CHAPTER II

PARIS, THE CRUCIBLE OF REVOLUTION

IN THE fall of 1835, Weitling had seen Paris for the first time. But he had remained only until the following April, when he returned to Germany and Vienna. Now, in the fall of 1837, he was back in France and, save for short trips to Geneva and the area around Strassburg, he remained until May, 1841, when he departed for Switzerland to spread into the cantons of the Alpine republic the communism which he had learned and developed in the French metropolis.

Weitling reached Paris at a time when a new world order was struggling to be born, not only in France but all over western Europe and to a lesser degree in the Americas as well. The challenge to the old order came primarily from the rise of the proletarian class and from the introduction of the factory system, which was destined to break down large segments of the middle class and start the movement of workers from the land into the cities.

In Germany during the 1830's, skilled craftsmen still were highly respected and relatively independent and self-sustaining members of the body politic. Yet the specter of "big business" and the factory system hung ominously over the skilled-artisan class. The population of Berlin was growing by 7,000 a year, because of an influx from the provinces; half the population of Cologne in the 1840's could be described as proletarians; and 50,000 of the inhabitants of Breslau belonged to the same class. Hunger and suffering in the overcrowded areas, a shortage of houses for the workers, low wages and long hours, and the spread of disease and prostitution were disturbing concomitants of expansion in industrial production and transportation. There is abundant statistical evidence that the economic revolution was on the march and that the ancient bonds which had held medieval society together were beginning to break. Moreover, labor was becoming more highly specialized and therefore more monotonous, and skilled workers already were being forced to yield their highly respected standing in the guilds to become mere cogs of a factory system. These developments still were in their earliest stages, and Germany lagged far behind England and France in this respect; but the march of "big industry" had started, along the Rhine, in Saxony, and in Silesia, and theories of laissez-faire economics and modern capitalism were beginning to replace the medieval concepts which had held the feudal and guild systems together in the German states.[1]

Aachen was the scene of workers' riots against the introduction of laborsaving machines in the early 1830's. Solingen and Cologne experienced serious labor troubles. The number of journeymen increased, but the number of masters remained stationary. Tailors complained about "ready-made" suits and consequent unemployment; workers in Bonn protested against the use of steam engines; and labor demonstrations in Breslau indicated the decline of the crafts and the rise of the class struggle.[2] The year 1844 brought the tragic insurrection of Silesian weavers. Goaded by the decline in demand for their products, and by low wages and exploitation under a "truck system" which forced them to accept inadequate food in lieu of wages, the starving and desperate workers attacked the factories and mills of their employers, only to have their dem-

[1] Erich Kunze, *Beiträge zur deutschen Literatur des Vormärz, 1840–50* (Breslau, 1938), 10–11.

[2] Eduard Bernstein, *Die Schneiderbewegung in Deutschland, Ihre Organisation und Kämpfe* (Berlin, 1913), I, 69–71; Max Quarck, *Die erste deutsche Arbeiterbewegung 1848–1849* (Leipzig, 1924), 2, 10, 21; see also Hugo C. M. Wendel, *The Evolution of Industrial Freedom in Prussia, 1845–1849* (New York, 1921), *passim.*

onstrations ruthlessly suppressed by the military. Long before Gerhart Hauptmann thought of making their tragedy the subject of one of his most stirring dramas, the sufferings of the Silesian weavers figured in the novels of the 1840's and in the poems of Heinrich Heine and Ferdinand Freiligrath. The year 1844 also produced an epidemic of strikes in the calico factories of Berlin, among the railway workers of Westphalia, and in Hamburg and Saxony. In 1843, a "society for the education of the children of the helpless proletariat" was organized in Breslau, and workers' organizations of several kinds were formed in leading cities of the German states, in vain efforts to solve the labor problem.

The problem of the emerging proletariat also had its sympathetic analysts among the German intellectuals. As early as 1800, Johann Gottlieb Fichte in his *Geschlossene Handelsstaat* had described the anarchy of *laissez faire*, which deprived the worker of the full product of his labor and gave an undue share of the profits to the owning class. In 1835, Ludwig Gall, sometimes called the first German socialist, issued a pamphlet in Trier which foreshadowed the class struggle and maintained that labor was the sole source of wealth. Georg Büchner, a dramatist of merit who died in exile, founded the "Society for Human Rights" in 1834 in Giessen, and Stephan Born published his first plea for the working classes when he was only twenty.

The mid-thirties also saw the beginnings of a spiritual revolution in Germany, against the church and the clerical class, and a plea for the return to the ethics of primitive Christianity. David Friedrich Strauss's *Life of Jesus* (1835) was one of the few books which Weitling owned, and it may be assumed that he was thoroughly familiar with its contents. Strauss's attempt to combine Hegelian philosophy with Christianity and to reconcile science and religion started a veritable spiritual renaissance in Germany and Switzerland. Karl Gutzkow referred to the book as "the yeast of Germany's intellectual ferment." [3] Ludwig Feuerbach's *The Nature of Christianity* represented a further challenge to ortho-

[3] Karl Gutzkow, *Rückblicke auf mein Leben* (Berlin, 1875), 140, 290–91.

doxy. Its author, at a time when the altar supported not only the throne but practically every other institution of the established order, sought to emancipate human beings from being "the valets of His Heavenly Majesty." The poet, Georg Herwegh, announced that he was ready for revolution and wrote

> Reiszt die Kreuze aus der Erden,
> Alle sollen Schwerter werden,
> Gott im Himmel wird's vergeben.

Alfred Meisner and Karl Beck were active along similar lines in Austria, the latter publishing a poem entitled "Why Are We Poor?" Also, radical ideas, which somehow managed to escape the vigilance of the censors, appeared in some of the papers of Rhenish Prussia, Hesse, Westphalia, and Frankfurt. These were the ingredients from which a social revolution could be fashioned.

Needless to add, such challenges to the existing order were labeled communistic and were carefully watched by the spies and stool pigeons with which every ruler of consequence surrounded himself in this age of Metternich's inquisition—censorship of the press and close scrutiny of the universities and of every other activity that might jeopardize the "public peace and order" of the existing "legitimate" governments.[4]

Because of the greater unity of the nation, the large amount of personal liberty which prevailed, and the more advanced state of invention and the industrial revolution, the reaction of the British to their "social question" assumed its own characteristic forms, but the underlying forces were much the same as on the Continent. The Luddite riots against the introduction of labor-saving machines had rudely shaken the tranquillity of the upper classes in Great Britain in the second decade of the nineteenth century. The years 1802, 1819, 1825, 1829, and 1831 marked the enactment of factory laws which inaugurated the effort to protect children from the worst forms of exploitation. The Parliamentary

[4] See also Georg Adler, *Die Geschichte der ersten sozialpolitischen Arbeiterbewegung in Deutschland* (Breslau, 1885), *passim.*

Reform Bill of 1832 had given additional political recognition to the British middle class, but the proletariat remained politically powerless though their number was growing rapidly. Chartism and the rising trade-union movement were further evidences of social ferment in the British Isles. A few enlightened employers like Robert Owen of New Lanark were aware of what was happening. Owen became an out-and-out exponent of a communist society, though his "Community of Equality," established at New Harmony, Indiana, hardly inspired confidence in the new ideology. Repercussions of the new social conflict may also be found in the novels of George Sand and in Kingsley's *Village Sermons* and Disraeli's *Sybil*. By 1831, moreover, there were 300 co-operative stores in England.

Italy had its *Carbonari* and the "Young Italy" movement, whose activities spread from the peninsula to the rest of Europe. Despite its major emphasis on political unification, "Young Italy" had many broader objectives suggestive of a general social revolution. Germans, Poles, Swiss, and Italians co-operated in the "Young Europe" movement. In the United States, the period was marked by the rise of a labor movement, the introduction of Fourierism by Albert Brisbane, the friendly interest of Horace Greeley's *Tribune* in the new radicalism, the antirent movement in New York, and the radical ideas introduced by hundreds of immigrants from Europe. Some conservative Americans thought the new radicalism could be killed by ridicule; others, like James Gordon Bennett of the New York *Herald*, expected "storms and tempests and tornadoes and earthquakes." [5]

Thus the whole Western world was more or less in ferment. Paris, however, was the intellectual center from which the new movements derived much of their sustenance, and Weitling was there during one of its most exciting periods. Moreover, the traditions of the French Revolution lingered on and provided the germs from which many of the economic and philosophical principles of modern socialism developed.

[5] See Henry Christman, *Tin Horns and Calico* (New York, 1945), 67.

François Noel Babeuf, an ardent revolutionist of 1789, had plotted among the soldiers and the workers of Paris to overthrow the government and establish community of property and had paid for his radicalism with his life. To men of his type the French Revolution was a mere precursor of the much greater upheaval which would end in the establishment of communism by force and by decree. Babeuf's ideas greatly influenced the French secret societies of the nineteenth century and were carried by his disciple, Filippe Michele Buonarroti, into Belgium and Switzerland.[6] Weitling so deeply admired Babeuf that many years later he named one of his sons after the great conspirator.

Saint-Simon, a count of noble lineage who had served under De Grasse with the French fleet before Yorktown, was another of the pioneers of planned economy. He spent the fortune which he had made in speculation on a program for a new social order based on a "physico-politics" and a "science of production" which would relieve the miseries of the poor. Saint-Simonism, whose champions spread their new gospel with the zeal of fanatics, was popular in the Paris of Weitling's day and became one of the sources of his own social theories. Louis Auguste Blanqui, prominent in the French Revolution of 1830 and a leader of the uprisings in 1839, was another who advocated revolution by secret societies and made plans to establish a dictatorship of the proletariat by force of arms.[7]

François Marie Charles Fourier, though not strictly speaking a communist and actually a defender of interest, profit, and inheritance, probably was the most influential of all the theorists of Weitling's time. He advocated a social order based on pure reason, which would end the waste of competition and establish a cooperative society composed of "phalanxes." Victor Considérant,

[6] See Filippe Michele Buonarroti, *Conspiration pour l'égalité dite de Babeuf* (Brussels, 1828), *passim;* E. B. Bax, *The Last Episode of the French Revolution, Being a History of Gracchus Babeuf and the Conspiracy of the Equals* (London, 1911), *passim.*

[7] See A. Thomas, "Blanqui im Jahre 1834," *Dokumente des Sozialismus* (Stuttgart, 1903), II, 205–14.

his best-known disciple, carried Fourierism to Texas; and Brook Farm in Massachusetts and the North American Phalanx at Red Bank, New Jersey, are American examples of the world-wide influence of Fourier's principles of association. Weitling apparently was introduced to Fourier's system through the work of Considérant.

To complete the list, mention must be made of two additional French reformers, Étienne Cabet and Lamennais. Not only was Weitling familiar with Cabet's program, but he knew the French Utopian personally, visited his colony in Illinois, and carried on a considerable correspondence with him while both were residents of the United States. Trained as a lawyer, Cabet in 1831 had established a paper, known as the *Populaire*. When his radicalism forced him into exile, he went to England, where he fell under the spell of Robert Owen and embraced communism. His *Voyage en Icarie*, one of the most charming of all Utopian fantasies, appeared in Paris in 1840. Weitling read it and referred to it frequently and later had an opportunity to watch the attempt of the Icarians to put their blueprint for happiness into practice on the American frontier.

Lamennais' *Paroles d'un Croyant* was another little book that made a deep impression on the embryo German communist during these Paris years. Its author was Hugues Félicité Robert de Lamennais, a frail little man with piercing, restless eyes, a priest who had turned socialist. A mild-mannered man, devout and strict in his daily observance of the Catholic ritual, he nevertheless broke with both the Papacy and the French monarchy. A champion of political liberalism, he put the red cap of liberty (to use Heine's phrase) on top of the cross. He issued the first edition of his book in 1834 and was promptly excommunicated. But Ludwig Börne translated his work into German, and eventually it went into a hundred editions. When Lamennais died in 1854, the New York *Tribune* pointed out that he had thrown "the halo of religion around the cause of political freedom and equality," for his real purpose had been to equate the cause of communism with primitive Christianity. His influence spread even to the United States. Orestes A. Brownson read the *Paroles d'un Croyant,* as well as the same author's *Le Livre du Peuple,* a book which Weitling translated under the title *Das Buch des Volkes* and which was published in Boston as *The People's Own Book.* Through the efforts of Brownson and others, it exercised some influence on the development of Jacksonian democracy in the United States.[8]

Thus, during the years which Weitling spent in Paris, revolutionary propaganda filled the air; and the ideas of Fourier, Saint-Simon, Considérant, Cabet, the communist priest, and many others already had affected the thinking of many people, and had seeped down from the intellectual groups to the workers, to whom Weitling belonged. He owed nothing to the universities, and he had the honest craftsman's contempt for mere theory. His contacts were largely with fellow workers, whose problems and reactions he understood because they were his own. He entered upon the path of social revolution through the door of the worker's movement by way of the secret societies to which he and many of his class belonged, for, after the suppression of the workers' uprisings in Paris and Lyons in 1834, there was no other place for radicals to go except underground.

Paris, in the first half of the nineteenth century, was the mecca for refugees from many lands, and particularly from Germany. Arnold Ruge, the intellectual, once wrote: "Leaving Paris is like leaving life, a complete retreat from the world"; and he paid tribute to French humanism in these words: "Paris is no less important for Germany than it is for the departments. Our victories and our defeats we experience in Paris. Even our philosophy, for the moment one step ahead of theirs, will never be a significant force until it makes itself felt in Paris and in the French spirit." [9]

But Paris also was the home of thousands of German craftsmen

[8] See also Victor Giraud, "Le Cas de Lamennais," *Revue des Deux Mondes,* L (March, 1919), 112–19.

[9] See Arnold Ruge, *Zwei Jahre in Paris: Studien und Erinnerungen* (Leipzig, 1846), I, 59, 431.

such as Weitling. The "independent dignity" of the working classes of Paris impressed Albert Brisbane on his first visit to France. At that time, France, like Russia for the present-day Marxist, was the spiritual and intellectual center of communism. Ruge and Karl Gutzkow estimated the number of Germans in Paris in 1842 at 80,000 or 85,000. Others put the figure even higher. Gutzkow wrote to his wife that German was spoken on every street.[10] The German colony in Paris consisted of refugees, workers, and intellectuals. At the outset there was little co-operation between German intellectuals and artisans. The latter had migrated to the French capital largely for economic reasons and in the early years were regarded as a threat to native craftsmen, whose resentment was so great that occasionally bloody battles were fought in the streets of the working-class districts. Gradually, however, these national antagonisms were forgotten in the coffeehouse society of the workers.

The French Revolution of 1830 was precipitated largely by secret societies of republicans and workers of the industrial and urban centers, but its results were far from satisfying to the groups primarily responsible. The regime of Louis Philippe turned out to be a government dominated by wealthy bourgeois, factory owners, and bankers, from which the old aristocracy and the workers were excluded. Widespread disgust with Louis Philippe made it possible in the France of the 1830's and 1840's to get a hearing for more revolutionary proposals. In 1834 a law was enacted which forbade secret associations and this was followed by restrictions on the press and trial by jury. The result was that the opposition was driven under cover, and Paris became the nodal point for a succession of secret revolutionary societies which fanned out over France. Bearing such names as *Société des Familles* and *Société des Saisons*, they led to the kind of rioting and street fighting described in George Sand's *Horace* and Victor Hugo's *Les Misérables*. The German secret societies paralleled the French

[10] Karl Gutzkow, *Pariser Briefe* (Leipzig, 1842), 276.

organizations and, though frequently founded and directed by exiled students and intellectuals, gave more and more emphasis to the demands of the workers.

The first secret society of German refugees established in Paris probably was the *Association patriotique allemande*. It was founded to promote the freedom and unity of the German states. In 1834 the Society of Exiles, or Banished (*Bund der Geächteten*), was organized. It is known that Weitling was a member of this organization during his first sojourn in Paris. Its leaders were Theodore Schuster, an instructor in law at the University of Göttingen and a friend of Buonarroti, and Jakob Venedey of Heidelberg, a Freemason who had escaped to France from a German prison and later served as a member of the Frankfurt Parliament of 1848.[11] The membership, estimated to number between 200 and 500, consisted largely of German journeymen organized in tents or huts (*Zelten*). The society demanded the liberation of Germany under a republic and operated in a fashion typical of secret organizations, demanding blind obedience to its official hierarchy.

In 1836, several hundred seceders from the Society of Exiles, under the leadership of the more radical Schuster, joined a new League of the Just (*Bund der Gerechten*).[12] Lamennais' *Paroles d'un Croyant* had considerable influence on the new League and was distributed in translation among the German workers of Paris. It was this League of the Just that attracted Weitling's interest and enlisted his active support on his return to the French metropolis in the fall of 1837, and it was as one of its members that he achieved fame in the early history of communist activities in France, Germany, Belgium, Switzerland, and England. He was not its founder [13] but he quickly became one of its most influential leaders. All the while, he was working at his trade as a tailor, sometimes

[11] See review of Wilhelm Koppen, *Jakob Venedey* (Frankfurt, 1924), in *Marx-Engels Archiv*, II (1927), 587–91.

[12] Max Beer, *Allgemeine Geschichte des Sozialismus* (Berlin, 1924), 434.

[13] Leopold Schwarzschild, *The Red Prussian, The Life and Legend of Karl Marx* (New York, 1947), 92, takes a contrary view.

as long as twelve to fourteen hours a day, and half days on Sunday. His earnings amounted to about 700 francs a year. Yet despite this exacting schedule he had time and energy, not only to read and master the growing literature of social revolt and to debate its content in meetings with his fellow workers, but also to organize a co-operative eating center for tailors where two plain but substantial meals were served each day for eleven sous; to translate Lamennais' *Le Livre du Peuple* into German; to produce a dozen songs for a worker's songbook (*Volksklänge*); and to prepare for publication his first treatise on social reform.[14]

The membership of the League of the Just was classified according to the varying degrees of responsibility which individuals exercised and grouped under such fantastic names as "*Brennpunkt*" (burning point), the very top of the hierarchy, "*Kreislager*" (provincial camp), "*Lager*" (bivouac or camp), and "*Zelt*" (tent). The society in its procedure used such symbolic terminology as "*Bürgertugend*" (virtue of the citizen), "*Beständigkeit*" (steadfastness), "*Tatkraft*" (energy), and "*Volksherrschaft*" (sovereignty of the people). It had its mystic signs and passwords, and the initiated recited certain sentences for purposes of identification. Each member, moreover, had a secret military name derived from history or from some personal characteristic, Weitling being known to the initiated as "Freymann." [15] Finally, the organizational structure also included *Gemeinde*, consisting of five to ten members, the *Gau* which included a number of *Gemeinde*, and at the apex of the pyramid, a *Volkshalle* and a commission of three, elected annually and subject to recall. Much of the terminology and plan of organization was similar to that of the earlier Society of Exiles and to Armand Barbès and Louis Auguste Blanqui's *Société des Saisons* which espoused the revolutionary principles of Babeuf.[16] Needless to add, the secret police made every effort

[14] Franz Mehring, *Geschichte der Deutschen Sozialdemokratie* (4th ed.; Stuttgart, 1909), 103.

[15] See Theodor Zlocisti, *Moses Hess, Der Vorkämpfer des Sozialismus und Zionismus, 1812–1875* (Berlin, 1921), 112.

[16] See also Charles Andler, *Le Manifeste Communiste* (Paris, n.d.), 20–32.

to penetrate the ritual mysteries [17] of all such subversive organizations.

Although Swiss, Scandinavians, and Hungarians also belonged to the League of the Just, its language of procedure was German. Associated in the leadership with Weitling, who reflected the point of view of the craftsman, were a group of intellectuals and refugees who had enjoyed considerable formal education. One of them, Karl Schapper, had studied forestry and had lived the life of a university man at Giessen. While a refugee in Switzerland, he had been prominent in the Young Europe movement and had fallen under the spell of Mazzini. In Paris he made his living as a typesetter. He quickly rose to the top in the administration of the League and was a member of its *Brennpunkt;* and, after his expulsion from France, he became a leader of the communists in London.[18] Dr. August Hermann Ewerbeck, an M.D. from Danzig, was a member of the League's *Volkshalle* and taught socialism to a small group who met regularly in a room in the suburb of Vincennes. He translated Cabet's *Voyage en Icarie* and succeeded to Weitling's leadership in the League when the latter moved on to Switzerland. Weitling credited Ewerbeck with leading the League into definitely communist lines. Other influential members were Dr. Germain Maurer of Rhenish Prussia, who later was employed as a teacher in Berlin and contributed to various German papers. Among the members who did not belong to the intelligentsia may be mentioned Heinrich Bauer, a Franconian shoemaker; Joseph Moll, a watchmaker from Cologne who became a Chartist in England and fell in the revolution of 1849 in Baden; a certain Weissenbach, who, according to Weitling, gave the League its name and later came to Peoria, Illinois, to live; and Heinrich Ahrends of Riga, who also immigrated to the United States, took up spiritualism in New York, and remained a lifelong friend of Weitling.

[17] See Dr. jur. Wermuth and Dr. jur. Stieber, *Die Communisten-Verschwörungen des neunzehnten Jahrhunderts* (Berlin, 1853), especially I, 177–87. The account consists largely of police and court records.

[18] August Wilhelm Fehling, *Karl Schapper und die Anfänge der Arbeiterbewegung bis zur Revolution von 1848* (Rostock, 1922), *passim.*

In Paris the young tailor developed rapidly into a militant communist and became one of the most eloquent orators and literary champions of the proletariat. In passionate language, suggestive of the style of an old-fashioned American revivalist, he undertook to give expression to the yearnings of the underprivileged for Utopia.[19] It was during his residence in Paris that Weitling read Jean Jacques Pillot's little book entitled *Ni Chateaux ni Chaumières, ou État de la question sociale en 1840*, translated into German under the title, *Weder Schlösser noch Hütten* ("Neither Castles nor Hovels"). In the workers' clubs which he frequented, he perused such journals as *Intelligence, Égalitaire, Tribune du Peuple*, and *Journal du Peuple*. Tailors, who could put their minds on other things while sewing at the bench, often made it a practice to employ someone to read to them while they worked, and this procedure also was followed in some of the Paris societies. Thus newcomers like Weitling could perfect their French. In the Paris journals he found discussions of the theories of Fourier, Saint-Simon, and others; and by 1840, the ideas of Robert Owen were beginning to reach the Parisian workers. In the long and excited debates in which the radicals tried to agree upon a set of doctrines, Weitling moved steadily toward the left, away from such moderate Utopians as Ewerbeck, who rejected the extreme tactics of revolution. Weitling developed into a good public speaker and became the recognized spokesman for the "tailor party," known to be more radical than the cabinetmakers and several other groups.

The most convincing evidence of Weitling's growing importance among the radicals of Paris and of the respect which his fellow workers had for his intellectual ability was the fact that in 1838 he was commissioned by the League to prepare its first major publication. It was the intention of the sponsors to produce a treatise which would formulate the principles for which the society stood, for circulation as propaganda material in France and

[19] See also H. D. Lockwood, *Tools and the Man, a Comparative Study of the French Workingman and the English Chartist, 1830–48* (New York, 1927), 76.

especially in Switzerland and the German states. According to Weitling's account, he won the assignment in competition with another contestant.[20] He received no pay for his literary labors, and the project had to be carried out in strictest secrecy. An edition of two thousand was financed by the German workers of Paris at great sacrifice. They worked at night as typesetters, printers, and binders; and their confidence in their leading propagandist was so great that several pawned their watches to help pay for the printing, and many accepted copies of the book as reimbursement in full for their financial contributions. The original edition was printed on a wooden press on poor paper and was so full of errors that slips of paper had to be pasted over some of the pages to provide the necessary corrections.[21]

The publication in question was entitled *Die Menschheit, wie sie ist und wie sie sein sollte* ("Mankind as it is and as it should be"). Weitling had written the manuscript while carrying a full load of work at the tailor shop. Copies were carried in 1839 to Frankfurt by Heinrich Jakobi, a shoemaker's helper, and by other traveling journeymen into the towns of France, Switzerland, Germany, and as far as the Scandinavian countries. In 1840 the little book was translated into Hungarian, and in 1845 a second edition was published by the radical printer, Jenni of Bern, Switzerland. Four years earlier the police had found copies in the baggage of journeymen in Hamburg, and the chief of Austria's elaborate police network instructed his subordinates in the provinces to confiscate all copies of this "highly destructive and dangerous" publication which preached "hatred and hostility to all higher authority" and was written so interestingly as to mislead the innocent reader.[22]

[20] New York *Die Republik der Arbeiter,* July 19, 1851. Hereafter cited as *Rep. d. Arb.* The Wisconsin Historical Society at Madison has a complete file.

[21] Karl Glossy, "Literarische Geheimberichte aus dem Vormärz," *Jahrbuch der Grillparzer Gesellschaft* (Vienna, 1922), XXI, 98 *et seq.*

[22] See Gustav Mayer, *Friedrich Engels: Eine Biographie* (Haag, 1934), I, 116; Emil Kaler, *Wilhelm Weitling: Seine Agitation und Lehre im geschichtlichen Zusammenhange dargestellt* (Zurich, 1887), *passim;* Frederick C. Clark, "A Neglected Socialist," *Annals of the American Academy of Political and Social Science,* V (1894–1895), 718–39; Brügel, *Österreichische Sozialdemokratie,* I, 42.

Die Menschheit was Weitling's first attempt to integrate the workers' movement in its broader aspects with the new program of communism, or socialism, interchangeable terms at the time. Heinrich Heine called the little book "the catechism of the German communists," and Sebastian Seiler, a fellow communist, hailed its author as "the new king of the tailors," who, "à la Münzer," would become the "founder of a modern sect of Anabaptists." [23] Both statements were exaggerations, but the first fruit of Weitling's literary labors nevertheless was a significant contribution to the literature of pre-Marxian communism. The book was written before its author had read Fourier, though it may be assumed that his long discussions with workers and friends in Paris had made him familiar with the general outlines of Fourier's plan for the reorganization of society. Though Lamennais is cited in *Die Menschheit* but once, his influence was greater than that fact would indicate.

Weitling's little book belongs in the Christian communist tradition. It reveals that its author was by nature deeply religious, whatever his violent altercations with priests and churches may suggest to the contrary. Weitling's communism was firmly grounded in definite moral precepts. It called for absolute equality among human beings and for a return to that happiness of which men have been deprived by the exercise of political and economic power for selfish ends. It was a vigorous protest against the existing state of society which profited through the support of an organized priesthood.

The remedy for such abuses obviously was revolution, thorough and complete, not partial or compromising. The break with the past must be so complete that the new age proclaimed by the new Messiah might begin.[24] Replete with Bible quotations, *Die Menschheit* advocated the reform of Christianity itself and a return to the original characteristics of its primitive stage, when men

[23] Hermann Buddensieg, *Die Kultur des deutschen Proletariats im Zeitalter des Frühkapitalismus und ihre Bedeutung für die Kulturidee des Sozialismus* (Lauenburg, 1923), 13; Seiler, *Der Schriftsteller Weitling,* 11.

[24] Joho, *Wilhelm Weitling,* 33.

loved their neighbors, lived in the happy days of communal property, and professed a religion which was in complete conformity with the law of nature. Weitling cited such leaders as Thomas Münzer, champion of the religion of the "inner light," who died a martyr in the Peasants' War after the battle of Frankenhausen; Johann von Leyden, the tailor of Westphalia who became a communist leader; and Lamennais, the communist priest, as examples of the kind of Messianic leadership that would be needed to make the Bible once more an effective document of revolution. Such passages suggest that Weitling already had visions of himself in the role of the new Messiah of the "second coming," an idea that developed eventually into a strong and strange fixation. The opening pages of *Die Menschheit* appealed for workers in the vineyards of the Lord, for laborers who would go into the harvest fields and whose sickles would be "whetted on the golden rule." Men were called to practice love, Christ's first law, and to combat the sins of selfishness, fear, and cowardice.

It was not difficult to point out the gross inequalities that flourished in the existing social order, in which the laborer, who created all wealth, enjoyed it least and in which many were employed in wasteful occupations, in the army, or in the production of luxuries, and the whole economic system seemed to pit the rich against the poor. Contrary to the views of some of his contemporaries, however, Weitling did not trace all the workers' woes to the introduction of power-driven machinery. He was aware that machines caused technological unemployment and created new inequities; nevertheless, he welcomed their greater speed and power and hoped eventually to harness them in the service of labor itself. Although workers blamed the machines, tradesmen the guilds, and farmers the seasons, he was sure that the real cancer gnawing at the vitals of society was the unequal distribution and consumption of goods, the unequal apportionment of the labor necessary to produce them, and the vicious monetary system which sustained and perpetuated these inequalities. Because money was the root of all evil and the cause of all envy, Weitling had no faith in any of the reforms suggested by the men of money and capital and maintained that a device such as a national bank, by making the money piles smaller, would only spread the poison of usury among a larger number of the population.

Weitling on many occasions preached moderation and temperance to his fellow workers. He urged them to seek after honor and knowledge, to cultivate the arts and sciences, to appreciate "the real treasures of a progressing civilization," rather than those that "moth and rust could corrupt, and thieves break in and steal," and he clinched his arguments by numerous citations from thirteenth Corinthians and from the Gospel of Matthew. He preached that the respect of one's fellows and the approval of history were the most precious rewards which any man could win on earth. They could not be bought with earthly coin. They were the cherished possessions of men who live by faith and for the spirit, not for the satisfaction of their creature comforts.

There followed a long exposition of the principles of Christianity and of the laws of nature and a plea that they might be made the basis of all human legislation, so that nationalism and sectarianism might be superseded by devotion to one common human brotherhood. In the new order equal work would be required of all, and all men would receive equal rewards, equal educational opportunities, and equal rights. Private property and inheritance would be abolished, democratic processes of election and recall would be adopted, and state officials would be the servants of the people and would enjoy no preferential treatment, either in the assignment of labor or the distribution of goods. Freedom of speech and action would be limited only by respect for the equal rights of others, and all would be free to develop their physical and intellectual gifts to the utmost. Criminals who violated the rights of others would have these rights taken from them and perhaps, in extreme cases, would be banished in disgrace, but there would be no capital punishment. Principles such as these, adding up to ten points in all, Weitling regarded as nothing more than logical elaborations of the golden rule to be taught all men as divine truths which derive from the "father of light" above.

Weitling rejected the pacifism of some of the early Christians and quoted Matthew to prove that Christ had come to bring not peace but a sword. He believed that the world needed leaders and martyrs who would not compromise with the enemy nor seek safety in cowardly evasion. At the same time, and perhaps because he was a little alarmed by some of the implications of his logic, Weitling hastened to tone down his statements by stressing the virtue of tolerance, pointing out that no generation had a monopoly of wisdom and that perfection could be achieved only by God. He cautioned against attacking what others regarded as holy, unless the enemy actually used these things as weapons in the battle against progress, and reminded his readers that for a while longer, until the harvest is ripe, good and bad will grow together.

Details of the political, economic, and social structure which Weitling offered the workers of Europe, in the form of his communist Utopia, will be discussed in a later chapter. Obviously, many of his proposals had been made by others and can be found elsewhere in the revolutionary literature of the period. Nevertheless, Weitling's eloquence and passion made his argument seem peculiarly his own. He was sure that communism was a sound and practical way of life and that the only problem that would need to be faced after its adoption would be what to do with the great surplus of products which would become available. He believed that under the new moral dispensation, intemperance would remain the only crime. Furthermore, he was convinced that the new society would be so stable and so powerful that it could defend itself easily in case of attack, and that three or four million communists occupying a small strip of Europe would be able to hold all their neighbors at bay and finally take the offensive in a great war for the liberation of all mankind. He envisaged a world held together by a universal language, and a society in which all workers would be educated and all the educated also would be workers. "Persevere," he exhorted the "children of light," for in three generations the earth could be converted into a Paradise in which theft, envy, poverty, and murder would be unknown!

Die Menschheit, like Weitling's later publications, revealed the soul of a man who in spite of his stress upon materialism, rationalism, skepticism, and anticlericalism, spoke with the fervor of a religious prophet. He wrote with the holy fire of an apostle and with a high moral purpose. In the final analysis he had faith in the potentialities of man. His life was a bundle of contradictions. He tried to be a rationalist in his public conduct, yet inwardly he was motivated by a deep-seated religious sentiment. He was the kind of man to whom the invention of "systems" came easily because he was naïve enough to underestimate the practical difficulties in the way of putting them into practice. His fundamental objective was to bring order out of chaos and to establish harmony and peace in the world, yet he was never to achieve that harmony and peace in his own inner self.

In May, 1839, the League of the Just became involved in a revolutionary uprising in the streets of Paris, directed by Blanqui and Barbès, disciples of Babeuf. Though the rioting was primarily a demonstration by French members of the *Société des Saisons,* Weitling, Schapper, and other Germans were involved to some degree; and German workmen fought bravely on the barricades around the Hôtel de Ville, side by side with their French comrades. Schapper and Bauer were thrown in jail and later, with Moll, escaped to England. Blanqui and Barbès had their sentences commuted to life imprisonment. Weitling was neither apprehended nor prosecuted, but his League of the Just was broken up, with the French societies, and was forced to shift the center of its activities to London.

German journeymen already had carried the seeds of communism into Germany, and, though the number of communists in the German states hardly exceeded a few thousand, the authorities were on the alert. Friedrich Engels, writing to Marx, reported hearing lectures on communism in his home town of Elberfeld-

Barmen, and he "stumbled over communists" in other parts of Germany.[25] Also, communist activities were brought to light at a trial held in Frankfurt in 1840. That same year, Weitling accepted a commission to carry the communist gospel of the League of the Just to the workers of Switzerland.

[25] Werner Sombart, *Der proletarische Sozialismus* (Jena, 1924), II, 325.

CHAPTER III

CARRYING THE TORCH TO SWITZERLAND

AT THE close of the 1830's, Switzerland was a center of revolutionary propaganda. The policy of most of the Swiss cantons toward political refugees was remarkably liberal. In the neighboring Italian, German, and Austrian states censorship of the press was rigid; in Switzerland the press was relatively free and, with few exceptions, the Swiss managed to maintain their liberal policies despite diplomatic pressures and international complications. In Zurich, Julius Fröbel published Herwegh's *Gedichte eines Lebendigen,* a powerful leaven for revolution in Germany. Switzerland also was the publishing center for other German liberals and radicals, such as Hoffmann von Fallersleben and Ludwig Seeger; for Arnold Ruge's atheism; and for Ludwig Feuerbach's assaults upon organized Christianity.[1] Though the impact for the revolutionary eruptions of 1848 in Germany came from Paris, Switzerland was the spiritual home in which many of of the German revolutionists nurtured their ideas to maturity.

Both the Young Europe movement and the Young Germany agitation centered in Switzerland, and Mazzini moved the headquarters of the Central Committee of Young Italy from Marseilles to Switzerland in 1834. All such movements had the common objectives of unifying the nations politically, uniting all men in a fraternity of freedom, equality, and brotherhood, and liberating the oppressed wherever they were held in bondage. Radical

[1] Werner Näf, *Die Schweiz in der deutschen Revolution* (Leipzig, 1929), 50.

journals advocating everything from mild republicanism to extreme communism circulated in Switzerland, usually without too much interference from the police. Fröbel, a professor at the University of Zurich, edited the *Schweizerischer Republikaner*. The home of August Adolf Ludwig Follen was a center for revolutionary literati, and his *Tafelrunde* (Round Table) in Zurich at one time or another included such distinguished guests as Freiligrath, von Fallersleben, Herwegh, Fröbel, and Mikhail Bakunin. Many cantons harbored refugees from Germany, Poland, France, Hungary, Austria, and Italy, some of whom actually planned to attack neighboring states from the friendly soil of Switzerland.[2]

A number of these revolutionary groups were seriously interested in enlisting the support of the working class. As early as the 1830's, for example, a group of radical students who left Göttingen for the new university in Zurich published a paper, known as *Das Nordlicht*, which was addressed primarily to workers and farmers.[3] By 1836 some of the Swiss cantons were so alarmed by the multiplication of workers' organizations among Swiss and German journeymen that an effort was made to control these *Handwerkervereine* whose agitation sometimes precipitated diplomatic crises with neighboring governments. Geneva, burial place of Calvin and birthplace of Rousseau, was a notable exception and managed to avoid such repressive measures.

While some leaders of the workers' organizations had moved on to Paris and London, the membership which remained behind in Switzerland continued to meet under the guise of harmless singing societies and reading clubs whose ostensible purposes were recreation and education. Geneva, for example, had in 1839 a *Bildungs und Unterrichtsverein* which operated its own eating hall, owned a fair library and a collection of maps, and provided its members with facilities for instruction in singing, natural science, history, geography, French, and drawing. The club solemnly had resolved

[2] Wilhelm Marr, *Das junge Deutschland in der Schweiz* (Leipzig, 1846), *passim.*

[3] Hermann Buddensieg, *Die Kultur des deutschen Proletariats im Zeitalter des Frühkapitalismus* (Lauenburg, 1923), 13–14.

"not to engage in politics," but that decision could have had little effect in view of the fact that radicals like Albert Galeer, the good angel for many a homeless refugee, were prominent members. In Geneva a reading room for German workers was founded by a Lutheran pastor, who stocked the warm room, where men smoked their pipes and drank a glass of wine, with the right kind of religious tracts.[4] By 1840 the number of such *Arbeiterlesevereine* (workers' reading circles) had grown considerably, and most of them ostensibly were nothing more than singing, study, and pleasure clubs.

The transformation of such organizations into centers for the serious discussion of internationalism, socialism, and other reforms was relatively simple. On his arrival in Switzerland, Weitling found that communist propaganda had not yet penetrated these societies to any considerable extent. The seeds of communism were already sprouting, but the Swiss groups had little connection with the headquarters of radicalism in Paris.[5] By the middle forties, moreover, they were being closely watched, and Metternich's police spies reported regularly on their activities and on the number of initiates. Nevertheless, a German translation of Lamennais was fairly well known in the German workers' clubs of Switzerland; Swiss papers occasionally published items sympathetic to communism; and a little communist journal, known as *Posthörnchen*, was printed for a time in Zofingen.[6] Communist tracts and books were available in Geneva in spite of the vigilance of a government which was becoming less and less tolerant. Lausanne had a communist club known as "*La Société du cygne*," and Considérant lectured in the town hall in 1846 to a sizable audience. Cabet's *Populaire* was available in the coffeehouses of St. Gervais; the followers of Fourier published their *Edificateur* here, and

[4] Seiler, *Der Schriftsteller Weitling*, 9.

[5] Otto Brugger, *Geschichte der deutschen Handwerker in der Schweiz, 1836–43, Die Wirksamkeit Weitlings, 1841–43* (Bern, 1932), *passim.*

[6] Brügel, *Österreichische Sozialdemokratie*, I, 20–21. See also Ernst Barnikol (ed.), *Geschichte des religiösen und atheistischen Frühsozialismus, nach der Darstellung August Beckers vom Jahre 1843* (Kiel, 1932), *passim.*

many of the watchmakers in the canton had been affected by communist propaganda. Zurich was known as a relatively conservative city, and in 1839 its clergy had demonstrated vigorously when it was proposed that David Strauss be called to a professorship in the University. Nevertheless, when Gottfried Keller returned in 1842 from Munich, where he had tried to become a painter, he found the city in ferment. "The times seize me in their iron arms," he wrote. "I am storming and seething inside like a volcano." [7] Though he later reacted violently against the new radicalism, he discussed some of its fundamental problems in his *Grüne Heinrich*.[8]

Weitling visited Switzerland in the summer and fall of 1840. Perhaps it was during that first visit, when he worked as a tailor in several cantons, that he discovered that the soil of the Alpine nation was ready for the seeds of communism. It is conceivable that he already had decided to try his propaganda on the German workers in Switzerland when the League of the Just in Paris gave him thirty francs and the promise of additional support and sent him on his way to propagandize Switzerland. He arrived there with something of a reputation as a labor leader and with a "system" which he was ready to demonstrate in practice.

Life in Switzerland was full of activity but it was neither comfortable nor easy. Weitling had to earn his living at his trade. He was employed in several establishments, including the ladies' tailoring shop of Master Konrad Wuhrmann of Zurich. Here he proved to be the same competent workman he had always been, and to his earlier accomplishments he now added a touch of Parisian style and elegance.

Weitling was ready to make every sacrifice for the cause. He slept in lodgings that were overcrowded and sometimes had three occupants to a room. He did his writing on a board spread across

[7] Emil Ermatinger, *Gottfried Kellers Leben, Briefe und Tagebücher* (Berlin, 1924), I, 129.

[8] See also Jonas Fränkel, *Gottfried Kellers Politische Sendung* (Zurich, 1939), *passim;* Hans Max Kriesi, *Gottfried Kellers Politische Lehrjahre* (Frauenfeld, 1917), *passim.*

his knees. He declined most social invitations because he was too poor and too busy to reciprocate, and he became something of an ascetic, purely for economic reasons. According to one of his friends, he lived so frugally that he went about without socks, gloves, and underwear, stopped buying sugar, soap, and wine, and lived on the simplest fare and much black coffee. Intermittently, he received small contributions from Paris. On one such occasion, he used seventy-five francs, which had been sent him to spend for clothes, for the journal he was publishing at the time. In the evenings, when he frequented the taverns, he often was asked to address the assembled workers, though there were also those who shunned him as a false prophet. He found relaxation in the German singing societies, for, though he knew little about music, he loved singing.

Weitling considered himself the confrere and the equal of many refugees in Switzerland who had enjoyed far greater educational opportunities, and he continued to correspond regularly with the leadership in Paris.[9] He had complete faith in his mission as he tramped from one group to another to spread the new gospel of salvation for the workers. In Zurich he was part of a group which assembled in the rear of Konrad Wuhrmann's tailor shop. The young Keller attended a number of their discussions and later rescued Wuhrmann from oblivion by making him the Master Hediger, one of the "seven upright," in Keller's *Fähnlein der sieben Aufrechten.* Wuhrmann's cupboard was stocked with files of the *Schweizerischer Republikaner* and Karl von Rotteck's *Weltgeschichte.* It was rifled by the police in 1843.[10] Weitling also attended the Zurich singing society known as the *Hoffnung* and often read aloud to its members from Heinrich Zschokke's *Stunden der Andacht* and other literary works.

For days at a time, however, the tailor dropped his needle to work feverishly with the pen. A Viennese spy reported that he

[9] E. Schmidt-Weissenfels, *Zwölf Schneider: Historische Bilder der bemerkenswerthesten Zunftgenossen* (Stuttgart, 1878), 73–86.

[10] Jakob Baechtel, *Gottfried Kellers Leben* (Berlin, 1895), I, 202–203, 208, 250–51.

dramatically tossed scissors and needle into Lake Geneva to symbolize his intention to work and die for communism.[11] Another member of Austria's network of spies met Weitling in a coffeehouse in Geneva and reported that the latter had tried to sell him a copy of Cabet's *Voyage en Icarie* and had taken him to a communist meeting where Weitling addressed the "brethren" from a number of the French cantons. The Austrian stool pigeon, if one may believe his rather fantastic report, was initiated into the secret fraternity and received "the kiss of brotherhood" from Weitling himself, who impressed him quite favorably because of his knowledge of history, his mastery of the Bible, and his ability to adjust to new situations. It is evident that Weitling stood out as the intellectual superior of most of his associates, and even the spy admitted that he was a man who could be introduced to any social group and who knew how to win the support of church people and former university men among the German colony in Switzerland.[12]

Weitling corresponded regularly with Dr. Ewerbeck in Paris, and he was careful not to sever his French connections as he made new contacts in Switzerland. In Zurich he associated occasionally with Follen, who was blessed with ample funds and lived in medieval splendor, with Fröbel, and with other university men. He wrote to Karl Gutzkow and tried to convert him to communism, with such men as Dr. Sutermeister, a physician of Zofingen; Dr. Wilhelm Schulz, a Hessian refugee; and others among the *bourgeoisie*.[13] He took Herwegh to several meetings of workers' clubs and hoped for financial support from the funds of the poet's charming and relatively affluent wife. He met Wilhelm Marr, son of a famous actor, who had come from Vienna. At twenty-two, he was a leader in the workers' clubs of Switzerland, though as a follower of Feuerbach he soon reacted unfavorably to the religious aspects of Weitling's communism. August Becker, who was

[11] Wermuth and Stieber, *Communisten-Verschwörungen*, I, 25–29.

[12] See Brügel, *Österreichische Sozialdemokratie*, I, 29–31.

[13] Mehring, *Deutsche Sozialdemokratie*, 222.

a journalist, teacher, and incomparable reader of Goethe, had been a student of Dr. Georg Büchner at Giessen and had served time in a Darmstadt jail for revolutionary activities. The son of a minister, he became a communist in Switzerland and was one of the most courageous champions of the new radicalism. Mehring, historian of socialism, called him "a good natured bum," but he was far more than that. He was one of Weitling's ablest followers and advisers, trying to dispel the factional strife among the workers and to unite them for one grand attack on private property. He endorsed most of Weitling's program and credited him with being an original thinker. Yet he also was one of the few who frankly told his friend the truth when the latter revealed signs of jealousy and envy, or ambition to become the "Communist Pope." [14] Among the outstanding workers with whom Weitling was closely associated were such stalwarts as Niels Lorenz Petersen, the son of a shoemaker of Copenhagen, who embraced communism in Switzerland; Simon Schmidt, a tanner from Liegnitz, who had worked in France, learned of communism from his Swiss barber, wrote essays under the name of "Sebastiano," and became an active organizer of worker's clubs in Switzerland; the tailor Bartels, whom Weitling met again in Louisville in 1851; Karl Joseph August Haetzel, a Catholic and a shoemaker, born in Neumarkt, near Breslau.

Like other radical groups, the communists have always had their lunatic fringe. Indeed, there were those who would have put Weitling himself into this category, especially during the later months of his stay in Switzerland. Among the most picturesque of these unbalanced extremists were Georg Kuhlmann of Holstein and the "Prophet Albrecht." Kuhlmann was an erratic physician who became a communist. He regarded himself as a prophet, wore his hair and beard long, lectured on "The New World, or the Proclamation of the Rule of the Spirit on Earth" and talked about establishing colonies in Turkey. The Prophet Albrecht came from

[14] See August Becker, *Was Wollen die Kommunisten?* (Bern, 1843); Brugger, *Deutsche Handwerker in der Schweiz,* 147; and *Dokumente des Sozialismus* (Berlin, 1902), I, 203–17.

Altenburg. His voluminous and fantastic correspondence with Weitling was couched mainly in Biblical allegory. Jailed in Germany in the 1830's with nothing to read but the Bible, he heard voices and saw visions and thereafter found the complete explanation for most human experiences in the Old Testament. In Switzerland he renamed one of the Alpine peaks Mount Sinai; wrote brochures on "The Restoration of the Kingdom of Zion," "An Appeal to the World of Women," and "A Challenge to the Priesthood"; published a collection of poems dedicated "to the altar of liberty"; and translated Cabet's communist creed. A few of the German communists were religious mystics and were ready to believe in a new Messiah. Weitling himself was not without faith in a kind of Second Coming and eventually came to conceive of himself in the major role of the deliverer.[15]

Of quite a different nature was Weitling's brief association with Bakunin, whose "Swiss interlude" in a stormy career happened to synchronize with our tailor's sojourn in Switzerland. Overwhelmed by the beauty of Zurich and by his debts, the embryo anarchist lived in one room overlooking the lake and the mountains, read George Sand, and translated Schelling. Through Herwegh, at whose wedding to the beautiful Emma Siegmund in Baden Bakunin was best man, he was introduced to the group of radicals in Switzerland. His biographer maintains that "the most important figure who crossed Bakunin's path during his sojourn in Switzerland was Wilhelm Weitling." The latter had called on the Russian, and the Russian legation had promptly reported to the home government that the two men were becoming congenial. Bakunin discovered that his new friend was something of an undisciplined fanatic, but he found him to be an honorable man and full of faith in the potentialities of the human race. Although his efforts to initiate Weitling into Hegel's philosophy proved in vain, Bakunin read Weitling's *Guarantees of Harmony and Freedom* when it appeared and considered it "a really remarkable book."

[15] See Johann Caspar Bluntschli, *Bluntschli-Bericht, Die Kommunisten in der Schweiz nach den bei Weitling aufgefundene Papiere* (Zurich, 1843), 46–47.

Indeed, he was sufficiently impressed to quote, in a letter to Ruge, Weitling's lines to the effect that "the perfect society has no government, but only an administration, no laws, only obligations, no punishments, only means of correction." It is more than probable that intercourse with the philosophical tailor may have turned Bakunin's thoughts from mere speculation to actual revolution and thus have helped develop the creed of anarchism which marks his later years.[16]

On his arrival in Geneva, Weitling had joined the existing *Arbeiterbildungsverein* (society for the education of the workers) and promptly had tried to convert its members to communism. He received mail in Switzerland under several party names, Freymann, Rogge, and Müller. To his great chagrin, he discovered that the Geneva society was dominated by the Young Germans, republican nationalists who had no interest in the cosmopolitanism of the communists. Failing in his attempt to establish a workers' co-operative dining hall which he had hoped to manage, Weitling left the organization and, with the help of men such as Becker and Schmidt, proceeded to promote new educational and singing societies and communal eating halls, all of which were used as screens for the communist activities of the League of the Just.

Operating under such innocent names as *Harmonie* and *Eintracht*, these clubs admitted new members only after careful scrutiny. The candidate had to be proposed two weeks in advance and had to receive the unanimous approval of the membership. Thereupon, he was allowed to pay an initation fee, was handed propaganda literature, and was given a membership card signed by the officers of the society. Each member who introduced a new candidate to the organization endorsed his name on the reverse side of the membership card, and all members were expected to sign the roster of the association. An appropriate address welcomed the initiate into the fraternity at the time when he took the

[16] See E. A. Carr, *Michael Bakunin* (London, 1937); Ernst Barnikol (ed.), *Gerechtigkeit; ein studium in 500 Tagen* (Kiel, 1929), 162–63; and F. A. Sorge *et al., Briefe und Auszüge aus Briefen* (Stuttgart, 1906), 12.

oath and received "the kiss of brotherhood." Henceforth he was addressed with the familiar "*du.*"

The order of business in these societies was fairly standardized. The reception of new members was usually the first item on the agenda, and the newcomers were thoroughly examined, impressed with the need for secrecy, instructed in the principles of the movement, and urged to secure at least one new member each month. Thereupon, each member reported on his propaganda activities since the last meeting. If he had been derelict, he was admonished to be more zealous. There usually followed a report on the propaganda in other areas, gleaned from foreign journals. Members were given an opportunity to ask questions, dues and contributions for propaganda purposes were collected, committees chosen, and announcements made about the travel plans of members. Finally, a substantial amount of time was reserved for reading, debate, and discussion, for all such organizations had a distinctly educational objective.

Weitling hated the prevailing *Kneipenleben* of the workers which made them the slaves of the taverns, where they drank too much, wasted their time and money in card games, quarreled with each other about inconsequential matters, and talked about nothing but wages. Violent feuds between members of various trades and crafts sometimes ended in drunken brawls and pitched battles. Weitling had higher ideals for his fellow craftsmen, and in his communist clubs he saw the cure for many of their vices. In these *Vereine* workers could get cheap and wholesome recreation and be educated for the responsibilities of citizenship and, eventually, public office. Weitling was eager to demonstrate what workers could accomplish, without police or judges, through the principle of free association. Like a Methodist revivalist he preached temperance and the virtues of self-effacement, brotherly love, and forgiveness, as he appealed earnestly to "the people of blouses, jackets, smocks and caps . . . the most numerous, useful and powerful group on God's earth," to live up to their possibilities.

In eighteen months, Weitling organized at least ten societies, with a total membership estimated variously from 550 to 1,100. He himself put the number of societies at seventeen, thirteen German and four French, and reported that they provided "the means of instruction" for a total membership of 1,300, the tried and true advance guard of the communist revolution. He asserted that the indoctrination of new members was proceeding at the rate of 600 annually. Johann K. Bluntschli's report on Weitling's activities in Switzerland estimated 750 German and 400 French members in these organizations. Whatever the exact number, it is known that Weitling founded or directed the activities of *Arbeitervereine* in Lausanne, Vevey, La Chaux-de-Fonds, Neuchâtel, Geneva, Zurich, Aarau, Winterthur, St. Gallen, Kreuzlingen, Bern, and Zofingen. The French societies seem to have been the stronger as a rule, partly because of the more liberal attitude of the authorities in the French-speaking section of Switzerland and partly because they received some support directly from Paris. In Lausanne the club of some eighty members met every evening and on Sunday afternoon. Whenever Weitling attended he opened the meeting with a parody of the Lord's Prayer. These societies attracted the attention of communists as far away as London, and the *Communist Chronicle*, published in London by Goodwyn Barmby, "president-in-chief" of England's Universal Communitarian Association, frequently referred to the progress of the movement in Switzerland, to the success of the circulating library in Lausanne, and to the translation of "Weiling's" [*sic*] work into French.[17]

Groups such as these were composed largely of the better-paid and better-situated workers, men intelligent enough to be attracted not only by the new propaganda but by the opportunity to further their education as well. The clubs subscribed for newspapers and journals, and at Lausanne the organization employed a teacher at two francs per hour plus free board. It issued a half-dozen numbers of a handwritten *Volkstümlicher Handwerker* which Simon Schmidt prepared and which carried the motto "Equality-Brotherhood-Liberty-Unity-Education-Moral-

[17] London *Communist Chronicle*, I, No. 5, p. 80.

ity-Labor-Order." With members of such caliber and ambition, Weitling expected to encounter little difficulty in launching co-operative dining halls on the model of the institution he had started for the tailors of Paris.

Organizations of this general pattern were founded in Geneva, Vevey, Lausanne, and Morsee. In Vevey a German workers' club raised 300 francs for a co-operative tavern and in Morsee, fifty members collected 200 Swiss francs to rent a house and garden where about 200 workers took their meals.[18] With his mania for figures, Weitling demonstrated to his own satisfaction that the undertaking in Geneva would yield a profit of no less than 14,400 francs a year, and he immediately made plans for spending a tidy surplus on a library, a new hall, social insurance, and the founding of colonies. He concluded that profits would come primarily from the sale of wine and from serving breakfast and supper, thus enabling the club to provide a noonday meal at exact cost; and he maintained that if each member would help the association to make a profit of only twenty cents a day, in two years it would be possible to pay each member a dividend of sixty-five francs for travel and to have enough left to pension forty aged and disabled colleagues. Indeed, it would only be a matter of a few years until the resources would be adequate to finance a colony in America! [19] Weitling was surprised when he encountered the opposition of innkeepers who defended their system of "free enterprise" against such co-operative undertakings.

As a matter of fact, though the police in some of the German cities were alarmed by the "triumph of the new spirit of co-operation," [20] these co-operative ventures were anything but a conspicuous success. Launched with great enthusiasm and sacrifice, they ended for the most part in debt and failure. In some cases, the membership was permitted to buy too much on credit, was too slow in payment, or defaulted altogether. In Geneva, where Weit-

[18] *Die junge Generation*, June and August, 1842.
[19] See *Der Hülferuf der deutschen Jugend*, September and October, 1841.
[20] See Zlocisti, *Moses Hess*, 119.

ling had offered to serve as manager without pay as long as there were no profits and had been rejected, the treasurer absconded with 9,000 francs. With few exceptions, the movement was a failure in Switzerland. Weitling tried to revive it later in the United States. In 1850, years after the founder had left Switzerland forever, F. A. Sorge, an early socialist, discovered a German workers' club in Geneva which had been for a time under Weitling's leadership and which he described as a place dedicated to serious discussion and wholesome recreation, "without envy or distrust." In 1854 a correspondent writing from Zurich to Weitling in New York reported that his labors had not been in vain, that a communist club still existed, and that copies of his books still circulated from house to house.[21] With such isolated reports Weitling had to be content. They provided the only evidence that his labors in Switzerland had not been entirely fruitless.

Weitling's experiences from the time of his arrival in Switzerland to the time of his arrest, confinement, and expulsion centered largely in the history of these communist workers' clubs. He created many of them, and they languished after his departure. He carried on an extensive, shrewd, and disarming secret correspondence with scores of the initiates, periodically visited the groups which he had founded, and was accepted as their "spiritual head" and chief theoretician. Harassed by the authorities, he moved from canton to canton to avoid arrest. He became involved in heated controversies with local leaders as he tried to keep the control of the movement firmly in his own hands. References in his correspondence to his "torn and bleeding heart," to "the shipwreck" of his plans, and to the "cross" he had to bear for others indicate a psychological strain that brought him close to a complete breakdown and manifest an increasing reliance on the terminology and comforts of religion.

Under pressures of this kind, it was perhaps inevitable that Weitling should become more vain and less amenable to honest

[21] See *Die Neue Zeit* (Stuttgart), 17. Jahrgang, II (1899), 320; and *Rep. d. Arb.*, June 24, 1854.

criticism. He read Simon Schmidt, one of his most faithful coworkers, out of the movement. He believed that by 1844 he would have 40,000 members—enough to start the revolution. He devised a plan to liberate professional murderers and thieves and to turn the "thieving proletariat" loose on society, to hasten the revolution for equality by "one violent push." For a brief moment, his mind also played with the idea of favoring the community of women. Correspondents in Paris, such as Dr. Ewerbeck, were horrified by such proposals and said so in no uncertain terms. Their reactions to such attempts "to found the kingdom of heaven by unleashing the furies of hell" [22] were violent indeed. The exchanges between Weitling and Ewerbeck became more and more acrimonious until his friend Becker felt called upon to remind the impatient revolutionist that the world could not be conquered with iron; that ideas were stronger than cannon; that all men shared the responsibility for the existing state of society; and that a true communist's revenge is forgiveness, and moral and spiritual conquest his chief weapon. Others, such as Bakunin and Johann Most, later advocated the use of the thieving proletariat for a similar purpose. Be it said to Weitling's credit that he quickly recovered his balance. Essentially he was a religious and moral man, and therefore the whole unfortunate episode may be dismissed as a temporary aberration of a highly overworked and unusually excitable individual.

Incredible as it may seem, Weitling had time left from these propaganda activities to publish a journal and to compose his most systematic treatise on social reorganization. In September, the first number of *Der Hülferuf der deutschen Jugend* ("The Cry of German Youth for Help") appeared in Geneva. Its editor invited contributions from members of all classes, whether workers or intellectuals, on the status of the workingman, suggestions for its improvement, and reports from physicians on the effect of various occupations on public health.

The new monthly was sold for three French francs a copy, and subscriptions were solicited in Paris by Bauer, the shoemaker, in

[22] See *Bluntschli-Bericht,* 106–11.

London by Moll, the watchmaker, in Geneva by Sandoz, and in La Chaux-de-Fonds by a baker named Zutter. All contributions were to be addressed to "Monsieur W. W., Chez Sandoz, rue de Pellisserie, N. 131," Geneva, who promised to work without charge and contribute any surplus which the paper might yield to the cause of labor. Though he was urged by some of his friends to devote himself entirely to propaganda, and though he received some help occasionally from Paris and London, Weitling continued to work at his trade, earning from thirty to forty francs a week.

Presently, because of the police, the new monthly had to be moved to Bern, and subsequently to Lausanne, Vevey, and Langenthal, each move necessitating new contracts with new printers. In its later issues the journal was known as *Die junge Generation*, although its format was identical with that of the first publication. A promise to print half of each number in French and the other half in German could not be kept for financial reasons. A few issues reached Berlin and North Germany, but the circulation never exceeded 1,000 subscribers, of whom 400 lived in Paris and 100 in London. When François Guizot ordered the paper seized at the borders of France and forbade transshipment to England, one half the subscribers dropped off. Another 100 readers, who belonged to Young Germany, canceled their subscriptions because the paper was too communistic.

Weitling's journal was the prototype of the paper he published later for five years in the United States. There can be no doubt about who wrote most of *Der Hülferuf* and *Die junge Generation*, for the material was presented in Weitling's unmistakable style and in many respects was a mere prelude to the *Garantieen*, the author's major book, in which much of the subject matter reappeared. The prospectus of the *Hülferuf* proclaimed that "We German workers also want to raise our voices in our own behalf and for the welfare of humanity, to prove that we understand our interests, and uninflated by Latin, Greek or other artful expressions, know how to describe, in good German, where the shoe pinches and what is to be done about it. . . . No one who has not himself been a worker, can judge the condition of the worker." [23] The journal's motto was: "Opposition to the interest of the individual, insofar as it injures the interests of all, and for the interests of all, without excluding a single individual." Gutzkow was impressed by the prospectus; and when he by chance received a package of the papers in Paris, he was greatly affected by Weitling's eloquent description of the lot of the journeyman as he wandered from place to place in search of employment. Gutzkow did not become a communist, but he became convinced that the workers were entitled to a careful and sober reply to their grievances and suggested the establishment of a department of national welfare, to combat socialism from above.[24]

Weitling wrote almost the whole first number of the new journal, which reiterated his familiar plea for the union of all workers, the emancipation of the whole human family, and the establishment of co-operatives. As usual, he quoted Scripture and referred to Jesus and his apostles as fellow workers; he demanded faith and courage and closed with the lines: "We pray constantly 'Thy Kingdom Come.' Well, it will come, the kingdom of the saints, promised 1800 years ago to those who live in communal harmony. The boundaries of the nations will crumble when the Son of Man comes to judge the quick and the dead."

In March, 1842, *Die junge Generation* restated its editor's well-known views about government, laws and punishment. In the second number of the *Hülferuf*, Weitling already had paid his respects to those who would divert attention from communism and brotherly love to mere political action. Now he went on to expose the illusions of nationalism and the folly of national hatreds. He thought the Rhine question and the controversy over Alsace-Lorraine eventually would be solved not by the sword but in the spirit of love. He ridiculed the admonition that workers be thrifty in order that the banks might profit by their self-denial. In other

[23] Quoted also in Beer, *Allgemeine Geschichte des Sozialismus*, 436.
[24] Gutzkow, *Pariser Briefe*, 260–62, 270–73.

issues he exposed the caste system of the German intellectuals and the inconsistencies between practical politics and the religion professed in the churches. He was sure that only a communistic universal brotherhood could destroy the nobility, who based their prerogatives on the accident of birth, and the aristocracy, whose power derived from the money bags. He advocated more and more discussion clubs, so that "the frightened diplomats, magistrates and usurers may become as accustomed to the clamor for communism as the sailor is attuned to the roar of the waves"; and he agreed with Pierre Josef Proudhon that "Property is theft." He did not shrink from a temporary dictatorship to establish communism, for it was his belief that popular sovereignty and universal suffrage were but a mirage and democracy only the accidental rule of the majority over the minority. For the trickery of elections and the logrolling of parliaments, he would substitute the rule of the talents and a plan by which voters could choose capacities, not individuals. He promised to explain all these ideas in "a greater work" which he expected to publish in a few months.[25]

In a leading article in the *Hülferuf*, Weitling developed another of his favorite themes under the title "The Communion and the Communists." In this essay he completely identified communism with the gospel of Jesus. If his references to the Last Supper seemed blasphemous to ardent believers, he cited Lamennais in his defense. Weitling contended that there was greater suffering in his day than in the time of Jesus. He challenged his readers to debate the true meaning of the Bible and referred sarcastically to Christian "charity" as actually practiced. He stanchly defended the institutions of marriage and the family, and spoke frequently of "higher and more perfect beings" beyond the comprehension of man. Citing Lessing in support of tolerance and brotherly love, he wrote, "We are all children of one father, and we all have a common destiny, to be happy here, and then forever after, in the great beyond." Almost every issue of the *Junge Generation* dealt in some way with religion, religious imagery, and symbolism, and

[25] *Die junge Generation,* June, 1842, pp. 83–96.

specifically called the readers' attention to such publications as Louis Hessberg's "Versöhnung der Welt mit Gott" ("God's reconciliation with the world"), and Scherzer's articles on "Ermahnungen zur Nächstenliebe, An die deutsche Jugend" ("Exhortations to brotherly love addressed to the German Youth"), and "Tagwache zum Ausbruch des Reiches Gottes auf Erden. Eine Hirtenstimme aus den Alpen" ("The vigil for the dawn of God's kingdom on earth; the voice of a shepherd from the Alps"). Scherzer had been a member of the League of the Just in Paris.

In addition to serving as a vehicle for the editor's propaganda, Weitling's journals contained a variety of other material, such as articles on the Peasants' War of Luther's time; the nuisance of passports and travel restrictions; the English factory system, with references to the "honored and beloved" Robert Owen; the Rappist colony of Harmonie, near Pittsburgh; extracts from philosophers; sarcastic observations on what was being perpetrated in Germany in the hallowed name of science and philosophy; translations from Proudhon, Socrates, Rousseau, Fourier, Chateaubriand, and Saint-Simon; references to Roger Bacon; articles on the progress of invention and science; an attack on Malthusianism; poems by Herwegh, Hoffmann von Fallersleben, and lesser poets from the ranks of labor; articles on astronomy; occasional book reviews; a fantastic description of Paris in the year 2000 A.D.; and violent diatribes against the soldiery, who in exchange for food surrender "all reason, understanding, conscience and free will." Most of these articles were unsigned. Almost all of their authors agreed that society was rotten at the core, though they could not always unite on the cure. The degree of tolerance manifested by the editor toward opinions at variance with his own was quite remarkable for a radical journal of this sort.

Weitling's magnum opus appeared in December, 1842, under the title *Garantieen der Harmonie und Freiheit*. It was issued secretly and was intended to provide the exposition of Weitling's complete "system." As a matter of fact, his theories, as will be demonstrated later, had changed little after 1838. Fourier had written about the "Guarantees of Harmony"; Weitling added "Liberty," or "Freedom." Some of his friends regretted the time and energy which he spent in writing books and told him in no uncertain terms that he should concentrate his efforts on propaganda and the founding of communist societies. Although Ewerbeck managed to send the author a thousand francs, the new book, as in the case of earlier publications, was mainly a labor of love and sacrifice. Weitling felt called upon to explain his "system" in language which the workers could understand, and he hoped that the gospel would spread to the comrades in Germany and Austria, where the distribution of books of this kind through dealers was a very precarious business.

The type for the *Garantieen* was set at the establishment of Alexander Michod, printer of the *Junge Generation,* and before long the author and printer were involved in a sharp disagreement over the cost of the publication. The book was sold by subscription, each subscriber agreeing to take at least two copies. Some took ten, and Simon Schmidt induced the Lausanne group to take two hundred. Workers invested their savings and carried the printed sheets into Paris, where they were bound. The venture was anything but a financial success, though the book later went into new editions, and 600 copies of the third edition were sold in Hamburg through the efforts of the workers' associations of that city. Metternich's spies promptly reported the appearance of this new instrument of revolution, noted that one copy already had reached Frankfurt (apparently Weitling had sent it to Gutzkow), and summarized its contents for the secret archives. The police were forced to admit that it was "written with great earnestness and profound research" and had made a serious impression, "even upon statesmen," in Lausanne.[26]

The title page of the first edition bore the often quoted words, "We want to be free! Free as the birds of the heavens; free to travel through life as they do, in happy flight and precious harmony"; and the author launched at once into his discussion of

[26] See Brügel, *Österreichische Sozialdemokratie,* I, 29, 30.

why the world was out of joint. His descriptions of the sufferings of the poor, in contrast with the happy lot of the rich, must have moved many of his readers to fury. They are not without their appeal to the reader of today. Weitling wrote with the rage and fire of the craftsman, the artisan, and the *petit bourgeois* who were beginning to disintegrate under the impact of large-scale industry and were struggling for deliverance from forces that were depressing them into the proletariat. The author was convinced that the battle was between a religion of brotherly love and the poverty and suffering which were the results of artificial class distinctions.[27] Though Weitling sensed the beginnings of the class struggle, he belongs among the Utopian moralists, rather than with the advocates of a class-conscious proletariat. His interpretation of history was simple. It was largely the story of the robbery and exploitation of honest men by crooks and thieves; and it recorded a steady decline from that happy golden age which Rousseau had described as the state of nature when the earth yielded abundantly, when there was no "mine" and "thine," and when all the children of God lived in harmony with the ordinances of Nature.

When Weitling wrote, he used the vivid word-images of the artist or the prophet, certainly not the rationalism and objectivity of the scholar. Though he displayed an amazing knowledge of many things, he wrote as a simple child of the people and a romantic, who sought to arouse and inspire. When he referred to God, he put the word in quotation marks; but he had a deep faith in man's intelligence, and in his capacity to build a harmonious world order in which all would be brothers working toward the common goal of happiness and virtue.[28]

Weitling attributed man's happiness in the "golden age" to the balance and harmony which had existed at that time between man's desires and his capacities to produce and to enjoy. Contentment had resulted from this harmonious balance. "The total

[27] See also Friedrich Muckle, *Die grossen Sozialisten* (Leipzig, 1920), 77–82.

[28] See also Charlotte von Reichenau, "Wilhelm Weitling," *Schmoller's Jahrbuch für Gesetzgebung, Verwaltung und Volkswirtschaft im Deutschen Reich* (Munich, 1925), XLIX, 293–328.

capacities of every generation are always in balance with its total desires, or needs," he wrote. But, he added, the desires and capacities of individuals are unequal, and no individual in a civilized state can satisfy his desires completely through his own capacities alone, but must trade his capacities for those of others. It was the function of the social organization to bring these qualities and capacities into harmony again. Furthermore, because desires developed with progress, harmony could be assured only by balancing mankind's total capacities to produce and to consume.

Weitling traced the evolution of society from a simple pastoral order to his own time, demonstrating the emergence of modern concepts of movable and immovable property. Like Proudhon, he regarded private property as the curse of mankind. He described how, as primitive man began to count his herds and to make special provision for his own family, he became aware of mine and thine. As long as Nature provided abundantly, however, the distinction did not prove serious or alarming: as yet there were no fixed boundaries and men could go where they pleased and use what they wanted and needed. But eventually the time came when men tilled the soil, coveted the best available land, and marked it off as their own. While population expanded, the amount of available land did not change; and thus there emerged the "loveless, fratricidal concept" of property, and men began to quarrel and fight, to compete for pasturage and the bounties of Nature, and to employ other men as laborers to help reap what they had not sowed. Land and its products increased in value; laws of inheritance were invented; and society divided into masters and slaves, workers and drones.

It is not necessary to pursue the historical argument through all its steps. Presently, Weitling arrived at the point where the violation of Nature's laws led to wars. The skillful use of weapons became a trade or a profession; tribes united into peoples, and boundaries became the "property" of nations. Peoples developed their own languages and began to speak of such "sweet delusions" and utter such "sanctified lies" as "fatherland," a concept that had no meaning for the propertyless classes. "The worker has no country, for he has no property." Yet men were marched off to kill, "like marionettes," not as creatures made in the "image of God," and war became simple murder. Weitling ridiculed the silly desire for ribbons and decorations that marked the soldier and the statesman and described the brutal barbarisms of the drill sergeant as he transformed free men into automatons. Because of the unequal distribution of labor, men had divided into workers and drones. The drones wanted booty; wars resulted, and, in their turn, led to human slavery. Weitling did not neglect an opportunity to excoriate the great republic across the Atlantic which boasted of its liberty and held the black man in chains. At the same time, he fiercely denounced a priesthood that preached happiness in the sky to those too poor ever to achieve it on earth.

It was the author's contention that the diversification of agriculture and the development of new desires had led to the invention of new implements, a new division of labor, and thus to commerce and trade. Because values were fixed by the law of supply and demand, men drove hard bargains, strove for monopoly, and eventually resorted to bloodshed.

In 1842, Weitling had translated Considérant's criticisms of trade into German, and now he incorporated much of this material in his *Garantieen.* Like Cabet, he regarded money as the curse and sin of mankind. He referred to property as "stolen" and to "the exchange of stolen goods" as "commerce." With the multiplication of products, trade had become more complicated, and mankind had invented money as a medium of exchange. Thus the basis had been provided for a new kind of slavery, for thenceforth men had no value except in terms of what they could buy or sell, and money not only produced inequality but was the means of sustaining it. Instead of stamping coins with the likenesses of crowned heads, the writer suggested that it would have been more appropriate to use symbols for labor, such as the hammer, anvil, saw, and chisel; or such words as "worth one loaf of bread," or ". . . one pound of meat," or ". . . [so many hours] of labor";

for money, he maintained, also was "a real product of labor."

Weitling's invective against the power of money knew no bounds. It was an "excrescence of hell." The lust for money had nailed Christ to the cross in exchange for thirty pieces of silver. Not satisfied with their ill-gotten property and with their money, its tainted symbol, men had gone on to create the titles and sinecures that mark the drones of society: the armies which were "lifeless machines without a will," the police, the priesthood, flags and national symbols, and all the false concepts of honor and morality. Weitling considered merchants who did nothing but sell and store the products of the labor of others as utterly worthless and the source of economic waste, deceit, speculation and adulteration. He closed this portion of his book with a long quotation from Victor Considérant, whom he called the "St. Paul of Fourierism." The second section of the *Garantieen* presented its author's plan for the reorganization of society and will be summarized in the next chapter which deals in detail with Weitling's "system."

The *Garantieen* in many ways was merely an elaboration of Weitling's earlier writings. It showed the influence of Saint-Simon, Owen, and Fourier. Its author derived his ideas from many sources, never completely assimilated them, and sometimes became involved in inconsistencies. It must be remembered that Weitling was a man of remarkable native intelligence and great facility with the pen, and what he knew he learned from life itself. Therefore he never acquired a detailed systematic knowledge of any subject, such as Fourier, for example, had of economics and trade. His ideas were born and molded in the clubs and taverns, largely from conversations and discussions with his comrades.

The *Garantieen,* as will become apparent in the next chapter, stressed a co-operative, handicraft system of production, despite the fact that industrialization was making rapid progress. It described a Utopia of skilled workers. Weitling's restless and active mind saw things too simply, but his heart could not find peace in a world torn by suffering, inequality, and injustice. Weitling viewed communism as an international movement that could not be confined within narrow national boundaries. Yet he feared a mere "barracks state" and therefore desired to substitute a form of administration that would regulate, but not command, and to establish a regime in which the wise and the good would rule.[29]

The *Garantieen* passed through several editions. The third, issued in Hamburg in 1849, contained minor variations, additions, and omissions. The greatest expansion appeared in the chapters about democracy and the *Kommerzstunden*, and in connection with a discussion of the proper kind of propaganda for a proposed League of Liberation (*Befreiungsbund*). These changes can be detected easily, but they make no substantial difference in the nature and content of the work. The preface to the third edition is interesting, for in it the author reviewed his associations with the many workers he had known and reflected on how long his faith and strength would sustain him. He noted progress among the workers and he was especially pleased with the great multiplication of books in which the learned spoke to and for the worker. He believed that communism was spreading "like a flow of lava" into many lands and he thought he noted a decline in national and craft antagonisms, as men began to envisage a truly universal goal.

The book eventually was translated into Swedish, Norwegian, and French. Christian Essellen, who later published the *Atlantis* in the United States, recommended it as a powerful proselyting document. Emil Girardin referred to it favorably in the Paris *La Presse*, and the Belgian *Le Peuple* advertised the French translation as the work of "the most celebrated and popular of the German Socialists." Feuerbach read the book and hailed the author as "a prophet of his class." Even Marx approved. Letters from otherwise unknown workers, in Hamburg, Liege, and far-off Brazil, were addressed to the "German Rousseau" and compared Weitling with Spinoza.

In the preface to the third edition, Weitling reprinted extracts

[29] See Joho, *Wilhelm Weitling*, 57, 61; and *Handwörterbuch der Staatswissenschaften* (Jena, 1894), VI, 668–71.

from the reviews of his book, both favorable and unfavorable, which had appeared in papers such as the *Aachener Zeitung*, *Die Schweizerzeitung*, the *Kölnische Zeitung*, the *Züricher Landbote*, the Paris *Vorwärts*, *La Patrie* of Switzerland, and the London *Times*.[30] Comments from men like Bruno Bauer and Wilhelm Marr were transcribed into the personal copy which Weitling carried with him to the United States.

Werner Sombart, in his monumental work on proletarian socialism, lists Weitling's *Garantieen* with Louis Blanc's *L'organisation du travail*, Proudhon's *Qu'est ce que la propriété?*, Cabet's *Voyage en Icarie* and Moses Hess's *Die europäische Triearchie*, among the "decisive works of the second period" in the evolution of socialist thought. As late as 1901, Juarès, the famous French socialist, was still citing Weitling's major work in the Paris socialist newspaper, *La Petite République;* and Morris Hillquit, historian of American Socialism, characterized Weitling's social theory as "the connecting link between primitive and modern socialism." [31]

[30] See Barnikol, *Weitling der Gefangene*, 256–60; *Rep. d. Arb.*, June 14, 1851; Mehring's introduction to Jubilee Edition of Weitling's *Garantieen*, xxiii; Karl Grün, *Ludwig Feuerbach in seinem Briefwechsel und Nachlass* (Leipzig, 1874), I, 365; London *Communist Chronical*, I (1843), No. 14, 151; and Bruno Bauer, *Parteikämpfer* (Berlin, 1874), *passim.*

[31] Sombart, *Der Proletarische Sozialismus*, I, 25; Morris Hillquit, *History of Socialism in the United States* (New York, 1903), 161; see also "Wilhelm Weitling und sein System der Harmonie und Freiheit," *Die Zukunft*, I (1878), 583–94, 606–15, in which the writer referred to Weitling as "one of the most important and generally forgotten authors." Mr. Harvey Goldberg has supplied the reference to *La Petite République*, December 28, 1901.

Chapter IV

WEITLING'S "SYSTEM"

NO SUBSTANTIAL change occurred in Weitling's principles or theories after the publication of the *Garantieen*, although the later *Evangelium des armen Sünders* provided some additional insight into the nature of the particular kind of communism which he advocated. Though he published millions of additional words during the remainder of his life, it can be said that, as far as contributions to the literature of social revolution are concerned, Weitling became intellectually "unemployed" after the appearance of the *Menschheit*, the *Garantieen*, and the *Evangelium*. The activities of Marx and Engels had no effect on Weitling. He remained completely isolated from the trends that marked the development of so-called modern, scientific socialism.

The main purpose of Weitling's writings was to help mankind find happiness and contentment, and these he believed were attainable only under a system which guaranteed equality for all. To produce a balance between the desires that are inherent in all men, and the capacity to satisfy those desires by mechanical and intellectual labor, he regarded a communist society as essential; for it was harmony between desires and capacities that produced good, and failure to provide that harmony was the cause of all evil. It followed that production and exchange, or production and consumption, would have to be administered in such a way as to ensure that desirable balance between desires and capacities. Weitling recognized that men were not equal in stature, intellectual powers, emotions, or in many other ways, and in this disparity among individuals he discovered both the source of trouble and the cause of progress. It was to ensure the balanced and equitable use of these powers that he advocated communism.

Weitling knew that without the economic emancipation of mankind, political action would fall far short of achieving the ends he had in mind. A free press, for example, he considered an impossibility as long as people were not free and editors were hirelings of the wage system. Universal suffrage, though perhaps desirable, would do little good as long as the rich remained rich and the poor, poor. Though political action was desirable and a republic more palatable than a monarchy, Weitling insisted on a complete social revolution. "The reign of the majority over the minority is as oppressive as the absolute command of a sovereign," he wrote on one occasion. "As republicanism will liquidate the monarchies, so communism will liquidate the tyranny of majorities. . . . Communism will be as strong and inescapable as the reign of God, and at the same time, it will perfect democratic self-government to such a degree that men will be unaware that there is a government because of the complete harmony that will prevail." And finally, because Weitling believed in the rule of science and knowledge and that "Science must cease to be a privilege," he was eager to perfect a system in which those best qualified for leadership would be in control of the administration of the state.

Weitling had a strange weakness for writing constitutions, and he wrote many, for a variety of purposes, during his lifetime. In his "Constitution for the Great Human Family," based on equal division of labor and equal consumption of goods, the unit of organization was a large one of perhaps a million people, who occupied a very sizable area. This union of families, known as the *Familienordnung*, was composed of *Familienvereine* (family associations) consisting of a thousand family units, governed by an elected board. Ten of these *Familienvereine* in turn composed a province, or *Familienkreis*, and each *Kreis* also was governed by an elected board. Each provincial board selected a representative to serve in the Congress of the *Familienbund*, and the latter, in turn, created a Senate and a governing triumvirate as the highest legislative and administrative body of the realm.

For this organization of families Weitling prescribed some of his most interesting proposals. The families were to be housed in common buildings erected in the shape of a pentagon, with the buildings of the *Familienverein* located at the center of population. Here were provided all the necessary facilities for storehouses, offices, schools, postal and telegraph offices, theaters, an observatory, a great hall with a speaker's rostrum, and quarters for transients. The interiors of these pentagonal structures were to be designed with careful attention to considerations of beauty, economy, and convenience. Glass roofs would keep out the dirt, windows could be moved for ventilation, and all rooms could be kept at an even temperature. No building and no organizational unit would be removed farther from the center of things than five hours' walking distance, and a railroad was to be constructed to connect the various *Familienvereine* so that all citizens could reach a common meeting place in a half-hour's time.

Parallel to this organization of families, the author of the *Garantieen* proposed an occupational organization, known as the *Geschäftsordnung*, which was intended to control and direct the economic activities of the society. It consisted of organizations for farmers, workers, and teachers; and an "industrial army." These groups chose representatives, by a complicated election procedure, to represent their interests in the various administrative bodies. In agriculture, for example, every ten farmers elected a *Zugführer;* these in turn chose a business manager for every hundred farmers, and at the top of the governing body for agriculture was an elected council (*Landwirtschaftsrat*) which chose "presidents" to supervise each phase of agriculture, and to represent the farmers in the ministry of the all-inclusive *Familienbund*. Weitling forecast the time when farmers would no longer trudge to the fields on foot, but would ride in comfortable wagons; and while they were working in the fields, tents would protect them from the sun. One milk wagon would replace a hundred milk-maids with their pails; fences and walls would disappear with the abolition of private property; each area would produce what it was best fitted to produce; and, as envy was banished from the earth and men worked for the sheer joy of helping their fellow-men, production would increase 300 per cent in a five-year period.

In a similar fashion, industry was organized into a *Werkstand* representing the manual laborers, artisans, and workers in the arts and in the factories. Based on the usual multiples of ten and a hundred, *Geschäftsführer* and *Meister* were chosen, every ten masters constituting a workers' council (*Werksvorstand*). This group would represent the leaders of each type of work. In addition, every area that had as many as a hundred of these councils also had a *Meisterkompagnie* (Master Company) composed of those who had made useful inventions and notable contributions to progress. This body, with the *Werkvorstände* of the area, chose representatives to a *Gewerbeausschuss* (Committee of the Trades) comparable to the *Landwirtschaftsrat* of the farmers and in turn integrated with the Ministry of the entire *Familienbund*. Weitling expected to develop a system of production in which most workers probably would follow several occupations, thus eliminating monotony by rotating the tasks assigned every two hours.

The Industrial Army was another prominent feature of Weitling's new society. All able-bodied members of the community between the ages of fifteen and eighteen were required to spend three years in training in the industrial army, under the supervision of overseers who had made the army their career or had been chosen from the better educated group because of their special talents. Failure to progress satisfactorily in the curriculum provided by the army might subject the delinquent to another three years of service. The Industrial Army was divided into corps according to the nature of the tasks which were being taught, and each corps was recruited by the volunteer method or by drawing lots. Every six months the personnel was transferred to a new corps to broaden the training program. Volunteers for the especially difficult tasks of an "honor corps" could complete their term of service in one instead of three years.

This unique organization was patterned on the military. Unquestioning obedience to the superior officer was enforced, and the rank and file were quartered in barracks or billeted upon the families of the district. Instruction included training for mining, railroading, canal, road, and bridge building; work in the building trades; and preparation "to colonize foreign lands." It was expected that this program of rigorous compulsory training would provide society with all the necessary labor and guarantee a singularly healthy race of men.

Unlike some of the proletarian leaders whom he knew, Weitling, as already suggested, had a deep respect for education and science, however disparagingly he might speak at times of the professors in the universities. He regarded every kind of work a potential science, and he had unlimited faith in what science could accomplish for the advancement of humanity. So he advocated a system of schools, ranging from art and trade schools to a great university for every million of population; and he favored an association of teachers and learned, known as the *Lehrstand*, to assist in making all appointments in agriculture and industry which required several years' special preparatory training. Professors in the faculties of the university were represented in the government of the *Familienbund*, and students chose ten of their number to sit with a council of the educated, the *Gelehrtenausschuss*. Every teacher was required to perform some manual labor, if time was available. Students were permitted to choose freely what they wanted to study, but only those who maintained the highest standards received work-time credit for their intellectual labors.

At the apex of the administrative pyramid was the *Trio* or *Dreimännerrath*, consisting of the top men in the three branches into which Weitling divided all science: the science of healing, which included the whole spiritual and physical nature of man, for he wanted both philosophers and physicians; physics, by which he meant a study of natural phenomena and the application of the laws of nature to the service of mankind in every field of activity; and mechanics, which included the theory and practice of all manual and machine production. Weitling's *Trio* suggests Plato's "philosopher-kings," the elite, who were masters of science and "the rudder of the whole administration." Only by such expert leadership, he believed, could harmony be introduced and maintained in the social system.

Immediately below this governing trio stood the *Zentralmeisterkompagnie*, consisting of the highest office-holders chosen by the various units in the society already described. It constituted a sort of Senate and Ministry which represented the Master Companies and other units farther down in the administrative scale. On the basis of reports coming up from officials and directors below, those at the top established general policies and apportioned the tasks among the heads of the various crafts and services, who in turn made the assignments and distributions farther down, finally reaching every member of the community. Those at the apex of the pyramid were expected not only to direct the work program but also to attend to all matters affecting the life of the society, such as health, housing, clothing, recreation, and the arts, and to administer them on the basis of equal benefits for all.

Alongside these various organizations dealing with organizational and administrative policy, Weitling's system established a series of "academies" and "health councils." Inventors would become members of the academies, and the health commissioners would be elected on the basis of their proved success in curing the physical and spiritual disorders of the body politic. The process for the selection of these various bodies was extremely complicated and their procedure hardly less so. It is unnecessary to describe the organizational and administrative pattern in all its details. It is so complicated and confused and reveals so many overlapping jurisdictions that Weitling's program obviously would work only in Utopia, though he insisted that it was a perfectly practicable design for a new society which could be realized rather speedily, if only a sufficient nucleus would undertake the social revolution.

As already suggested, Weitling favored a system which would bring the recognized leaders in the field of learning and science into the top administrative posts. No mere counting of heads would bring this about. He cited evidence to show that money and smooth oratory had defeated government by the people many times in human history. Despite the communal ownership and administration of all material things which he advocated, he was eager to ensure the recognition of genius, reason, and superior talent. Because he believed that only those who were themselves of this class could select leaders who possessed these qualities, he proposed a complicated method for judging ideas and plans anonymously. Thus men's status and powers in the new organization would depend on ability evaluated scientifically, without reference to personalities. To ensure this impartial and unprejudiced choice of the highest capacities, inventors were expected to submit their drawings and writers their writings in a competition conducted by academies, which offered honors and prizes in order to stimulate progress. Among other things, Weitling hoped to encourage the invention of a universal language, progress in air transportation, and "pouring" buildings in one piece from the ground up.

Thus the selection of the most competent would be made by a group of experts who themselves were eligible for the highest administrative posts. No office carried with it a definite term of service, however, and it was expected that men would yield their places of power and influence gracefully whenever better men appeared. Elections turned on plans, models, and inventions submitted anonymously to the board of expert judges. "If much is invented," the author blithely observed, "there will be frequent elections" and the examinations will be made more and more difficult. Thus knowledge and intelligence, not privilege and power, would govern the new society. No one, however able and talented, "can represent the people who refuses to give his possessions for the common good." On the other hand, men of such extraordinary gifts were not bound to fixed schedules of work, though they were expected to devote at least a third of their time to teaching others their special skills. Thus, in a society dedicated to equality, inventors, on whose "eagerness for progress" men must count to ensure maximum benefits for the masses were the only group for whom Weitling proposed special privileges.

Of greater importance than this intricate and confusing administrative and governmental structure were some of the general regulations which the author laid down for his new communist society. It was his desire that each family have its own dwelling place and garden, though kitchens, storehouses, and orchards would be common property. Theoretically, women were to have equal rights in voting and holding office, but they were to be assigned to the easier tasks and organized into female companies. No woman, however, was to be eligible to election to the supreme *Trio* until existing differences between male and female had disappeared. Weitling believed that divorces should be made easy and marriage freed from existing artificial economic and social limitations. "Love is the kernel," he wrote, "marriage the shell," and "the money system is the worm which eats its way into the kernel." His sentimental review of woman's suffering under prevailing inequalities ended with the prophecy that some day "the golden dawn of the morning of emancipation [will] break, to kiss the hot, bitter tears of slavery out of the weeping eyes" of women. Children, after they reached the age of six, were expected to leave home and attend schools designed to train them for living in a communist society.

Weitling's state guaranteed the right of every traveler to go wherever he pleased, and equal guest privileges wherever he stopped, provided he did not stay too long. In that event, the local authorities could put him to work. In the matter of dress, the materials for clothing were selected by the administration. The cut of the clothes, however, could be determined much lower down in the hierarchy to satisfy local tastes, provided not too much labor was required to keep up with changing fashions.

Since crime was regarded as a social disease fed by the false standards of existing society, Weitling expected it to vanish in his new order. He denounced existing penal methods, the American and British systems of judicial procedure, and the "Pennsylvania system" of dealing with prisoners. He advocated the choice of judges by a panel form of election. In a properly ordered society he believed there would be no theft—indeed, its persistence would be the best evidence that perfection in the social structure had not yet been attained—and he insisted that, though offenders might have to be quarantined, hospitalized, and in extremely rare cases banished, they must never be punished.

Weitling was convinced that equality of labor and equal enjoyment of goods could not of themselves guarantee permanent happiness and indeed might lead to unbearable monotony; and he was further certain that in the new society the subdivision of labor would be so great and the hours of work so few that many would find it possible and desirable to work at several jobs to escape boredom. He therefore sought a device which would avoid the blighting effects of the existing monetary system and at the same time give the spirit of man an opportunity for self-expression and individual pleasure. Though the state might furnish recreation, education, and public festivals, he realized that there still would be many who would be unhappy "if they cannot follow their own will and desires." One might decide not to work on a certain day; another would not be satisfied with the common furniture or dress goods; and perhaps another would desire a gold watch, or food or drink not available on the common menu. Weitling was keenly aware of the necessity for preserving individual initiative, and he knew that new desires would appear continually, as men reached a higher state of evolution. As the workday became ever shorter, the gratification of individual desires would become more imperative. Such considerations clearly posed the question, How could the principle of equality be combined with the desire for personal freedom and individual satisfaction? Perhaps when "love and concord" ruled the world that problem would resolve itself, but in the meantime, it needed a scientific solution.

Weitling found that solution in what he called *Kommerzstunden.* In addition to the tasks required of all able-bodied men and women of the community to satisfy the demand for the products and services that were essential, he argued, an individual should be given the opportunity to work voluntarily at some job of his choice, beyond his regularly assigned duties. By such additional work, he could accumulate credit for extra hours of work and service, and these extra hours would be recorded in a *Kommerzbuch* specifically designed for the purpose. Such labor credit then could be exchanged for the products produced by others in a similar manner. Because *Kommerzstunden* also could be earned by extra labor in the Industrial Army, Weitling made them available even to the most untrained and inexperienced members of the community.

Like some distinguished economists, Weitling clearly adhered to the "time theory" of value. He believed it was the universal measure for determining the value of labor, whether manual or machine; and he proposed to exchange labor for labor, eliminating the middleman and the banker from the economic system. Value was to be estimated according to the amount of labor expended in the production of all items; and goods were to be exchanged through a *Tauschsystem* (a method of exchange) by which money would be eliminated, or, perhaps it would be better to say, one form of currency would be exchanged for another. Specie would be melted down and used to produce tangible, useful goods, and the *Kommerzbuch* would perform the functions once performed by money.

Weitling realized, of course, that such utilization of the extra time of private individuals to satisfy their individual whims and desires, and the exchange of their extra products for those similarly created by others, would have to be controlled in the interest of the community as a whole. Production and consumption would have to be kept in balance and an adequate labor supply assured for the performance of the necessary services in the community and the production of the essential products. The solution for that problem he found by stipulating that if too many workers chose to work on the same tasks at any one time, such occupations would be denied any further labor credit by the policy-making administrators until the existing surplus was exhausted. Moreover, if raw materials were needed for the production of necessities, and the manufacture of luxuries had become too great, the "hour cost" used in computing the production of luxuries simply would be raised above the value of the actual work expended, or a temporary embargo could be placed on the production of such surplus items.

Thus each individual could "satisfy his particular wants without destroying the harmony between the desires and capacities of all." Weitling expected the family *Vereine* and the organizations of the *Kreis* to open factories and warehouses for the production of such additional articles as would satisfy the tastes and desires of individual members, and to display them to prospective buyers or "exchangers." In case of death, all articles obtained by this system of exchange would revert to the common storehouse, to be offered for sale a second time. Weitling anticipated such a surplus of production, and so large a balance in the *Kommerzbücher*, that the last week of each year could be set aside for a "week of carnival," and all members of the community could be given a vacation. To provide for the aged and the infirm, extra hours of labor were assigned to the able-bodied, thus ensuring a kind of old-age pension. Inventors, literary men, and the like received hours of credit at once for their creative work. Here again it was the duty of the academies to make sure that no capacity or talent was lost to society, that "all products of labor for the refinement of the pleasures of the senses" were evaluated properly, and that public exhibitions were arranged to display attractively all goods produced beyond the mere necessities of life. In the category dealing with "the refinement of the pleasures of the senses," Weitling included the theater, dancing, music, liquor, tobacco, and fireworks.

By this system, individual initiative and desire would be blended and reconciled completely with the objectives of communism.

Weitling thought he had anticipated every possible objection to his plan. Unfortunately, it does not seem to have occurred to him that his theory emphasized only the time spent on the job and overlooked what was accomplished in that given time. Thus the door was left open to exploitation of the talented and the industrious by the stupid and the lazy; conceivably, under a system of equal pay for all work, the ablest might seek the easiest jobs and the most stupid the most difficult.

The *Garantieen* closed with eloquent chapters on the superiority of communism to all other systems and described the happiness and prosperity that would result from a planned economy regulated by science and motivated by a sincere feeling of brotherhood. The author knew that Utopias may spring full-grown from the mind of man, but that they never are realized in a day. And so he offered suggestions for a period of transition, such as free public education, a free press, poor relief, tax reform, co-operatives, and extensive social legislation. These, however, were mere palliatives. What was needed was a revolution, not necessarily a bloody one, although twenty years of chaos would not be too great a price to pay for an entirely new social order based on equality, justice, and brotherhood.

It was in this connection that Weitling reverted to his earlier suggestion of "justification of theft" and referred to the social revolution as the "last theft," when it would be honorable and permissible to rob the rich to help the poor. He was sure that good would issue eventually from an excess of the bad and a period of disorder. He talked about "a war without mercy" and prepared a plan to be enforced after a few weeks of tumult and "the first victory." Provisions were included to disarm the rich, arm the proletariat, grant amnesty to all prisoners, and create a people's militia. A provisional "revolutionary paper money" would be used until the *Kommerzbuch* system could be established; thus the wealthy would be forced to join the revolutionaries because their gold would no longer buy so much as a loaf of bread. Yet Weitling offered to pension the rich who would surrender their possessions to the state; he admitted that they were only the victims of a bad economic system and not inherently wicked; and he pointed to Owen, Babeuf, Cabet, Hess, and others to prove his argument that communism could be made to appeal even to the propertied classes.

Weitling's system clearly shows the influence of Saint-Simon, Owen, Fourier, and others. It also invites comparisons with the Stalinist Russia of today, although the analogies are not too clear and should not be pushed too far. The complex system of representation in Weitling's ideal society and the organization of its various power interests for purposes of government clearly recognize the decisive significance of economic and occupational groupings and, to this extent, suggest a clear parallel with the theory underlying the Soviet state today. Furthermore, although he was a genuine humanitarian and a man of great compassion who emphasized the moral worth of each individual and believed in the redeeming power of love, Weitling was never impressed with democratic methods and procedures. One wonders, for example, what might have happened if his scheme for the selection of the talented inventors and creative artists and the men of novel ideas had actually been put into practice. Although designed to be completely objective, it may be doubted whether the plan would have produced intellectual and creative leaders willing to give free reign to progressive ideas who were altruistic enough to step aside for men of greater talents. One can more readily imagine the development of an inner ring who would undertake to force all intellectuals to conform to an ironclad mold of uniformity, perhaps with periodic purges of dissident elements. Apparently in the modern state which professes to be modeled upon Marxian communism, purges have occurred several times in the fields of music, literature, art, and science.

Weitling's plans for the new society contained many elements of authoritarianism, in spite of his professed hatred for the methods of the dictator and his belief that dictatorship was only a temporary, though perhaps unavoidable, expedient on the road to Uto-

THE NEW CURRENCY OF THE SOCIAL REVOLUTION

pia. It is a fact also that there were several purges in the *Arbeiterbund* which Weitling created in the United States in the early 1850's. Finally, it is not without significance that as time went on, Weitling's utterances revealed an increasing concern with a "new Messiah," "greater than the first," who would come to lead mankind out of its misery. No one who has read his major works can doubt who that Messiah would be. Nevertheless, Weitling believed that in the end, when the transition period was over and the social revolution was complete, its prophet and leader would surrender his authority to the people and dwell thenceforth among them as the humblest of them all.

CHAPTER V

A MARTYR'S CROWN

IN *Das junge Deutschland in der Schweiz*, his volume on Young Germany in Switzerland, Wilhelm Marr, who knew Weitling in Zurich and was thoroughly familiar with the political cross-currents that engulfed the Swiss cantons in the 1840's, made the observations that communism was a manifestation of the futility of the will; that communists lacked faith in themselves and in each other; and that their doctrine had become "a social theology" which "has its own sacred books, its prophets, its Messiahs and its heaven." There was much truth in Marr's conclusions, for sects actually were developing within communism itself. Before long, each had its special Messiah, and, though the various groups professed to agree in their major objective, they fought furiously when it came to putting their theories into practice.

Weitling felt the urge to publish a confession which would make clear to himself, his friends, and his enemies just where he stood in this matter of communist theory and practice, and, specifically, how he related religion to the new gospel. Friends and foes demanded clarification on this point. His friend Becker referred to him as "a communist without and in spite of the Bible" but tried to show that Weitling nevertheless wanted to "prove that one could be a communist with and according to the Bible." Becker contended that an honest and sincere communist nevertheless could take the position that those who were loath to abandon their old religious faith would find nothing in the Gospels, if properly interpreted, to refute the social and economic theories of the most radical reformers. Seiler reported many conversations on this subject with Weitling and testified that although the latter regarded the religion of revelation preached by church and priests as the basis of all superstition, he revered Jesus of Nazareth as a genuine reformer.

To Weitling, German philosophy seemed utterly futile: "the quintessence of German nonsense . . . presented in learned figures of speech, and artificially fashioned out of a metaphysical hocus pocus." Its highly abstract terminology left him completely befuddled. Although he read Feuerbach with understanding and appreciation, his short excursion into Hegel, under the tutelage of Bakunin, ended after their first session in "fog" and disgust. Weitling feared lest these "foxes and asses of German philosophy" should lay obscene hands on communism and confuse the common people; and he insisted that communism must derive its power not from "artificial, school-perfect, flowing words," but from "the noble sentiments of the heart."

Perhaps that was Weitling's main reason for wanting to utilize "religious feeling" as a motivation for communism. He certainly did not want to make religion the enemy of his movement. He went so far as to suggest that a religious person in a communist society could preserve his ritual and his faith and might even go to church and to Mass, after working hours, provided that he did not try to force his views on others of a different persuasion. He would tolerate bishops, priests, and Jesuits, provided they performed useful work in addition to their religious duties and preached for the common good, not for self-aggrandizement; and like Milton, he did not fear the outcome when truth and error entered the lists in a fair encounter.

There is ample evidence to show that Weitling was being carried away by his dreams of an earthly kingdom of a thousand years of peace, to be ushered in by a new Saviour. Such a Messianic hope had been part of the old Jewish tradition, and it intrigued many of the early Christians, such as the Waldensians, the Lollards in England, and certain groups in the Hussite movement. Weitling belongs in this same tradition of chiliastic sectarianism.[1]

The result of his long reflection on communism and religion and their proper relationship was a new book, entitled *Das Evangelium des armen Sünders* ("The Gospel of the Poor Sinner"). Weitling started working on it while he was still in Lausanne. In May, 1843, he had appealed for advance subscriptions and in a table of contents and prospectus had explained his purpose: to prove that the religion of Jesus, the prophet of love and freedom, need not be condemned or destroyed by the social reformers, but could be used to great advantage for the emancipation of mankind.

Weitling had taken up residence in Zurich, in defiance of the advice of some of his best friends. The prospectus of the new book, in which the author readily admitted he had not worshiped in a church for years, was enough to convince the Church Council of the city of its blasphemous character, and the police commissioner of Bregenz reported to Vienna that the new work would prove far more destructive and dangerous than the *Garantieen.*[2] Fröbel probably declined to take the manuscript for his own press; Follen refused a plea for financial aid; and Ruge angrily turned down Moses Hess's request for twenty francs. After considerable difficulty, Weitling came to terms with a printer in Neumünster near Zurich, but when the latter discovered the real contents of the *Evangelium* he refused to proceed with the printing unless he were guaranteed against liability and prosecution. After a sharp quarrel, the author carried home that part of the manuscript which already had been printed and decided to find a new publisher.

Apparently, Weitling had resolved to move to the canton of Aargau to avoid a crisis. But before he could carry out his decision he was arrested by the Zurich police, at 3 A.M., June 9, 1843, while returning from a meeting of the *Hoffnung*, a society which met

[1] Karl Kautzky, *Vorläufer des neueren Sozialismus* (Stuttgart, 1909), I, 35–55.
[2] Brügel, *Österreichische Sozialdemokratie*, I, 31–33.

regularly at the *Gasthaus zum Pfauen*. His room and the printing establishment were raided by the police; a part of the manuscript and some of Weitling's correspondence and other papers were confiscated; but some of his material, including part of the *Evangelium*, apparently had been removed or burned by friends before the police arrived. Among others arrested in this purge of the radicals were a shoemaker from Homberg and three German tailors. Although released rather promptly, they were kept under police surveillance, with other journeymen, for a long time. According to the report to the Vienna police, sixty-six dangerous characters were under suspicion, though the police could make no specific charges at the moment.

Before proceeding with the events of the trial of the conspirator against Christianity and the social order, the contents of this dangerous manuscript should be examined. Through the good offices of friends, it finally was issued in Bern by Jenni, publisher of many radical treatises; and after Weitling's release, a second edition, enlarged and revised, was published in Birsfelden. The book went through a fourth edition in New York in 1854, with a preface proclaiming "the gospel of liberty," which would give the poor and despised new courage, "plant the kiss of forgiveness on the cheek of the criminal," light the way to hope, and bring the warm glow of love and liberty into the hearts of sinners everywhere.

The *Evangelium* opened with a discussion of the "trinity of all religions," faith, hope, and love. Faith in God, "the concept of highest perfection," the author defined as that "acute" emotion which man's reason cannot comprehend, but which a suffering and feeble humanity will not relinquish. Weitling had no desire to rob men of this "anchor" in the storm of life which was a "comfort, support and trust," even for men of science and education. Preserve "a holy spark of faith," he pleaded. No one has unraveled the riddle of the universe; and man needs religion when mental and physical sufferings become too heavy to bear. At the same time, he pleaded with his fellows not to hope for help *from* heaven or *in* heaven, but to strive for a good society on earth, anchored in love. "God and Love are the eternal riddles," he concluded, but Christ said "God *is* Love!"

Thereupon the writer proceeded to analyze the life and character of the founder of Christianity. He described Jesus as a genuinely human being who was the most perfect image of the unfathomable God, but who was not a supernatural phenomenon. He pointed out how the Bible, a product of weak and fallible men, had evolved from manuscript to manuscript through the centuries; and after the manner of the "higher criticism" of the theologians, he presented considerable textual analysis to prove his conclusions.

Weitling deplored and condemned the sectarian quarrels and religious wars that had resulted from the narrow, literal interpretations of Holy Writ; and he described the Gospel of Jesus as a simple appeal to the heart of man, an expression of man's innate sense of justice, concluding that even if Christ had not been a historical personage at all, the New Testament would remain one of the most significant documents in human history.

The *Evangelium* then proceeded to demonstrate that doubt was natural to man, and skepticism a useful cathartic; that even the best of the disciples were sinful men; and that Jesus himself had all the desires and frailties common to man. Weitling explained and more or less condoned the treason of Judas Iscariot on the ground that Jesus had distrusted him; a sharp rebuke administered, not in private, but before all the other disciples, had driven him to murder and suicide. Jesus appears in the *Evangelium* as the plain carpenter's son, a simple worker who had to earn his own living, who had brothers and sisters like other men, whose character was not without its little human flaws. Later generations had enveloped him in the supernatural mysteries characteristic of the lives of the founders of other great religions. The miracles were disposed of as unessentials which every man might explain in his own way. The parables were interpreted as shrewd tales to outwit the Pharisees. After the fashion of rationalist attacks on the Bible, the *Evangelium* directed attention to its many anachronisms, contradictions, and inconsistencies; and the book of Revelation was disposed of summarily as a mere confusion of words, in which "whatever is intelligible . . . is not worth preserving."

The next section of the book was the most important, for it purported to elucidate the "true doctrine" of Jesus. From a wealth of citations and quotations which revealed extraordinary knowledge of the Scriptures, Weitling pictured the kingdom of heaven as an ideal human society founded in brotherhood and maintained by good works. He directed special attention to Jesus' compassion for the poor and to his strictures on the rich who lay up treasures on earth. He apparently took delight in pointing out that Jesus was an "illegitimate child" and, drawing on his own experience, referred to the "bitter ridicule" which he must have had to endure through life on that account. On the subject of marriage, however, he found the founder of Christianity too vague to be satisfying, and he restated his own favorite thesis that family and marriage relations would improve when property was abolished, and "mankind as a whole" would become more important than individual families. He apparently felt it necessary specifically to repudiate all theories suggesting community of wives.

Weitling concluded that communism, coupled with the new medium of exchange which he advocated, would usher in an ideal society in which men would seek their own well-being only through the well-being of all, and good will would be as important as intelligence. Like other writers before and after his time, Weitling speculated on whether Jesus actually had belonged to the Essenes, the religious community of Jews which developed apart from the main stem of Jewish life, and, according to Josephus, "despised riches," considered commerce the source of all greed, and prescribed that "every one's possessions [be] intermingled with every other's possessions" in "one patrimony among all the brethren." [3] He restated his views on crime and punishment and supported them with Biblical proof. He identified the Holy Spirit with "the spirit of truth" made manifest in men like Keppler, Copernicus, Newton, Bacon, Columbus, Gutenberg, and, in its most perfect form, in the career and character of Jesus of Nazareth. The sin against the Holy Spirit was the use of power for selfish ends, to perpetuate existing inequality and injustice.

Jesus emerged from this long analysis of the record as a revolutionary at war with all the forces of Mammon, the indomitable champion of man's unrelenting struggle for the necessities of life against the forces of special privilege. Weitling interpreted the parables to support this thesis, and though his interpretations may conflict sharply with the conclusions of the theologians, they make interesting and provocative reading. For his specific purpose the author marshaled the incidents in Jesus' career which revealed him as a foe of property and a consorter with the sinful poor. Jesus is presented not as an obscurantist or ascetic, but as one who had "picked as many flowers of joy in his short life" as possible, and who took leave of his boon companions in a final feast of lamb and wine. The *Evangelium* closed with the statement that the Christian Gospel is "one of freedom, equality and love; man has made it into a gospel of tyranny, subservience and deceit."

In an appendix to a later edition, Weitling tried to summarize his view of Christian morality and conduct. As essentials of Christian living, he stressed temperance, patience, loyalty, honesty, modesty, good will, and mercy. He admonished his followers to look for the best in people, and to give every man the benefit of the doubt in this respect. He added that in the communist state "we will love our enemies as soon as we have conquered them" and will treat them as we would be treated. He cautioned against speaking or writing in anger; demanded charity for the poor, com-

[3] See W. Wiston (trans.), Flavius Josephus' *The Wars of the Jews* (London, 1915), 134; Emil Schürer, *A History of the Jewish People in the Time of Christ* (Edinburgh, 1885), 190–218; W. O. E. Oesterley, *The Jews and Judaism During the Greek Period* (London, 1941), chap. xxi; and Ch. Guignebert, *The Jewish World in the Time of Jesus* (New York, 1939), 172–90.

passion for those in sorrow, and pity for criminals who had fallen victim to passion or the maladjustments of society; and advised his followers never to borrow money nor to expect to collect loans made to a friend in distress. Weitling recognized that he himself fell far short of practicing these high principles of moral conduct, and he copied them and hung them on the wall, to serve as a constant reminder of the frailties which he and other men had to overcome.

The *Evangelium* marked the end of the period of Weitling's major productivity, which covered the half-dozen years from 1838 to 1844, though he still had a long period of activity before him in Europe and the United States. By modern standards, it is difficult to find much in the *Evangelium* that could be considered blasphemous. Yet even Lamennais repudiated the book when it appeared. Its offensive passages may be overlooked when we recall the author's high purpose to develop a gospel that would have vitality and meaning for the common people for whom he spoke. The book revealed an amazing familiarity with the great literature and characters of world history. Besides a thorough knowledge of the Bible, indicated by many specific citations to chapter and verse, the author referred to Rousseau's *Confessions*, which he had read, to Josephus and Seneca, and to Pythagoras and Socrates and Homer's *Odyssey*. He recounted incidents from the lives of Zoroaster, Castor and Pollux, Alexander the Great, Perseus and Romulus; referred to Mithraism and additional material in the field of comparative religion; and cited an array of modern writers beginning with Proudhon.

The little book attracted some attention outside Switzerland. Barmby, writing in his London communist journal, likened the "sensation" created by the *Evangelium* to that which marked the appearance of Lamennais' *Paroles d'un Croyant* and requested a speedy translation into English. In 1851, a correspondent from Paris informed Weitling, then living in New York, that his old associate, Ewerbeck, had published a work in French on religion and the Bible and had reprinted a 43-page extract from the

Evangelium. In the same year a humble clerk in a Pennsylvania town wrote the author to ask for an English edition, to be circulated among the miners and farmers of his neighborhood. Although there was a rapid decline in the workers' organizations of Switzerland after Weitling's expulsion and a reversion to the "medieval slumber" or to the beer hall conviviality of earlier days, Weitling's friends reported that the libraries of their once active societies still contained some of the old radical literature. "People still inquire about you," wrote a friend from Zurich in May, 1854, and "many an *Evangelium* still finds its way from house to house, and from hut to hut." "Be comforted, old man, you did not sit in the Zurich jail in vain. . . ." "Do not forget your friends in Europe, for they have not forgotten you. Send us several numbers of your *Republik der Arbeiter*. . . ." [4] To the end of the 1880's, long after the communist movement had forgotten its erstwhile leader and Weitling had died in the United States in poverty and oblivion, some of his publications still were banned by the Austrian police.

At the time of Weitling's arrest, Switzerland, and Zurich in particular, was in a turmoil over communism, the Young Germany movement, atheism, and other radical doctrines which refugees from all over Europe had brought with them to their new asylum among the Alps. Radicals have never been noted for their unanimity of opinion or for their ability to co-operate, and there was much friction and strife among the Swiss refugees. They not only intrigued against each other, but occasionally reported their rivals to the police. The secret societies were weakened by factional controversies, dissolutions, and expulsions based on trials to determine the orthodoxy of the members and their complete allegiance to the official doctrine. Such factional strife became an issue in the domestic politics of some of the Swiss cantons, and there is evidence to show that the trial of the author of the *Evangelium* was used by Bluntschli and other conservatives in Zurich to embarrass their political opponents, and particularly to break the

[4] See *Rep. d. Arb.*, June 24, 1854; also July 26, 1851, and January 7, 1854.

power of Fröbel, who had shielded some communist extremists. There also is evidence that the pietists and orthodox churchmen of Zurich welcomed the trial as an opportunity to attack German philosophical writers as a whole.[5] On the other hand, the methods used by the police, arresting Weitling in the dead of night and rifling his personal papers, aroused liberal groups in Zurich who had no special reason to champion communism.

Weitling was charged by the prosecution with inciting to riot, with advocating attacks on property, with blasphemy, and with being a public nuisance generally. The trial was made the occasion for a thorough airing of the radical communist movement, and Johann Caspar Bluntschli, with several associates, was commissioned to make a full report on the activities of Weitling and his followers. The extensive document produced by the commission and based largely on an analysis of the publications and private papers of the prisoner remains the most important source for the trial. As an official document it could be legally circulated, and communists welcomed this advertisement for their cause.[6] Moses Hess publicly thanked Bluntschli for the report, and the Prussian minister in Paris believed that it had helped to recruit 300 new members for the communist movement.[7]

The trial was conducted in an atmosphere of great tension. While Weitling was in jail some of his colleagues, such as Seiler, published pamphlets in his defense; anonymous letters were addressed to the court from Mainz and Cologne threatening a march on Zurich and bloody revenge if the prisoner should be sentenced. The words "liberty and equality" suddenly appeared on the walls of buildings, where they were inscribed during the night by persons who escaped the vigilance of the police.

In presenting the case the prosecution reviewed the history of

[5] See Paul Nerrlich (ed.), *Arnold Ruge's Briefwechsel und Tagebuchblätter aus den Jahren 1825–1880* (Berlin, 1886), I, 315.

[6] See also Johann Caspar Bluntschli, *Denkwürdiges aus meinem Leben* (Nördlingen, 1884), I, 342–45; and Friedrich Vogel (ed.), *Memorabilia Tigurina* (Zurich, 1853), 273–76.

[7] Zlocisti, *Moses Hess*, 123.

the assault on property rights since the days of Babeuf; analyzed Weitling's theories as revealed in the *Garantieen*, the *Hülferuf* and the *Junge Generation;* quoted from the writings of associates, such as Becker; read into the record the correspondence which the prisoner had carried on with confreres in France, Germany, and Switzerland; traced the history of workers' societies and co-operatives in Switzerland and elsewhere and the role of the accused in their establishment and development; and tried to prove that the movement had many international ramifications and a special technique for infecting all literature with the poison of communism. Julius Fröbel, a political foe of Bluntschli, was portrayed as a communist sympathizer, although he had strongly advised Weitling against coming to Zurich; and the prosecution tried also to implicate Herwegh, Follen, Gustav Siegfried of Zofingen, and Swiss newspapers which occasionally carried radical articles. The books found in Weitling's room when he was arrested hardly proved very incriminating. Besides his own *Garantieen*, they included an English dictionary (Karl Fröbel had been giving him English lessons), a copy of Strauss's *Life of Jesus*, a work by Adam Smith on economics, and a commentary on Plato.

Bluntschli's report undertook to convince the court that Weitling's brand of communism meant revolution, guerrilla warfare, and social chaos. The learned Swiss doctor made the most of the prisoner's unfortunate earlier references to the "thieving proletariat" and quoted a damaging letter from Seiler, in which he expressed a desire to "set all Europe in flames." The letter contained the lines, "Up to now you have shot only with vapor, we want to load with bullets." [8] The commission of experts closed their review with the recommendations that Weitling be expelled from the country; that new arrivals be scrutinized more carefully there-

[8] As evidence of the intensity of feeling, see also a poem included in a letter to Weitling, referring to a beggar who has just been run down in the streets:

> Der Peter will sich fliehend schützen,
> Er stürzt—sein letzter Ruf ist Brod!
> Ich seh sein Hirn aufs Pflaster sprützen,
> Gott Lob—der Vagabund ist tod!

after and watched more closely by the police; and that a special commission be created to study the problem of the poor. Better educational facilities should be provided, and better instruction in the meaning of religion and the comforts it can provide for the unfortunate and the underprivileged.

The prisoner at the bar was defended by a Zurich attorney named Rüttimann. "Staatsanwalt" Huber, a Liberal, had declined to take the case, "for health reasons." The chief strategy of the defense was to attempt to prove that Weitling's work lay wholly in the realm of theory, and that no evidence had been introduced to prove a conspiracy against the state. When the prisoner took the stand, he reviewed the main events of his life. Weitling referred to his lowly origin, reported that his stepfather had died ten years ago and that he had received his last letter from his mother a year or two ago. He believed that she was living in Magdeburg on poor relief. As far as his own activities were concerned, Weitling solemnly affirmed that his sole purpose had been to improve the social order by oral propaganda, not by force.[9]

On September 16, 1843, Weitling was found guilty by the criminal court of Zurich. Two days later his case was appealed, and final sentence was not passed until November 23, 1843, after the prisoner had been held in jail for several months. On the occasion of his final appearance in the court of appeals, the prisoner made a dramatic plea for acquittal. His attorney and some of his friends had tried to dissuade him from addressing the court, and he was deeply hurt when he learned that they regarded his performance as "mere vanity." Weitling's remarks were reported promptly to Vienna as an attempt "to encourage and give an example to his followers in and out of Switzerland, rather than to prove his own innocence." [10]

The prisoner at the bar confined his remarks to an attempt to refute the charge of blasphemy. He denied all intention to undermine the religious foundations of the state, or to rob the people

[9] Barnikol, *Weitling der Gefangene,* 137–45.
[10] Brügel, *Österreichische Sozialdemokratie,* I, 33–36.

of the faith which sustained them. He quoted again from the Bible to prove that his system was entirely compatible with the fundamental tenets of Christianity. He reviewed the history of religious liberalism, with a shrewd reference to the reformer Zwingli, of whom Zurich was particularly proud, and contended that since the Reformation it had been illogical to regard differences in interpretation of the Bible as synonymous with hostility to religion, which he defined as "a spiritual possession, an inexhaustible treasure in heaven," not subject to "compulsion."

Thereafter the speaker turned to a discussion of the social reformation, for he realized that he really was being tried for communism. He tried to show that in the charges filed against him property and religion had been combined improperly. With many a reference to Luther and the Peasants' War, to Voltaire and Rousseau, and to Calvin, who had Servetus burned at the stake, he maintained that one could attack the evils of the system of private property without necessarily becoming the enemy of religion. He cited the New Testament as proof that Christianity itself had repudiated usury and private property, and that the first Christians had lived in communal harmony and happiness. His views about law, courts, crime and punishment were elucidated, and the judiciary was accused of blindly ignoring the causes and conditions which made men criminals, and of being unwilling to treat the unfortunate offenders as socially diseased. He did not retreat from the views expressed in the *Evangelium* about the life and nature of Jesus, and he frankly admitted that one purpose in writing the book was to expose the supernaturalism and superstition that had gathered around the legend of this "prophet of freedom and love," who had died before his work was finished and whose mission must be carried forward by those who came after him. In short, communism, defined as "not a faith but a universal science," must carry Christ's message to full fruition and, to achieve that end, must turn to the Bible as one of its most effective instruments.

Weitling was in a highly emotional state when he appeared the last time before the court. He was not unmindful of his opportunity to play a dramatic role, and he closed his address with such sentences as "I have celebrated my resurrection, now you hold the last judgment," and "may the Holy Spirit enlighten you and grant me a mild sentence." He was disappointed that the crowd that filled the courtroom did not overflow into the streets outside. Already his mind was full of weird and fantastic notions about loyal followers who would break into the courtroom or the jail and rescue the new Messiah and martyr of the working class. He wept as he was led back to jail and discovered that no rescuers were at hand. "Happy the unfortunate," he reflected, "who can find some comfort in the most terrible moments of his life, from the faithfulness of a dog, the love of a mother, or faith in God." The court exonerated the defendant on the charge of seeking to destroy religion and on practically all other counts, save the one that he and his movement constituted a public nuisance. For that offense he was given a ten-month jail sentence, the four months already spent in confinement to be credited to his account. The sentence also stipulated a five-year exile from Switzerland.

The *Communist Chronicle* of London promptly printed the appropriate note of sympathy. "Our dear brother, Weitling . . . is now a martyr. But what of that? The blood of the martyrs is the seed of the church. The bruised geranium leaf smelleth more sweetly. . . . Meanwhile, although not free in person, the thoughts of Weitling are commingling with ours, and flying abroad like down-winged seeds over our common earth of green and gold." [11] "Since the French Revolution of 1792, we enumerate three illustrious communist martyrs," the article continued, "Babeuf of France, Joshua Jacob of Ireland, and Wilhelm Weitling of Germany. . . . Blessings upon them, as far as they should be blest." Such notoriety and expressions of sympathy provided little comfort, however, for a prisoner who was deprived of newspapers and had no way to follow the course of events while in jail. This British tribute to his martyrdom did not come to his at-

[11] London *Communist Chronicle,* I, No. 11, p. 121.

tention until well after the days of trial were over, but he preserved the files of the *Communist Chronicle* among his papers in America.

Weitling had achieved the martyrdom to which he had alluded frequently in his writings. But now that it had come it almost broke his spirit. He proved to be a difficult and unruly prisoner, and he was disciplined several times. His long confinement and his complete inability to adjust to jail conditions made him so neurotic that he never entirely recovered. A morbid concern with his role as the "second Messiah" and a certain megalomania, already apparent in some of his earlier writings, now developed into a serious persecution complex.

Some years later, a trunk was discovered in Hamburg which contained a diary covering the period spent in the Zurich jail. Unearthed in the archives of Hamburg in 1926, and ably edited by Professor Ernst Barnikol, the manuscript was published in Kiel in 1929, under the title, *Gerechtigkeit: ein studium in 500 tagen. Bilder der wirklichkeit und betrachtungen des gefangenen.* Barmby, the London communist, had indicated as early as 1844 that Weitling was at work on "a lengthy history of his imprisonment." The author himself reported, after his arrival in the United States, that some of his papers had been confiscated in Hamburg in 1849 when the police invaded the home of a paper hanger with whom Weitling had stayed, and carried off a trunk full of papers. An inventory of the contents revealed, among other things, material dealing with other publications like the *Garantieen*, and the *Urwähler*, which Weitling had started in Berlin during the revolution; his *Notruf an die Männer der Arbeit und Sorge*, issued in New York in 1848; books and papers dealing with the organization of the League of Liberation; a few volumes on philosophy and grammar in French, German, and English; a hundred copies of A. Scherzer's *Musestunden und Schweisstropfen* (Paris, 1847); and nine writing pads which comprised the manuscript for his treatise on *Gerechtigkeit* (Justice).

As the result of a brilliant piece of textual criticism and analysis, Professor Barnikol concluded that the manuscript, based on the

348 days which Weitling had spent in prison (from June 8, 1843, to May 21, 1844), was written in London during the author's first brief sojourn there, probably after August, 1844, and before February, 1846. It was intended to be a piece of accurate reporting of the author's prison experiences, reconstructed from a rather remarkable memory, in the form of day by day entries. Weitling labeled his account "pictures of reality," and the editor of *Gerechtigkeit* believes that he was successful to a remarkable degree in reconstructing accurately the story of his imprisonment in Zurich. It is significant that he left in the manuscript passages which might well have been deleted because they reflected unfavorably upon the author, and that letters which he could not have seen for at least a year were quoted with remarkable accuracy.[12]

Whatever its origin, the *Gerechtigkeit* is a most important source for the months which its author spent in prison. The manuscript reveals that Weitling studied English from a grammar sent to the jail by a friend, and that in about two months he was able to read the language fairly well. One reason for his studiousness was the fact that he was preparing to migrate upon his release either to England or to the United States. The *Gerechtigkeit* indicates that he spent much time going through the Bible again with a fine-tooth comb, and that he discovered new pearls of wisdom. A considerable portion of the manuscript deals with a recapitulation of the main events of his life to the time of his arrival in Zurich. But its most valuable features are the character analysis of the author which it provides and its alarming revelations of a psychological deterioration so serious that it brought Weitling to the brink of insanity.

Throughout his life, Weitling never had a real sense of security. The forces that make for security in the lives of most people had passed him by from the earliest years of his childhood. An illegitimate son and an emigree from his fatherland, he easily became suspicious of others and was always on the watch for intrigues against him. Perhaps it was equally natural under such circum-

[12] Barnikol, *Weitling der Gefangene, passim.*

stances to take flight from misery and deprivation into the world of introspection, and to seek refuge in an imaginary paradise supported by a God whose name he hardly ventured to pronounce. These prison recollections reveal an egocentric, persecuted mind, ready to draw strange analogies between the Passion of Christ and the martyrdom of the prophet of communism. They bring to a focus the puzzling contradictions in Weitling's character. His sensitive nature broke under solitary confinement in a dark and narrow cell. He became unruly and irritating and quibbled often with his jailers. Alone with his thoughts and with nothing else to occupy him, he began to reveal symptoms of paranoia. He was depressed because his arrest made so little impression on the movement which he led, and called forth no popular demonstrations for his release. He began to identify himself with earlier martyrs, such as Thomas Münzer. He raged against the prevailing system of justice and predicted a day when, "of an evening," workers and peasants would settle their disputes over a pipe of tobacco without lawyers or courts.

Weitling became so depressed that he was tortured with thoughts of suicide and the fear of insanity. He accused his jailers of depriving him of letters which he had carried for a dozen years, containing strands of the hair of his mother and grandmother, though the facts indicate that the letters were returned by the prison officials and that he himself had taken out the hair and hidden it in his clothes. The prisoner wrote to the authorities of Zurich to protest against his treatment and charged that he had been stripped and searched no less than eight times; that he had been four times confined in a dark cell for periods ranging from eighteen to forty-eight hours, and that he was being watched through a peephole by an Austrian spy, a lawyer from Vienna, who was quartered in a neighboring cell.

There followed tales of mysterious rappings at night on the walls of his dark cold cell, of hunger and despair, of the terrors of the night with its weird sounds, and of the thoughts of the prisoner about death and a great task still unfinished. As Weitling became increasingly psychopathic, he became convinced that there was a plan in the making to murder him. The doctor who gave him a powder in response to his plea for help was suspected of trying to feed him arsenic. When the jailer stripped him of his shirt, the prisoner concluded that it would be used to strangle him, and the incident reported as a suicide. He counted his pulse dozens of times a day and developed rapidly into a hypochondriac. He pushed a table in front of the cell door at night for protection, and his tortured mind fluctuated sharply between the deepest depression and the most ecstatic expectations.

Occasionally, the prisoner was given a little tailoring, ironing, and copying to do to break the unbearable monotony of his confinement. Sometimes he got a letter from a friend, who guardedly suggested that he was not forgotten and enclosed a few francs to buy extra food or wine. Siegfried, a manufacturer of Zofingen who was interested in his theories, sent him a shirt. Several times the prisoner conversed with the pastor assigned to the jail; he attended church services, wearing a red cap made out of a handkerchief, and heard the minister discourse on those who languish in jail for truth's sake. A letter, allegedly from his mother, was rejected as a forgery. Weitling frequently complained of chest pains, and sometimes became hysterical. His mind played with wild schemes for a jail delivery by his friends; he began to look for rocket signals and was alternately buoyed up by the hope of freedom and depressed by the thought that relief would come too late, or that he himself might prove inadequate to exercise the leadership which his martyrdom had thrust upon him. When Fröbel wrote to inquire when he would be released and added that "50 francs are here for you," Weitling immediately concluded this meant that fifty men were waiting outside to rescue him.

More and more, the tortured, introspective prisoner assumed the role of a Messiah. "A magic fire" burned in his breast: he would revive Christianity for the regeneration of mankind. As the communist Messiah, had he not carried "his cross" to Zurich, the area of greatest danger, as Jesus had ridden into Jerusalem to make his last sacrifice? Communism became for him a substitute religion as Weitling enacted the double role of one persecuted by the world, torn by doubt about the progress of his own cause, and at the same time transported into a golden dream world of the future. "Danger and pain have become a necessity for me," he wrote. "I have found a new criterion of truth which must not be lost. . . . You do not dare to let me, a tailor, address the people for even a quarter of an hour, lest your power crash into ruin." One day he was the Messiah, confident of his role as deliverer and sustained by his faith; the next day he was ready to give up in despair, certain that he was losing his mind and utterly crushed by the unbearable loneliness that overcame him because he believed that he was completely forgotten by "those outside." It was on such occasions that time weighed upon his unsettled spirits "like a hundred-weight."

Obviously, such manifestations of persecution and delusion did not make it easy for his jailers to deal with the prisoner in any rational way. There is no convincing evidence to prove that the authorities in Zurich deliberately planned to abuse their prisoner or to break his mind and body. He probably was treated no differently from scores of other prisoners in a time when penal reform had made little progress. Weitling received poor prison fare like all the other prisoners, but he also had his allotment of wine, which he frequently refused for fear that it contained poison. He had some visitors, and the number included Dr. Bluntschli, who found his conversation intelligible and clear, despite his hostility to the prisoner's false doctrines. Why Bluntschli came at all is not clear, but Weitling concluded it was because he really was interested in his theories. Karl Fröbel brought the prisoner a copy of Proudhon's *De la création de l'ordre dans l'humanité ou principes d'organisation politique*, which had just appeared in Paris.[13] The Zurich jailers seem to have been as considerate in their dealings with a troublesome, unco-operative, and overwrought prisoner as

[13] See Ernst Barnikol, *Klassifikation des Universums von Wilhelm Weitling* (Kiel, 1931).

could be expected under the circumstances. The prisoner not only was certain that he had a mission in life, but spent much of his time trying to outwit jailers, whose diabolical schemes seem to have been largely the product of the prisoner's own distorted imagination.

CHAPTER VI

A LONDON INTERLUDE

THE day of release from the real and imaginary terrors of the Zurich jail finally arrived, with Weitling in a state of tension and excitement approaching hysteria. Karl Fröbel, who had visited the prisoner on several occasions, called again to urge him to go to the canton of Aargau immediately upon his discharge, and to request a passport from the Prussian minister for England or America. Friends offered financial help, and were ready to pay the balance of the costs of the trial. Apparently Weitling seriously considered the suggestion to leave the Continent altogether, but in the end was unable to reach a decision. He was invited to join an emigration society founded by Andreas Dietsch, who was about to start overseas to establish his "Thousand Year Kingdom," but though Dietsch offered to take his fellow Utopian to the United States without cost, Weitling could not make up his mind to go.

According to the prisoner's own account, he was aroused at 2:45 A.M., May 21, 1844, and ordered to dress. Plans had been made to push the troublesome prisoner across the border into Germany. When he emerged from the jail escorted by police, Weitling expected the conspiracy for his liberation, of which he had dreamed so frequently, to go into action. So he called for help at the top of his lungs, shouting that he was about to be surrendered to the German police. When no rescuers appeared, he threw down his bundle and refused to go any farther. Apparently he was afraid either of another plot against his life or of deportation into Germany. In the scuffle which ensued, his coat was torn and he was roughly handled by the police, who finally led their unruly prisoner back to jail. There they tried to extract a promise that he would leave quietly, but the terror-stricken and disillusioned communist refused to make any commitments. Thereupon he was tied and shackled, gagged, and thrown into a carriage headed for Schaffhausen. En route Weitling kicked out the windows of the carriage. The party reached its destination about noon. Later he recalled that it was a market day and asserted that his rescuers had arrived in Zurich fourteen hours too late. Still later he modified his account by fixing the interval at eight hours.

Weitling was surrendered to the German police at a little frontier town in Baden, "seven hours" from Tuttlingen. From there he was pushed on by the police of Baden, via Stuttgart, until he could be delivered to the Prussians. Recounting his experiences in later years he described how he was passed from one jail to another; the kind of food he received, in comparison with conditions in Zurich; the kind treatment he received in Württemberg, and the bad treatment in Bavaria. In Würzburg he watched the Corpus Christi day procession, and in Erfurt he spent six days in the jail. After crossing the boundaries of several of the little German states, he finally was discharged from the custody of gendarmes and permitted to proceed to Magdeburg.

The police of his native city were not eager to welcome their new guest, and Weitling claimed that they tampered with his mail, tried to keep him away from the taverns where workmen assembled, and forbade him to visit his mother. Nevertheless, he saw his mother in Beynedorf, about two and a half hours' walk from Magdeburg, where she was keeping house for a schoolmaster. The reunion of mother and son after an interval of at least fourteen years was dramatically described in the *Gerechtigkeit.* The mother, now married and known as Frau Bern, did not recognize her son immediately; then both were dissolved in tears. Weitling reported regularly to the police, as was expected of transients, and was permitted to remain in Magdeburg, on condition that he stay away from the hostels of the journeymen and not leave the city without permission from the authorities.

For a month or six weeks, Weitling remained in his boyhood home. Friends in Magdeburg, Hamburg, and elsewhere sent him small amounts of money, and he borrowed a little more from a local bookdealer. It was at this time that he was rejected formally as unfit for military service, an obligation which he had managed to dodge for ten years by means of a false passport. Once, as a vagabond, he was transported across the border into Brunswick, only to be returned promptly to the police of Magdeburg. Prussia tried in vain to get him to surrender his citizenship, and when he finally was permitted to leave Magdeburg he did so without having renounced his Prussian allegiance. Fröbel advised him to stay in Germany, claim his legal rights as a Prussian citizen, win friends who could help him financially, and abandon the role of the lone martyr which he had assumed in Switzerland.[1] But Weitling had other plans. Promising to provide him with funds and a steamship ticket for England or the United States, the police finally got rid of their troublesome fellow townsman. Weitling proceeded by boat down the Elbe to Hamburg. He claimed that he was escorted to the dock by a large number of citizens, but this seems extremely doubtful, unless the crowd simply wanted to witness the departure of one whose presence had become extremely embarrassing to the authorities.

Weitling arrived in Hamburg on August 18, 1844, and departed on the steamer *Neptun* five days later. In this short period of less than a week, he lived at the *Gasthof zur Stadt Wilster* under police surveillance but otherwise unmolested. Two events made the brief stay in Hamburg of some importance. One was an unexpected meeting with the poet Heine; the other was the publication of a small collection of poems.

The meeting with Heine occurred in the bookstore of Julius Campe, owner of Hoffmann und Campe, who were publishers for a number of the Young Germany group, including Heine and

[1] Barnikol, *Weitling der Gefangene*, 228–30.

Börne. Heine referred to his encounter with Weitling in a letter to Marx, written on September 21, 1844. According to Heine's version of the incident, the tailor introduced himself as a "colleague" who championed "the same doctrines of revolution and atheism" as the poet. During the conversation Weitling remained seated, tailor-fashion, on a bench. He did not remove his cap and he held his right leg in one hand, pulling it up near his chin, and rubbing it constantly, presumably to stop the itch caused by his prison chains.

Whatever his earlier radical sympathies may have been, Heine by this time hated communism as "an artist, poet and learned man," and believed it would destroy the very flower of civilization. Essentially Heine was a literary snob, and by no stretch of the imagination can he be described as a democrat. He always felt uncomfortable among "the people, these poor kings in rags," and now he was both embarrassed and insulted to have a tailor, posing as a social philosopher, refer to him as a "colleague" and show such "complete lack of respect." Yet despite his fury at the moment because of this "repulsive familiarity," when Heine recalled his encounter with the "forgotten leader" of the men of toil some years later, he referred to him as a "man of talent," and characterized his *Garantieen* as "the catechism of the German communists," whom he regarded as "cohorts of destruction," "sappers whose axes threatened the whole social edifice, . . . in whose methods there is madness." When the poet's strictures were brought to Weitling's attention several years later, he professed to be genuinely amused, though he considered Heine's satire "somewhat ill-mannered" and commented sharply on "the aristocratic vanity of the poet." [2]

The same publisher in whose office the two men had met published Weitling's *Kerkerpoesien*, a little 72-page volume of jail poems. In a preface, the author explained that they were written

[2] See *Rep. d. Arb.*, November 4, 1854; and Ernst Elster (ed.), *Heinrich Heine's Sämmtliche Werke* (Leipzig), VI, 42–45. Heine's letter of September 21, 1844, to Marx was reprinted in the *Berliner Zeitung*, July 12, 1947, a paper published in the Russian zone of occupation.

while he was a prisoner, partly to comfort him in his physical and mental torment and partly to while away the hours spent in a solitary cell. "It was not dislike for my craft, nor ambition, nor personal interest that induced me to try to be a writer," the craftsman commented apologetically. "I found an appalling gap in literature . . . and went to work because I realized no other German writer would undertake to fill it." Having turned on several occasions from needle and shears to the pen, he explained that he did not write for a living, but lived to write so that he might help society along its slow road to progress. He admitted, however, that he had sold the collection of poems for a little necessary cash, adding drily, "Even the communist who is working to abolish money, cries for it."

Weitling's poems are not great poetry, and they would lose all vitality if an effort were made to translate them. They are somewhat in the style of Friedrich von Schiller, whose poems the author frequently quoted, and of whose "Bürgschaft" he was especially fond. They give a vivid, if exaggerated and overdramatized, picture of the mental and physical sufferings which a sensitive soul experiences in prison. Although they made little impression either in literary circles or among the workers, their author liked his work, carried copies with him to the United States, and from time to time made marginal corrections and additions in his personal copy. Some were published in the Paris *Vorwärts*, which also printed Heine's "Die armen Weber" and "Wintermärchen," but the poems were read by comparatively few people. Nevertheless, the police of Breslau seized the first four copies to reach that city, and Magdeburg forbade their sale as dangerous and incendiary literature.[3]

The following titles suggest the direct bearing which these poems have on their author's prison experiences: "Conscience," "Temptation," "The Betrayer," "To My Judge," "To My Prosecutor," "Hope," and "The Monster," the last referring to a spy planted in an adjoining cell. Several poems, though influenced by

[3] *Marx-Engels Archiv*, II (1927), 606.

the writer's reflections while in jail, were simple lyrics that conceivably might have been written at any time and under very different circumstances. "The Little Bird," "The Sun," "The Moon," and "The Birthday" fall into this group. Another poem was an allegory, based upon the relative advantages enjoyed by animals in their animal kingdom, and "Priests" was a poem of the familiar sort written by rationalists when they attack priests and clericalism.

"Forty-eight Hours in the Dark" was a horrible description of the fantasies and illusions that run through a prisoner's mind as he suffers from hunger, anxiously counts his pulse, notes the rush of blood to his head, hears the coughing of the sick in neighboring cells, and reviews the horrors of solitary confinement:

> Da steh' ich wieder in dem finstern Loch
> Und stosse an die unsichtbaren Wände,
> Bald mit der Nase, bald mit Fuss und Hände!
> Gott Lob! Nun kenn' ich diese Strafen doch!

"Night" pictured the loneliness of a cell when darkness descends and the prisoner counts the hours till dawn. He hears the jailer on his rounds, rattling his keys:

> Denn lichter sprudelt die Gedankenquelle
> In stiller Einsamkeit und finst'rer Nacht.

"Morning" described the first faint beams of light that hail the day, and ended with the lines,

> Schöner Morgen, mir ein schöner Traum!
> Schöner Abend, mir ein süsses Hoffen,

as the prisoner dreamed of the day that would bring his release from prison cells.

"Wounds and Balsam" was published with a footnote which explained Weitling's sufferings in detail, his despair because his correspondence with friends had been intercepted, and the disciplining which he expected as a result of violating prison rules.

The author also expressed the fear that the great new "system for the testing of truth" which he had discovered (perhaps his universal language) might be lost to the world. Every stanza of the poem revealed the increasingly neurotic state of the prisoner.

The poems entitled "The Christmas Tree" and "Do Not Despair," on the other hand, revealed a new optimism about the prisoner's fate, referred to a mission still to be performed, and appealed to God for strength and for the sanctification of the New Messiah through suffering. Two selections will suffice to illustrate this characteristic theme. In the poem "The Night," written in January, 1844, the last stanza contained these lines:

> Ich will durch Kerkernacht, durch Dunkelheit und Tod,
> Durch alle finst're Schattenbilder dringen,
> Ein kühner Bräutigam, die stolze Braut erringen,
> Hurrah! Du meiner Freiheit Morgenrot.

Finally, in "Exaltation," written toward the end of December, 1843, the prisoner definitely turned to God in prayer, and appealed for protection against the forces that threatened to engulf him and for strength to bear his cross:

> So hilf mir nun, O Gott, den Kampf bestehen!
> Der Wahrheit Schätze soll ich dir bewahren,
> Die lässt du nicht versinken in Gefahren,
> In Kerkersnacht und Tod nicht untergehen!—
> Ringt in Gethsemane ein Herz sich wund,
> So stärkt dein Engel es, macht es gesund,
> Und will ans Kreuz man einen Märt'rer schlagen,
> So kommt ein Simon, es zum Berg zu tragen.

Increasingly conscious of the great truth he had to proclaim, the excited prisoner in another poem cried out in morbid stanzas, with frequent references to his mother,

> Ruf mich noch nicht! O Mutter, lass mich hier,
> Dies Feuer darf im Kerker nicht verlodern,

Der Spiegel nicht an meiner Leiche modern,
Der heil'ge Geist der Wahrheit sagt es mir.

Weitling departed by boat for England in the summer of 1844. His heart must have beat faster as his ship approached the shores of the island kingdom, for he was familiar with the main events in the history of the British working class and he had been greatly interested in the English Industrial Revolution. In May, 1842, the lead article in his *Junge Generation* had dealt with "Progress in the Social Systems in England." It carried a tribute to Robert Owen, "father of English Communists," and pointed with pride to England's sixty-five "communist associations," each of which had a "Social Hall" where their members met each Sunday evening in a spirit of equality and brotherly love, to sing songs and to discourse on communism and the labor movement. Other issues of Weitling's paper printed extracts from letters and reports from the German Democratic Society of London, bearing the signatures of old associates like Schapper, Bauer, and Moll and describing the proceedings of the London group as a model to be followed by workers in other countries. At the same time there were occasional caustic references to the class system in English society, where hunting dogs got more meat than workers and children toiled nineteen hours a day in the factories.

Weitling's name, as already suggested, was known in England before he arrived. Goodwyn Barmby, founder of the Universal Communitarian Society, was the editor of a paper published in London, first as the *Promethean* and then as the *Communist Chronicle*. Bronson Alcott was one of his American correspondents, and Ralph Waldo Emerson the contributor of an essay on communism and individualism. In that strange monthly the name of the German communist had appeared rather frequently. A letter from Lausanne, published in the *Communist Chronicle*, reported the progress of workers' libraries in Switzerland and called attention to Weitling's *Garantieen*; other issues printed extracts from the "Select Scriptures" of the philosophical tailor, recounted the story of his arrest and prosecution, and recommended his three major works as the creation of an "intelligent, clear and contemplative theorician." [4]

Weitling's arrival in London near the end of August was celebrated by a "festive welcome" attended by workers representing several national groups. Addresses were made by the leader of the French section, by Karl Schapper for the Germans, and by the English publisher of the *New Moral World*. The guest of honor responded with an optimistic account of the spread of communism in Germany, stressed the international character of the movement, and predicted its ultimate success from Berlin to Vienna, from Cologne to Königsberg, and from Prague to Langenbielau.

Barmby called promptly on his German co-worker in the vineyard of communism. He reported that he was an impressive leader, of "middling stature, clear full eyes, broad forehead and expressive features," vigorous and effective in speech, but with a still "defective" knowledge of English. Although Weitling already had begun to write his prison memoirs, he expressed a readiness to translate English articles for the German communist press. Shortly thereafter he was invited to visit Joshua Jacob and Abigail Beale in Ireland. To the invitation, which was couched in strange religious jargon, the German leader replied in a letter "slightly anglicised in spelling" by his new friend Barmby, expressing the writer's sympathy and that of all foreign communists for the principles advocated by the Beales, commending them for their tolerance of various religious faiths, but declining the invitation to visit the Emerald Isle.[5]

[4] *Promethean,* March, 1842, p. 54; *Communist Chronicle,* I, No. 5, p. 80; No. 13, p. 144; No. 14, p. 149; also *Young Germany, An Account of the Rise, Progress and Present Position of German Communism* (London, 1844), *passim.*

[5] Extracts from Weitling's letter indicate his progress in English composition and his peculiarities of style. He wrote, in part, "I am to say you, that I partake the same opinions, belonging to the aim of the principles. . . . I am delighted to hear that you are not a community sterile, but also are expanding your principles by writing and printings. I was heartily pleased to hear from your letter, that you had invited brother Barmby to bring me over to Ireland, for to see you. Take hereby the expression of my sympathy and therefore the sympathies of all for-

Weitling was absorbed quickly into the life of London's West End. He realized a few pounds from the sale of some of his earlier writings and friends in France and Switzerland sent him small amounts from time to time derived from the sale of the *Garantieen*. Once they raised a collection of 500 francs for him. Small amounts occasionally came from sympathizers in Germany also, such as Georg Schirges, editor of Gutzkow's *Telegraphen* in Hamburg.[6] To supplement these uncertain sources of revenue, Weitling worked a little at his trade and pressed women's straw hats on a machine which he developed.[7] He did not go to the Prussian consulate to collect the passage money for America which had been promised, and he rejected a proposal to issue a journal. English socialists took notice of his presence but did little to help him meet his living expenses.

Weitling himself was so absorbed in an invention for a lathe, in the preparation of the manuscript for the *Gerechtigkeit*, and in the outline for a universal language, that he had little time for other things. Strangely enough, though he remained in London for nearly a year and a half, he did not seize that opportunity to study the progress of industrialism in England or to become identified with the Chartist movement. Instead, having been only moderately successful with his plans to revolutionize society, he turned to attempts to revolutionize science by working on inventions and a world language.

According to the not too reliable reports which Prussian agents sent regularly to Berlin, Weitling spent many evenings in a German coffeehouse on Leicester Square and lived better than would be expected from a man of so little visible means of support. Occasionally he attended gatherings of German and French com-

---

eign Communists for it. I am sorry to be obliged to refuse your request. Perhaps in the next spring it will be, if the circumstances permit it. I will close, fearing you might not seize the understanding of this forcign style. . . ." Signed—"Your Brother, W. Weitling, Oct. 14, 1844, Bateman's Building, Soho, London." (Letter in possession of Terijon Weitling.)

[6] *Marx-Engels Archiv*, II (1927), 593.

[7] Barnikol, *Weitling der Gefangene*, 209–33.

munists at the Red Lion, but in his lectures to the assembled workmen he spoke more often of the progress of his mechanical inventions than of social revolution. Most of the time he sat peacefully among his comrades, smoking a pipe, drinking his beer, and joining in the singing of French and German songs. On one occasion he attended a public debate between a minister of the gospel and a woman who was an avowed atheist, and concluded that the lady had failed in her effort to explain all creation by the simple term "nature."

On September 22, 1845, Weitling spoke at a great "Festival of the Nations" commemorating the birth of the French Republic in 1792. The program consisted of instrumental music, choral singing in many tongues, and formal addresses. Representatives of the German, French, Italian, Polish, and Swiss colonies in London were present, plus a Hungarian and a Turk; and the speaking was done in English, French, and German. Thomas Cooper, a leader of the Chartists, presided, and the editor of the Chartist *Northern Star* spoke for the British. Dr. Berrier-Fontaine, a disciple of Cabet, spoke for the French and Weitling for the Germans. Internationalism was the theme which characterized all these addresses. Each speaker denounced national rivalries and pledged, as part of a Young Europe movement, to work for the extermination of tyranny everywhere. Weitling was received warmly as the martyr from the Continent. He pleaded for brotherhood, denounced militarism, and maintained that if soldiers in opposing armies could only be given an opportunity to speak to each other across the battle line before the firing began, wars would turn into meetings of friends and brothers. No less a person than Friedrich Engels commented, in the *Rheinische Jahrbücher*, on the international character of this fraternal demonstration.[8]

Not much more is known about Weitling's London sojourn except for his part in the lively debates in the London society of communists, to be noted presently. He took credit for increasing

[8] Buddensieg, *Kultur des deutschen Proletariats*, 21; Adler, *Erste sozialpolitische Arbeiterbewegung in Deutschland*, 80–82.

the membership of that society from 70 to 130 in ten months, and for the discussion meetings held twice a week. While in London he became acquainted with a certain Newton, who planned to acquire an ironworks in Liverpool and to operate it as a co-operative. Weitling later reported having attended a meeting of workers in London addressed by Charles Kingsley, in which the speaker was said to have linked Christianity with the working-class gospel.

The most significant development during Weitling's London interlude, however, was his controversy with the leaders of the *Deutscher Bildungsverein*, sometimes referred to as the *Londoner Bildungsverein*, which Karl Schapper had founded in London in 1840 after his expulsion from France. The club, led at one time by Marx and Engels, is important in the history of the international labor movement. It survived to the time of World War I. Moll was its president, Schapper acted as secretary, and Heinrich Bauer of Franconia was another prominent member. One night each week the members talked politics, on another they practiced chorus singing, and still other evenings were reserved for lectures on a wide variety of subjects. Many of the members had been associates of Weitling in the League of the Just in Paris.[9] Toward the close of the 1840's, the membership was estimated between four and five hundred, and included a number of non-Germans. In addition to its activities in the field of propaganda, the society provided sick benefits, owned a co-operative hall where food and drinks were served and tobacco could be bought for a penny a package, and made its large piano available for musical entertainment. Schapper, a giant in stature, acted as the genial host of the club.

It did not take long to discover that Weitling and Schapper and some of the other German communists in the club were traveling along different roads. Schapper's followers, perhaps under the influence of Chartism, were becoming more practical both in theory and tactics. Weitling, fresh from his martyrdom in Switzerland

[9] As late as 1859, a follower of Weitling, A. Scherzer, was president of the club. See F. P. Schiller, "Friedrich Engels und die Schiller-Anstalt in Manchester," *Marx-Engels Archiv,* II (1927), 483–84.

and still deeply affected by his prison experiences, clung stubbornly to his role as a prophet and proclaimed a religious, sentimental, primitive-Christian brand of communism. Whereas Schapper's group became increasingly opportunistic, and was content to accept a slow and gradual evolution, Weitling continued to advocate revolution to change the whole structure of society in one brief cataclysmic uprising against property and the inequalities of the existing order.

The discussions sponsored by the society resulted in a sharp clash between the newly arrived leader of Continental communism and the group already established in London. Weitling refused to give ground. He emphasized the emotions and the primitive-Christian virtues as important factors in social reform, and insisted upon his plan to crush the old order by a temporary dictatorship of a well-organized revolutionary minority. Schapper took sharp issue with his former Paris colleague about religion, and Weitling resented all attacks on Christianity, especially by those who rejected faith and relied wholly on cold science.

Only Hermann Kriege, whom Weitling met in London and whose friendship was to prove important for his later career, sided with him in shouting "down with reason, if it means the suffocation of all feeling." Schapper favored the slower processes of education; Weitling maintained that the times already were rotten-ripe for change and he would wait no longer. "Revolutions," he argued, "come like a thunder storm, no one can foretell their effects." He insisted that enlightenment by peaceful means did not make for unity but that revolution, with its appeal to the heart for sympathy for suffering brothers, did! "Reason," he added, "will play a pitiful role . . . the greatest deeds will result from the power of emotion." "It is nonsense to preach enlightenment to the hungry." "The crown of thorns of the martyrs wins more hearts than all the laurel wreaths of poets and orators," whereas "the eternal propaganda for peaceful evolution merely stultifies men's courage and zeal" for reform. Weitling defended his position with all the eloquence he could muster and professed a readiness to accept the aid of all classes whenever the time should arrive for a temporary dictatorship to usher in the new society.

Another cause of friction between the Schapper-Bauer faction and Weitling was the latter's interest in emigration societies and model colonies. Schapper denounced such impractical and romantic proposals with the caustic reminder that his opponent had once proposed community of wives and the use of the "thieving proletariat" to bring about revolution. Again, only Kriege came to Weitling's defense. From major differences of this kind the dispute degenerated into discussions of minor matters. One was the question whether books or papers were the better form of propaganda. Weitling preferred books, and Bauer promptly reminded him that "Lycurgus and the first Christians had no books." Bauer opposed the creation of additional "systems" and preferred to stick strictly to oral propaganda. From such trivialities the debaters moved again to more profound issues, such as the question of individual liberty in a communist society and an analysis of Owen's "system," which Weitling declared the "best of all" and which Schapper rejected along with Cabet's *Icarie* and the *Garantieen*, on the ground that they established a "barracks state" utterly contrary to the nature of man.

Not much historical imagination is needed to sense the fire and heat with which these radicals and former members of the same persecuted league in Paris now debated their differences in the smoke-filled rooms of their London clubhouse. As was the custom in workers' clubs, a vote was taken at the end of each discussion and Weitling consistently lost by a heavy majority. He never reacted calmly to opposition, and now he became embittered and suspected intrigue and treachery. At one period he stayed away from the meetings of the society for nearly two months, though this may have been the time when he was serving incognito as an assistant editor of a paper in Trier, the *Trierische Zeitung*.[10] When he returned to resume the discussions he found that Schap-

[10] See *Marx-Engels Archiv*, II (1927), 594. There is much confusion about this stay in Trier which it has been impossible to unravel.

per, during his absence, had specifically attacked his pet proposals for a *Tauschbank* and *Kommerzstunden,* which he regarded as the very essence of his "system."

In January, 1846, the harassed champion of Utopian communism made his last speech in London. In it he recapitulated and rephrased his familiar criticism of settling issues by the democratic counting of noses, contrasted the relative advantages of republics and monarchies, and referred in passing to the accomplishments of Napoleon I toward unifying Europe. Two weeks later, the society voted to discontinue the discussion and to turn to the consideration of Friedrich Feuerbach's *Religion of the Future*, and of any scientific question which any member might like to introduce.

The vote clearly indicated a victory for Schapper, Bauer, and their group. In due time the Marxians won further control over the London group, and, in turn, Schapper, August Willich, and several others broke with Marxian orthodoxy after a number of factional fights in the 1850's. Weitling meantime had departed for Brussels, where his decisive conflict with Marx was about to take place.[11]

[11] On these factional battles in London, see Max Nettlau, "Londoner deutsche Kommunistische Diskussionen, 1845," in *Archiv für die Geschichte des Sozialismus und der Arbeiterbewegung* (Leipzig, 1922), X, 362–91; Carl Grünberg (ed.), *Die Londoner Kommunistische Zeitschrift und andere Urkunden aus den Jahren 1847/48* (Leipzig, 1921), *passim;* Gwenda David and Eric Mosbacker (trans.), Boris Nicolaievsky and Otto Maenchen-Helfen's *Karl Marx, Man and Fighter* (Philadelphia, 1936), *passim.*

Chapter VII

WEITLING AND MARX

The controversy in London between Weitling and Schapper foreshadowed the inevitable break with Marx in Brussels in 1846. Weitling was then far better known in communist circles than the young man who was destined to become a world figure as the oracle of modern scientific communism. As yet, Marx had been relatively unproductive and some of his best friends had accused him of laziness. Weitling, on the other hand, had published three major works in the field of Utopian communism, and had edited a journal for a brief period. His name was well known among the workers in Germany, Switzerland, France, and England.

Two years before their encounter in Brussels, Marx had referred to Weitling's *Garantieen* as superior in theory to the writings of Proudhon and as the "brilliant, literary debut of the German working class." "Where can the bourgeois, including their philosophers and literary leaders, point to a similar work?" he wrote in the Paris *Vorwärts* in comparing "the giant baby shoes of the proletariat" with "the pigmy, well-worn shoes of the bourgeoisie." Engels probably learned about Weitling from Gutzkow, who had seen copies of the *Hilferuf* and the *Junge Generation* in Paris. By the summer of 1842, Weitling's publications had penetrated the literary circles of Berlin, and Gutzkow reprinted an article from the *Junge Generation* in his own paper. We know that Engels read the *Garantieen* of the "social-democratic tailor," as he called him, and considered it worthy of translation into English for the British socialists, and that he referred to Weitling's organizing activities as "the first independent movement of the German proletariat." [1]

Weitling has been forgotten; Marx and Engels remain world figures. Yet the philosophical tailor also is entitled to his place in history. No proletarian author ever described the miseries of the poor more eloquently or contrasted the life of the rich and the poor more vividly. Weitling compared the growing threat of industry with "an iron bodice crushing the tender forms of children." He had initiated the workers of Germany into the propaganda for communism and in 1845, Engels commented excitedly on "the break-through of communist literature in Germany." In June, 1845, the Police Commissioner of Bregenz referred with alarm to the spread of communism in Switzerland and in the neighboring German states, and to its infiltration into the workers' organizations in Switzerland, France, England, Germany, and Holland. Friedrich Kapp, a "proletarian" and a "communist" who was then planning a colony in North America, and who later became one of the few Forty-eighters to return to Bismarck's Germany, wrote in 1845, "A new spirit is stirring among us in Westphalia. The reading society which I founded has sixty members . . . a local Jewish merchant, an excellent person, is reading aloud to the people at the inn from Friedrich Feuerbach's *Religion of the Future* and from Weitling's *Garantees and Harmony of Freedom* [sic]." In 1846, Weitling's books could be found in the library of the Communist Club of Berlin where they were read eagerly. Marx and Engels still regarded his program as "the only existing German communist system," [2] and a recent historian of the socialist movement has called Weitling "one of our greatest and best

[1] Gustav Mayer, *Friedrich Engels: Eine Biographie*, I, 116–17; and Friedrich Engels, *Die Entwickelung des Sozialismus von der Utopie zur Wissenschaft* (Berlin, 1907), 26.

[2] See Max Adler, *Wegweiser-Studien zur Geistesgeschichte des Sozialismus* (Vienna, 1931), 287–313; also Brügel, *Österreichische Sozialdemokratie*, I, 42–43; and Edith Lenel, *Friedrich Kapp* (Leipzig, 1935), 48–49.

. . . an excellent, constructive head, and an unselfish character, the only really great communist of pre-Marxian times." [3]

In the search for an explanation for the final break between Marx and Weitling, it is clear that the religious phase of the latter's communism was bound to prove extremely distasteful to Marx. Whether Marx attended any of the discussions previously described is not entirely certain, though it is known that Marx met Weitling in London and received reports of the London debates from his friends. It is also known that long before the Brussels conference Marx had begun to work on a plan to divorce communism from religious sentimentality and reduce it to a scientific doctrine. Weitling, the simple-minded Utopian, knew nothing about a law of economic determinism and did not have the formal education which would have enabled him to follow Marx's learned excursions into history and prophecy. He realized that men could not be spiritually free while held in economic bondage, but such a conclusion was relatively simple for a man who had to work with his hands. Weitling appealed to the emotions and the heart. He rejected the doctrine that made self-interest the sole motivation of life. He believed that man had an inner desire to do good and a potentiality for self-sacrifice which could be developed by training in morality and religion; and he desired to use religion to achieve a kind of communism which would be like the good life of the genuine Christian, and give men a faith which would help them to penetrate the black night of their despair.

Weitling was not an avowed atheist like Ludwig Feuerbach, nor a materialist like Marx or Karl Heinzen. He was not a churchman either. But he wanted to use Christian faith to stir the emotions necessary for revolution. "Cold reason has never produced a

[3] Max Beer, *Karl Marx: Sein Leben und Seine Lehre* (Berlin, 1919), 435-39. Two French scholars have pointed out Weitling's influence on the Communist Manifesto. See Charles Andler, *Le Manifeste Communiste de Karl Marx et F. Engels* (Paris, n.d.), 6, 162; Caille, *Wilhelm Weitling*, 73; and C. Bougle, *Socialisme français de "Socialisme utopique à la Democratie industrielle"* (Paris, 1933), 136.

revolution," he repeatedly said, and "there is as little reason in atheism as in deism." Knowledge alone would not solve all human problems nor completely satisfy the craving of the human spirit. Much of life remained a mystery, and like most men Weitling groped in vain for a solution for the riddle of the universe. He believed that "the mysterious emotions of love" often prove more powerful than reason, and lead men to comprehend that "image of highest love" which they seek in their search for God. "Only when the last riddle of human existence has been solved," he wrote, "can we know what God is." In the meantime, he preferred to have man take God on faith, rather than to "sink his thoughts into empty space."

Weitling was an agnostic, but his bruised spirit yearned for the balsam of religion, and he was not prepared to dismiss the whole world of religious experience as a mere opiate for the people.[4] He was conscious of an impenetrable mystery surrounding the origin of life, and to him that mystery suggested an "eternal, omnipotent, unifying cause." Though his extravagant references to religious terminology irritated Marx and his followers, Weitling refused to abandon his efforts to unite "intelligence and morality," "head and heart," the joint products of "the harmony of creation," in the quest for the communal society.

Weitling, the prophet with a mission to perform, undoubtedly was something of a fanatic, but in many respects he was a more lovable person than Marx. He belongs in the same category as that other lovable Utopian, Moses Hess, the son of a pious and learned Jewish rabbi, who was Weitling's colleague in the League of the Just and the pioneer of socialism in the Rhineland. His name also may be linked with that of Karl Grün, the philologist and journal-

[4] It will be recalled that Heine, who was in daily contact with Marx in Paris, once wrote,

Wir wollen hier auf Erden schon
Das Himmelreich errichten . . .
Den Himmel überlassen wir
Den Engeln und den Spatzen.

ist who taught Proudhon German philosophy, though both Hess and Grün had far more learning than the self-educated tailor. Like them, he believed that communism must be steeped in love, human kindness, and justice. His gospel, to use the words of Louis Blanc, was "*L'Evangile en action*," a secular faith comparable to that of the Anabaptists, the Moravian Brethren, and the Levelers and Diggers of England. It was a gospel to be proclaimed. It did not need to be scientifically demonstrated.[5]

Weitling began his career as a journeyman tailor, and he remained a champion of journeymen throughout his life. He wrote before the days of Darwinian evolution and modern industrial capitalism; he did not understand the role of capitalism as an instrument of progress in the modern world; and he had never seen any large-scale industry. His psychology was that of the guild craftsman who sensed that his livelihood was challenged seriously by new forces which he did not understand fully, but which threatened to reduce him to the level of the unskilled city proletarian.[6]

Despite a warm heart and a winning, kindly personality, Weitling, as a spokesman for his class, could bitterly denounce the ruling exploiting employer class. He typified many of the best qualities of his group: he was a man of courage and self-sacrifice and a believer in an honest day's work for an honest day's pay. He was not so much the inventor of new ideas as the eloquent voice that gave expression to the many real grievances of his fellow workers. He dreamed of a state controlled by skilled workers; and though he attacked violently the existing differences between employer and employee, he did not preach the class struggle, but made his appeal to men of good will in all classes. He was ready to propagandize the rich and powerful, as well as the poor and im-

[5] See Sombart, *Der proletarische Sozialismus*, II, 192. Weitling continued the same theme in *Die Republik der Arbeiter*, published in New York.

[6] See Adolf Douai, "Wilhelm Weitling und die Sozialdemokratie der Gegenwart," *Des seligen Schneider's Weitling Lehre von Sozialismus und Communismus* (New York, 1879), 271–81.

potent. He admitted that communism was partly a matter of the stomach; but he insisted that it also was a matter of practical ethics dealing with a Utopia above and outside the state, rather than with a state which would be nothing more than a mere tool of social revolution.[7]

Still another essential difference between Marx and Weitling must be emphasized. The former was a university man who had enjoyed all the advantages of higher education, which culminated in a doctor's degree from the University of Jena. Marx was a pedantic neo-Hegelian, who even on minor questions could mobilize "his whole artillery of logic, dialectic, stylistic and learning." Weitling could not find his way around in the "fog" of Hegelianism, and he referred to Schelling and Schleiermacher with equal disdain. Metaphysical abstractions did not interest him. He believed that experience was far more valuable than books. He had what Engels correctly called a "hatred of the learned" (*Gelehrtenhass*), and like the true craftsman, he believed "science and skill" were of equal importance. He would have agreed with Heinzen's comment that Marx could not write half a page without footnotes.

Though Weitling is properly labeled a Utopian, actually he stood perhaps midway between the Utopians and the Marxists. But however he may be classified he certainly was not "scientific" in the Marxian sense, and he stubbornly refused to accept a theory of economic determinism which made man only a figurehead in the interplay of external, economic forces. For him, man was the actor and maker of the drama of history. To be sure, progress was the law of nature, but man, by his conscious effort and planning, was needed to help work it out.[8] Not unlike the Marxian-Hegelian system of dialectics, Weitling believed that all things have in them the germ of change and revolution, but he believed also in the

[7] See Veit Valentin, *Geschichte der deutschen Revolution von 1848–49* (Berlin, 1930), I, 281; and Karl Heinzen, *Die Helden des deutschen Kommunismus* (Bern, 1848), *passim.*

[8] Karl Mielcke, *Deutscher Frühsozialismus: Gesellschaft und Geschichte in den Schriften von Weitling und Hess* (Stuttgart, 1931), *passim.*

ability of man to build a better world according to the principles of Christian self-sacrifice and brotherhood.

Marx, a Hegelian since 1837, became a communist half a dozen years later. At a time when Moses Hess, who joined Weitling in opposition to "Jupiter Marx," already had made the transition from Hegelianism to communism, Marx was still a bourgeois democrat. In the fall of 1843 he and his young wife had moved to Paris to help edit Arnold Ruge's *Deutsch-Französische Jahrbücher*. Here he read the French radical literature and became familiar with the writings of Fourier, Proudhon, Cabet, and Weitling.[9] Marx had attended meetings of the League of the Just when Weitling was a prisoner in Switzerland. He belonged to the group of literati in Paris which included Herwegh, Heine, Ruge, Hess, Grün, Louis Blanc, Proudhon, and others who, "armed with Hegel" and Feuerbach, favored an intellectual alliance between Germany and France. In the end, Marx poured a lot of old French socialism into new German-Hegelian bottles.

Marx considered Weitling's Utopianism "a dogmatic abstraction." He rejected the state of nature, primitive Christianity, and even social ethics as appropriate bases for communism. He wished to divorce the labor movement altogether from the ritual and pattern of secret societies and instead to weld the workers into a political movement. With the able collaboration of Friedrich Engels, son of a well-to-do manufacturer and a sympathetic and keen student of the condition of the working class in England, he slowly evolved a scientific basis for his philosophy of economic determinism, materialism, the class struggle, and the ultimate and inevitable proletarian revolution. Between 1843 and 1847, Marx mixed his Hegelianism with large doses of Feuerbach's materialism. Thus Marxism was derived from the French Revolution, great German philosophers such as Hegel and Feuerbach, French theorists such as Fourier and Saint-Simon, and English industrialism.

[9] In the 1840's, one of the few differences between communism and socialism was that the former was primarily a proletarian reform movement, the latter, bourgeois. See also Arthur E. Bestor, Jr., "The Evolution of the Socialist Vocabulary," *Journal of the History of Ideas*, IX (June, 1948), No. 3, pp. 259–302.

In the hands of an inflexible theorist, it was developed into one of the greatest orthodoxies of the modern world.[10] Engels was quite ready to admit this derivation of Marxian socialism, and he expressed great pride in its ancestry.[11] According to "scientific communism" à la Marx and Engels, the economic structure of society was decisive for all social institutions, moral, legal, political and religious; and even "moral theories" were the product of "the economic stage which society has reached" at a particular time. In short, even morality and religion were determined by the processes of production and the exchange of goods.

In view of the ideological conflicts, the break between Weitling and Marx was inevitable. It represented the clash between a master of economics, scientific abstractions, and Hegelian dialectics, and a simple-minded prophet of the brotherhood of man who had no other formula for world betterment. It marked the collision between a champion of the class struggle determined by scientific economic laws, and a new Messiah who had faith in a kingdom of love and science. Marx discoursed on scientific concepts and concrete doctrine; Weitling dismissed such cold "closet analysis with contempt." "I see nothing in Marx's head except a good encyclopedist, but no genius," he once wrote to Hess.[12] Strangely enough, Marx always managed to avoid direct contact with the proletariat about whom he wrote so feelingly. Weitling was no such closet philosopher; he knew the hardships of the worker from personal experience. Moreover, he was ten years older than his competitor for leadership of the communist movement.

When the break came, Weitling undoubtedly was irascible and violent in argument, but Marx was notorious for his arrogance and intolerance. He never could brook opposition to, or the slightest deviation from, the gospel which he had evolved and proclaimed; and he had an overwhelming urge to dominate. Carl Schurz spoke of his "offensive, insufferable arrogance." Karl

[10] Mehring, *Deutsche Sozialdemokratie*, 3.

[11] F. Engels, *Die Entwickelung des Sozialismus von der Utopie zur Wissenschaft* (Zurich, 1882).

[12] Quoted in Joho, *Wilhelm Weitling*, 112.

Heinzen, a friend of the early days who later turned into an enemy, considered him a sophist and mere dialectician, who hopped like an "ape" from one Hegelian thesis and antithesis to another.[13]

Brussels in the 1840's harbored many refugees. Among them were Freiligrath, "the trumpeter of the revolution"; Heinzen, who was in exile because of his attacks on the Prussian bureaucracy; Joachim Lelewel, a Polish refugee; Heinrich Bürgers, a communist, and many others. Marx spent three years among this group in Brussels, and it was here that he met Engels, destined to become his alter ego. Before discussing the violent differences that developed among these expatriates, it is pleasant to recall that they also had the capacity to enjoy the lighter side of life. They gathered frequently in the city's coffeehouses, not only to discuss their plans for reform and to issue revolutionary brochures, but also to enjoy the camaraderie of such convivial occasions. Several witnesses attest that Marx enjoyed his liquor but did not hold it well, and according to Heinzen, he had to be taken home by his friends on several occasions. Joseph Weydemeyer, an ardent disciple, in a letter to his fiancée written in February of 1846, described the gay hours spent in the taverns or in sitting up all night playing cards, and reported that in a four-handed game played by Weydemeyer, Marx, his brother-in-law, and Weitling, the last-named generally "got tired first."

Weitling arrived in Belgium shortly after he had lost his encounter with Schapper in London. He must have realized that his influence was declining, and his prison experiences had made him unusually suspicious of treachery in the ranks. Engels described him as "no longer the naive journeyman tailor, astonished by his own talents," but "a great man, persecuted by the envious, surrounded by rivals, secret enemies and plots," the prophet harried from country to country, carrying the recipe for the complete

[13] See Carl Wittke, *Against the Current: The Life of Karl Heinzen* (Chicago, 1945), 237–39. See also Bakunin's comments, in Tim Klein, *1848: Der Vorkampf deutscher Einheit und Freiheit* (Munich, 1914), 98.

transformation of society in his pocket. On the other hand, Paul Annenkov, a Russian friend and creditor of Marx, pictured him as a "handsome, fair, young man, whose coat had a somewhat foppish cut, and whose beard was foppishly trimmed," and "who resembled a *commis voyageur* more than the dark, bitter worker, oppressed by the burden of his labor and his thoughts."

Weitling knew that Marx was organizing a communist party with himself at the head. He could not have been ignorant of the fact that Marxism was making inroads among his erstwhile followers, such as Philippe Gigot, Ferdinand Wolff, Louis Heilberg, and Sebastian Seiler, though in the final realignment, the last two stood with him. With the help of Gigot and Engels, Marx was carrying on a correspondence in three languages with communist leaders in many places, hoping to find a common doctrine which all could accept. He was eager to "purge" the party of its "sentimentality" and to crush both the artisan communism of Weitling and the philosophical communism of Hess. Proudhon refused to co-operate with his plans; Louis Blanc, on the other hand, kept in touch with the committee of correspondence in Brussels. Schapper and Ewerbeck replied from London, and letters were exchanged with others in Kiel, Silesia, Cologne, and elsewhere.

Weitling could hardly be ignored in the launching of the new party, and so he was invited to participate in the preliminary discussions. The group consisted originally of seventeen of the faithful, the majority of whom definitely belonged to the *bourgeoisie*. Among them were Freiligrath, Hess, Marx's brother-in-law, Edgar von Westphalen, Weydemeyer, a former artillery officer, Seiler, Heilberg, Gigot, an employee of the Brussels library, Ernst and Ferdinand Wolff, two German typesetters, Ernst Dronke, later editor of the *Neue Rheinische Zeitung*, Weitling, and several others. The group met twice a week under the name of a workers' educational society for discussion and debate, amateur theatricals, singing, and lectures.[14] It was this small group who eventually

[14] Eden and Cedar Paul (trans.), Otto Rühle's *Karl Marx, His Life and Work* (New York, 1929), 145.

hammered out the communist doctrine which became the great force in world history it is today.

In earlier correspondence Weitling, using the familiar *du* form, had expressed his gratitude for Marx's favorable reviews of his literary output in the Paris *Vorwärts*, and on one occasion he wrote from London to offer his friendship and to send greetings to Mrs. Marx. Not long thereafter, Weitling apparently was offended because Marx and Engels failed to help him financially with a project to publish the treatise on a universal language on which he had been at work in London. It is probable that the refusal was couched in the brusque, sarcastic style of which both Marx and Engels were masters, and the incident undoubtedly heightened Weitling's distrust of intellectuals.

Curiously enough, the actual crisis in the relations between Marx and Weitling came because of the activities of Hermann Kriege in America. Kriege, a friend of Robert Blum, who fell in the Revolution of 1848, was an ardent disciple of Ludwig Feuerbach. He had founded a "reading circle" in Berlin to create interest in democratic reforms and after trouble with the Prussian police had gone to the United States. Here he became the leader of a Young America group, and published a paper in New York, known as the *Volkstribun*. This little radical journal, printed in German, had some circulation in Europe, and its editor corresponded regularly with communists on the Continent. As spokesman for the old League of the Just, Kriege founded a local of the organization in New York. Never noted for great stability in his reform activities, he had embraced the program of the Land Reform Association, which advocated free homesteads and accepted the support of Tammany Hall. Kriege never hesitated to appeal for contributions to a rich man such as John Jacob Astor when he needed money either for his paper or to aid needy immigrants who had just arrived in the city.

Though the *Volkstribun* championed the doctrines of the communists about labor and money, the editor did not feel bound to follow any party line. His paper was anticlerical, anticapitalist, and antirent, and Kriege defended vigorously his program of opportunism and piecemeal reform on the ground that the democratic United States presented a very different problem from autocratic Europe. Unfortunately, the *Volkstribun* was written in the extravagant style of the sentimentalist who loved all humanity, and before long Kriege was charged with making communism laughable by the methods of a crackpot. By the end of 1846, the paper had suspended publication. Thereafter its editor became a Democrat, published three volumes on the "Fathers of the Republic," went back to Europe to participate in the Revolution of 1848 in Berlin, returned to the United States to edit the *Illinois Staatszeitung* in Chicago for a short period, and died, insane, in New York at the age of thirty-one. In accordance with his specific request, Kriege was buried with an American flag draped across his breast,[15] and the New York *Tribune* eulogized him as "one of the most sincere, upright and generous men with whom it was ever our fortune to be acquainted."[16]

To the Marxians, however, Kriege was nothing but a source of embarrassment for the party. There had been a time when Engels considered him a "splendid agitator" and had sent him material to use as an official emissary of the League of the Just, but before long, Engels repudiated his co-worker in communism, though he was inclined to blame his eccentricities on "the crazy Harro Harring," a veteran of the Greek and Polish wars of liberation who had migrated to the United States in 1834 and later had written articles for Kriege's *Volkstribun*.[17] Marx was convinced that the renegade from orthodox communism must be called to account, and in this light, Kriege's case was presented to the party conference in Brussels.

[15] *Belleviller Zeitung*, January 23, 1851.

[16] New York *Tribune*, January 1, 1851.

[17] Engels to Marx, February 22, 1845, in A. Bebel and Ed. Bernstein (eds.), *Briefwechsel zwischen Friedrich Engels und Karl Marx, 1844 bis 1883* (Stuttgart, 1921), I, 15, 18, 39, 43, 49; also Quarck, *Die erste deutsche Arbeiterbewegung*, 324; and B. A. Uhlendorf, "German-American Poetry: A Contribution to Colonial Literature," *Jahrbuch der Deutsch-Amerikanischen Historische Gesellschaft von Illinois* (Chicago, 1912–1913), XXII–XXIII, 214.

The quarrel between Marx and Weitling began at a meeting attended also by Gigot, Weydemeyer, Seiler, Heilberg, and Edgar von Westphalen. "Jupiter Marx" sat at the head of the table, with pencil and paper in hand. The discussions began innocently enough with a consideration of the kind of propaganda best suited to Germany. As Marx's desire to rid the movement of all sentimental appeals to emotion became more and more apparent, the debate became heated,[18] and suddenly Marx turned on Weitling, bluntly demanding a summary of his program for the future and arguments in defense of his methods of agitation. Confused and ill at ease, and really without a definite program, the older man made repetitious statements, expressed entire satisfaction with his program and his methods, and indicated that he felt his influence and achievements were not appreciated properly. Marx angrily interrupted the speaker to denounce a fantastic propaganda calculated to arouse the people without first giving them a definite basis for social action, and sarcastically observed that Weitling's ideas might be suitable for a country such as Russia but were wholly inappropriate for Germany, whose workers needed a doctrine which would be both scientific and specific. Marx argued in favor of his evolutionary concept of communism, while Weitling stubbornly insisted that no mere intellectual could comprehend the sufferings of the common people.

The dispute ended with Marx stamping up and down the room, and making caustic references to his opponent's ignorance. Weitling in a letter to Hess admitted that he too lost his temper. He accused Marx of turning for support to people with money. It is interesting to note, however, that after the quarrel Weitling sent Marx an article which he had promised, and that the latter invited Weitling to lunch. Hess wrote to Marx, "You have made him completely mad, and then you are astonished because he is mad." [19]

In May the final break came. The immediate cause was Kriege,

[18] Weitling to Hess, March 31, 1846, in Barnikol, *Weitling der Gefangene,* 269–70.

[19] Zlocisti, *Moses Hess,* 225–27.

whose sentimental aberrations in the *Volkstribun* infuriated Marx, perhaps even more than Weitling's Utopianism. He accused the youthful editor of violating communist principles by endorsing land reform, of giving away his paper instead of selling it, and of accepting money from the *bourgeoisie* of New York. Weitling alone refused to sign the circular letter which was prepared to read Kriege out of the party. Copies of the document went to England, France, Germany, and the United States, however, and the indictment was published in the *Westfalische Dampfboot.* Weitling insisted that Kriege must be allowed a reasonable amount of freedom to adapt his techniques to American conditions. The resolutions of censure appeared in the *Volkstribun,* together with Kriege's reply. The latter was inclined to blame Engels rather than Marx for his difficulties.

Moses Hess, the "communist rabbi," had not been present at this critical meeting, but when informed of what had happened he expressed sympathy for Weitling. Eventually he broke with both Engels and Marx, writing to the latter, "With you personally I would still like to associate, but I want nothing more to do with your party." [20] Weitling received some support from letters that came from London. He wrote promptly to Kriege to give his version of the break with Marx, and in this letter he represented the attack on the New York editor as really an attack on himself. He honestly believed that the charge of "reactionary" which was leveled against him was intended primarily to rid the Brussels group of a dangerous competitor. Weitling formally proclaimed the *Volkstribun* as a proper organ for the spread of communist doctrine, and deplored all attempts to sow dissension between European and American communists. This letter also was reprinted promptly in Kriege's paper, along with a new statement elucidating the power of love in the affairs of men. In a fury, Engels wrote to Marx "about the infamy of brother Weitling" and repudiated all connections with the "warm brotherliness," "gentleness," and "meekness" of prophets of this kind.[21] The anti-

[20] Mayer, *Engels,* I, 249.
[21] Bebel and Bernstein (eds.), *Briefwechsel, Engels und Marx,* I, 49–50.

climax came on July 4, when Kriege took down the slogan at the masthead of the *Volkstribun* which read "Up with the workers. Down with capital," apologized for the name "communist," and rejoiced that Tammany Hall had embraced the cause of the Social Reformers with whom he now was identified completely.[22]

Having won the initial round at Brussels, Marx and Engels decided to follow their victory with a purge of all elements in the communist agitation who deviated from the doctrine announced by the *Pontifex Maximus*. Engels proceeded to Paris to break whatever influence Weitling still had among the German workers there. He painted him as a reactionary and, what was worse, intimated that he was not the author of the books which he had published. Weitling heatedly denied the charge as a malicious libel, and Engels produced no evidence to prove his case. Instead, he appealed to Ewerbeck to join the Brussels group, tried to get "the little tailor clique" expelled, and reported with satisfaction that the carpenters of Paris would not accept Weitling's leadership and frequently were at odds with the tailors.[23]

In 1848, in a letter to Marx, Engels ridiculed the small following which their rival still had among London journeymen, a group which he described as "asses." Two years later Marx attacked Weitling's sentimental methods in the *Neue Rheinische Zeitung*. In 1853 the same tactics still were being followed, but to the list of the unfaithful the Marxists now had added such names as August Willich and Fritz Anneke, who also had dared to differ with them and were editing German liberal papers in the United States. Along with Weitling, they were denounced for "trying to sow dissension in our ranks." [24] Weitling occasionally fired back at Marx in his *Die Republik der Arbeiter*, and Marx and Engels continued to watch for "the poison of this king of the tailors, and dictator of the colony, Communia." [25] When Weyde-

[22] See also John R. Commons *et al.* (eds.), *A Documentary History of American Industrial Society* (Cleveland, 1910), VII, 91–93, 225–31.

[23] Bebel and Bernstein (eds.), *Briefwechsel, Engels und Marx,* I, 23–29, 40, 88.

[24] *Ibid.*, I, 398, 422; and *Rep. d. Arb.*, January 7, 1854.

[25] Bebel and Bernstein (eds.), *Briefwechsel, Engels und Marx,* I, 145, 171, 384.

meyer came to New York and seriously considered taking over the paper edited by the "king of the tailors," Marx advised strongly against it. As late as 1879, eight years after Weitling's death, when a new edition of the *Garantieen* came off the press, Marx watched eagerly for the book and wrote to his friend Sorge to say that it had not yet arrived.[26]

It is interesting to speculate on what might have happened in the history of communism and in the history of modern Europe if Weitling's suggestion of bridging the gap between materialism and humanitarianism had been accepted at the Brussels conference. Marx and Engels demonstrated that they had the intelligence, the education, and the determination necessary to develop a system that was destined to become a powerful force in world affairs. Weitling lacked the qualifications for such a task; his head was not equal to his heart. But he saw clearly that a system which eschewed all considerations of morality, social ethics, and religious emotionalism, and frankly proceeded on the amoral principle that the end justifies the means, might be turned into the devil's own philosophy leading to a new form of tyranny.

Late in the spring of 1846, Weitling went to Bremen. As usual, he was short of funds, and he talked about getting a job on the railroad. Early in January, 1847, he was reported in Paris, traveling with a false passport. There is no way of reconstructing the story of his activities during this period. Apparently, some of the German workers in Paris gave him money when he talked of going to America to assume the editorship of the *Volkstribun*, by invitation of his friend Kriege, and it is known that the New York *Sozialreform Verein* furnished some additional funds for the journey. According to Weitling's own account, he landed in New York on the last day of 1846. Other evidence, however, fixes the date at January 25, 1847.

A number of the newspapers of Germany took notice of the departure of the famous communist. The *Vossische Zeitung* and the *Trierische Zeitung* commented on his career, and the *Telegraph*

[26] F. A. Sorge *et al.*, *Briefe und Auszüge aus Briefen*, 162.

für Deutschland spoke highly of his services to the common man in Europe and expressed confidence that in the free atmosphere of America he would be able to do even more for the benefit of mankind. Scherzer published a *Nachruf* ("farewell") in his *Musestunden und Schweisstropfen,* issued in Paris, which is further evidence of Weitling's reputation at the time:

> Freund lebe wohl, jetzt wo das Licht der Sonne
> Dich frei umstrahlt dort in der neuen Welt,
> Dort werde dir das Glück, das Heil, die Wonne,
> Und bleibe stets ein Kämpfer und ein Held.
> Lass dich durch nichts, sei's wass es will, umstricken,
> Betrete ruhig deine neue Bahn,
> Und das Bewusstsein wird dich stets beglücken,
> Was du für's Wohl der Menschheit hast getan.[27]

On his arrival in the land of liberty and opportunity, Weitling learned to his dismay that the *Volkstribun* was in bankruptcy and had just suspended publication. Poor but undaunted, as usual, Weitling promptly started to agitate for his principles in the United States. He received a little financial support from the *Sozialreform Verein,* which had helped bring him to America; and he raised additional dollars from the sale of his books, including a third edition of the *Evangelium* which he had printed in New York on credit. He traveled about to make contacts among the German workers, and the expenses for these journeys were probably met locally. On July 5 he addressed a national festival of German-Americans in Philadelphia at Lippincott's Woods, "on 2nd Street three miles north of Vine Street." The celebration, marked by singing, dancing, speeches, and good German food, was a completely happy one until sixty rowdies from the Richmond and Kensington districts started a fight and had to be driven off by force.[28]

[27] Quoted in Barnikol, *Klassifikation des Universums von Wilhelm Weitling,* 50.

[28] C. F. Huch, "Die Deutschen in Philadelphia ums Jahre 1847," *Mitteilungen des Deutschen Pionier-Vereins von Philadelphia,* XVII (1910), 13–21.

Weitling issued new appeals to his countrymen in Germany, and printed a pamphlet entitled *Ein Nothruf an die Männer der Arbeit und Sorge* ("A Cry of Distress to the Men of Labor and Sorrow"), which he distributed personally upon his return to Germany. His most important activity during this first brief sojourn in the United States, was the launching of a new League of Deliverance, or Emancipation, the *Befreiungsbund*. He made a tour of the country as far as New Orleans, on behalf of the *Bund*, which he apparently regarded as the successor of the League of the Just, and he claimed to have established lodges in New York, Newark, New Orleans, and Philadelphia, and as far inland as New Braunfels, Texas.

Shortly after news of the German Revolution of 1848 reached the United States, Weitling called a meeting of the German workers in Philadelphia for April 29, 1848. His call indicates that he regarded the events in the German states as a revolution for the "social emancipation" of the workers and not merely a struggle for a change in the political forms of the state. An *Arbeiterverein* was organized in Philadelphia and a constitution adopted and officers elected on May 3. Ten days later the new organization held its first formal meeting.

The constitution of the Philadelphia *Arbeiterverein* defined its membership broadly enough to include all who rendered useful labor, whether manual or intellectual. It demanded that the state provide full employment and care for the aged and the infirm; denounced the drones in modern society; and called upon all Americans, regardless of language or origin, to unite in the crusade for a genuine democracy of freedom and equality.

The society met every Saturday evening. It elected officers twice a year and collected dues of three cents a week. At its meetings the membership debated such issues as land reform and national workshops, endorsing the former and rejecting the latter; denounced the tariff and advocated free trade; and urged the abolition of inheritances and interest on capital. An auxiliary organization was created to serve as an employment agency and to provide sick and death benefits. On August 15, 1849, while Weitling was in Europe, the society resolved to devote one night each week to a discussion of the German Revolution and decided to conduct raffles to raise money for the Revolution and for the support of the refugees who were arriving in Philadelphia. In the same year, a building and loan association (*Bau-Verein*) and a singing society were organized. It is interesting to add that this organization founded by Weitling lasted until 1899, when it amalgamated with the Philadelphia *Harmonie*.

In New York a similar organization established in February, 1849, adopted a constitution demanding free homesteads, a rural credit system, free public education, a mechanics lien law, hard money, direct taxes, and the abolition of the protective tariff and banks. In both New York and Philadelphia the membership made plans for a *Tauschbank* according to Weitling's theories, before the latter had returned from his labors for the German Revolution.[29]

A discussion of the American phase of Weitling's career must be postponed to a later chapter, however, for with the outbreak of the Revolution of 1848, Weitling, like other prominent German liberals and radicals, hurried home to the fatherland. His return voyage was financed by contributions of $60 from his *Befreiungsbund*, $100 from the New York *Revolutionsverein*, and smaller amounts from Philadelphia, Cincinnati, and other towns.[30]

[29] C. F. Huch, "Die Anfänge der Arbeiterbewegung unter den Deutschamerikanern," *Deutsch-Amerikanische Geschichtsblätter, Jahrbuch der Deutsch-Amerikanischen Historische Gesellschaft von Illinois* (Chicago, 1910), X, pp. 244–55.

[30] According to the reminiscences of a Philadelphian, written late in life when his memory was not too accurate, Weitling bade farewell in a speech in the *Turner* Hall of Philadelphia. In his address he spoke disparagingly of the American republic, and of the failure of the workers to comprehend his mission. He announced his intention to work for a German republic that would be greatly superior to its American counterpart. At that point he was greeted with threats against his person, and finally left the hall "unnoticed." "Reminiscences of L. A. Wollenweber," *Mitteilungen des Deutschen Pionier-Vereins von Philadelphia*, XV (1910), 23–24.

CHAPTER VIII

THE GERMAN REVOLUTION OF 1848–49

THE events of the German Revolution of 1848–49, so pregnant with fateful consequences for that unhappy country and for the world, need not concern us here.[1] The uprising was marked by many serious divisions in counsel and strategy and had more of the earmarks of a romantic adventure than of a practical, well-planned revolution. In larger communities of the United States which had sizable German populations, it was hailed with mass meetings, resolutions of sympathy and support, and campaigns to raise funds for the revolutionists. For several years after the collapse of the revolution, societies such as the Social Reformers of New York continued to send money to refugees who had been forced to flee the country and to mark the anniversaries of the revolution with appropriate celebrations.[2]

Though it was in no sense a revolution for socialism or communism, many varieties of radicals hurried back to Germany filled with new hope for the cause which happened to represent their particular panacea. Marx came over to the Continent from England. Engels and Freiligrath published the *Neue Rheinische Zeitung* in Cologne, confident that parliamentary reform would ripen into a full-fledged proletarian-communist revolution. Workers' organizations in Germany took on new life, though there was

[1] The best account is Valentin, *Geschichte der deutschen Revolution von 1848–49, passim.*

[2] *New Yorker Staatszeitung*, December 15, 1849; March 2, 1850.

no communist party as such, and Heinzen later accused the Marxian communists of sabotaging the revolution.

Weitling arrived in Paris on a Sunday, two days before the end of the June revolution in France. He reported that he and his traveling companion were locked into their hotel because street fighting, of which he claims to have heard while still on shipboard, was still in progress. According to his own account, he saw the National Guard entraining for another descent upon the heart of Paris; and when he shouted to them, "*Messieurs! il ne faut pas tirer sur les ouvriers,*" he immediately was thrown to the ground and overpowered by "*mouchards*" (spies). Whatever the facts may have been (and his report seems exaggerated, to say the least), we know that the German communist did not remain long in France. As he moved on into his native land, passing through Frankfurt and Heidelberg, he had revolutionary pamphlets printed and distributed, including the *Nothruf* which he had issued originally in New York. Weitling also spoke at a meeting in Cologne at which he demanded a thoroughgoing reorganization of all political and social institutions. As he moved eastward he found the Mecklenburgers quite responsive to his type of propaganda, for in this area of large estates there were many survivals of medieval feudalism, and some Mecklenburgers were talking hopefully about a peasant uprising.

We know comparatively little about Weitling's associates on this barnstorming trip for revolution. Hermann Kriege came over from the United States and, when the Frankfurt Parliament became more and more conservative, joined in the call for a democratic congress in Berlin which he and Weitling attended.[3] Johann Christian Luchow, a tailor and former colleague, published a labor paper known as the *Werkstatt* in Hamburg and distributed revolutionary poems and pamphlets. Seiler, another friend of Weitling's, took part in the uprisings in Baden and Westphalia in 1849. Christian Friedrich Mentel, a tailor, and Karl Joseph Haetzel, a

[3] See Wilhelm Bolin (ed.), *Ausgewählte Briefe von und an Ludwig Feuerbach* (Leipzig, 1904), I, 115–16.

shoemaker, friends who had been active in the League of the Just in Paris, started the first workers' organizations in Berlin in 1847 and later were among the defendants in the first communist trial held in the Prussian capital. One of the specific charges levied against them was that they were avowed disciples of Weitling.[4]

The cause of reform found expression in many revolutionary poems, and among his papers Weitling preserved the manuscript for five such poetic efforts. It cannot be established whether they ever were published. One, entitled "Es gilt noch einen Kampf auf Tod und Leben" (A Battle of Life and Death), was a call to fight anew the battle against tyranny,

> Soll Deutschlands junge Freiheit, kaum erwacht
> Wie unser Staub in Nacht versinken modern? . . .

Others, like "Kampfgesang" (Battle Song) and "Hilf dir selbst" (Help Yourself), were appeals to his fellow countrymen to take up the sword and to have faith in their own strength. The "Call to Battle," a stirring, martial rhythm in seven stanzas, called for an end to all Habsburgers, Hohenzollerns, and Wittelsbachers. Another poem was a diatribe against the frequently inebriated King of Prussia who "seeks courage in drink," and the last of the series told the story of a crippled veteran with "decorations on his old soldier's coat," playing a hurdy-gurdy and begging for alms. It included stanzas of violence and fury against the inequalities that existed between king and pauper.

The philosophical tailor saw no action in the revolution and smelled no powder. But he worked feverishly with his pen to bring about the kind of revolution of which he approved. "It is easier," he comforted himself when others referred to their military adventures, "to expose one's breast to the rain of bullets in a time of great excitement than to work for a plan, year in and year out, undaunted by all kinds of discouragements and all the little blows of fortune."

[4] Valentin, *Geschichte der deutschen Revolution,* I, 85, 280; II, 96–99.

Weitling was not a member of the famous Parliament that met in St. Paul's Church of Frankfurt. Though that body received numerous petitions from workers' groups in Germany, few of its members were aware of the impact of the industrial revolution on the German states. It adopted generalities about the rights of man modeled on the French Constitution of 1791; but its leftist members, who were badly divided, were unsuccessful in securing the adoption of such radical demands as Gustav Struve's proposal for a ministry of labor, and their discussion of such issues evaporated very quickly in high-sounding phrases.[5]

Despite the failures at Frankfurt, the revolution did succeed in bringing many dormant workers' associations back to life. Generally speaking, these societies did not have a comprehensive program for revolution. They were content, for the most part, with piecemeal reforms. In Berlin, for example, the organized tailors seized the opportunity to demand a twelve-hour day and no Sunday work; requested that masters refrain from training and employing women tailors; and petitioned for recognition of the right to organize, for national workshops, and for better educational facilities for their children.[6] A printers' strike in Berlin resulted in a call for a workers' congress; and *Der Volksfreund*, a paper launched in the Prussian capital, "in the year one of liberty," offered a program of reform which included breaking up the large landed estates, abolishing titles of nobility, and establishing people's banks, workers' factories, public education, and a long list of purely political reforms.

In response to a call issued by a central committee of the workers of Berlin, a "workers' parliament" met in that city on August 23, 1848, and remained in session for ten days. Its deliberations resulted in the founding of a workers' brotherhood (*Arbeiterverbrüderung*), with headquarters in Leipzig, and in a program of reform which advocated changes in the banking system, im-

[5] "Die Arbeiterfrage im Frankfurter Parlament," *Die Neue Zeit,* I (1883), 38–46.

[6] Bernstein, *Die Schneiderbewegung in Deutschland,* I, 81.

provements in the conditions of labor, and the establishment of co-operatives. About forty delegates, representing thirty-five societies drawn largely from northeastern Germany, attended the sessions of this Congress. Delegates came from Berlin, Hamburg, Königsberg, Leipzig, Breslau, Munich, Hanover, and other cities, as well as from the Rhineland and Westphalia.

Weitling appeared at the opening session, armed with a passport from Magdeburg. He found Berlin greatly changed. "Every street corner is plastered with caricatures and signs denouncing the existing order," he wrote back to America. He reported that newsboys were distributing radical papers in all the beer halls, and that speakers' platforms had been erected on many vacant lots. He visited the taverns and was favorably impressed with the quality of the political discussions which he heard there, though he also reported hearing a lot of ranting about democracy.[7]

The first general workers' congress convened in Berlin on August 23. Nees von Esenbeck presided and Stephan Born served as vice-president. Weitling apparently failed utterly to grasp the psychology of the congress. Its members were not revolutionists, and they had no plan to remake the world. Their main objective was to secure the recognition of their right to organize and to establish a better scale of wages. Weitling took the position that a "social parliament" must precede all such demands and advocated the creation of a "social chamber" to prepare and present a complete program of reform to a "political parliament." He urged that the members of the social chamber be chosen from all existing classes, by a plan of voting that would ensure representation by occupations. When the congress voted to create various committees before turning to Weitling's proposal, the latter left, angry, disappointed, and deeply hurt because his suggestions were not accepted immediately. The congress itself accomplished nothing of lasting importance, though it selected Leipzig as the headquarters for its central committee; created district committees and local committees in twenty-two cities; planned a parallel

[7] See Columbus (Ohio) *Der Westbote*, September 8, 1848.

organization for working women; and petitioned the Frankfurt Parliament to recognize the right of workers to organize.[8]

In October, Weitling issued a prospectus for another paper, to be known as *Der Urwähler*. It was printed by Rudolf Liebmann, in Berlin, Friedrichstrasse 18. The paper, which sold for a few cents a month, never secured more than 150 subscribers and died after the fifth issue. As its masthead it carried the symbol of a cock crowing to greet the sun and the words, "No division of goods, no forced labor, but rewarding work and honest trade for all," a rather mild slogan for a communist!

Although Weitling advocated such relatively moderate reforms as the repeal of all protective tariffs and the establishment of complete free trade, and discussed such problems as emigration, recreation for the workers, and the techniques of political elections, the new paper was devoted essentially to the principles of co-operative association. Weitling's major concern was the abolition of existing laws of inheritance, the destruction of the prevailing monetary systems, and an attack on the evils that arose from private property.

"The future belongs to us," the editor proclaimed optimistically in the first issue of *Der Urwähler;* "our little band has grown into a great army and we can accomplish great things." He called upon the national assembly at Frankfurt to enact a thorough program of political reforms based upon liberty and justice for all, freedom of the press and the protection of minorities, a three year moratorium on all mortgages, and state support for co-operative societies.

For the enlightenment of his readers, Weitling discussed the concepts of democracy, republicanism, socialism, and communism, and described the red flag as "the banner of agitation and suffering," "a symbol of the blood that is shed for the salvation of mankind, . . . the banner of fanaticism and faith, of hope, love and revenge . . . a flag of fanatics, ultra-radicals, revolutionaries,

[8] See Ricardo Huch, *Alte und neue Götter, Die Revolution des neunzehnten Jahrhunderts in Deutschland* (Berlin, 1930), 375–403.

anarchists and communists, but . . . also the banner for universal freedom in a European social republic."

In number five, the last issue of his ill-fated journal, the editor once more summarized his "social economy." He demanded jobs for all and stressed the obligation of every individual to labor for the benefit and in the service of society. He pointed out the need for constantly increasing production in order to raise the level of consumption and well-being and insisted that to this end science and invention must be steadily encouraged. To ensure maximum prosperity for all, however, he advocated the creation of a "ministry of social economy" whose duty it would be to provide a completely planned economy in which the state would become the sole purchaser of goods and services. Thus the evils of the capitalist system would be eliminated and an adequate standard of living would be guaranteed for all. This was the "end result" toward which all his propaganda was directed.

Weitling had as yet had little opportunity to study firsthand conditions in the United States, but he already was sharply critical of American democracy and referred to it as "that anarchy of liberty" under which the richest, the most powerful, and the most cunning derive the greatest benefits. It apparently had been the editor's hope to use the new paper as the official organ of the *Befreiungsbund*, the fraternal organization of workers to provide sick benefits and old-age pensions which he had advocated during his first trip to the United States, but of course the early collapse of this publishing venture ended all such ambitious plans. As a matter of fact, *Der Urwähler* revealed little of the early fire of the reformer, and took a position far more moderate than the program advocated in Weitling's earlier books.[9]

A second "Congress of Democrats" was held in Berlin on October 26. This was a larger and more heterogeneous body than the first assembly which Weitling had attended. Among the 234

[9] See Heinrich Leonard, "Wilhelm Weitling und seine Zeitung '*Der Urwähler*,'" *Neue Deutsche Presse* (Monatsheft des Verbandes der Deutschen Presse, Berlin, 1948, Nos. 9–10), 18–19.

delegates, purported to represent 260 societies in 140 cities, were Ruge, Otto von Corvin, Gottfried Kinkel, Fritz Anneke, Ludwig Bamberger, Stephan Born, Nees von Esenbeck, the aged socialist from Breslau, a professor from Marburg, Dr. Ewerbeck, Weitling, the shoemaker Haetzel, and Kriege. Weitling acted as the official representative of a New York group. His following, however, was almost negligible, a fact which he explained by pointing out that many of his co-workers already had left in the great migration to America. His own attitude, as a Utopian revolutionary, made little impression on a Congress composed so largely of bourgeois elements and agreed on little more than the desire to establish a united, German Republic. It is interesting to note that although Weitling had traveled far and wide as a journeyman and a propagandist and therefore had firsthand knowledge of the nuisances of petty boundaries, frontier guards and customs officers, he regarded the unification of the German states as a mere side issue; in contrast with Marx and Engels, who favored unification, he paid little attention to the question. He steadfastly adhered to his original plan for a truly international movement to liberate all peoples, regardless of political boundaries.

The Congress met in the "English House" on the Mohrenstrasse, in a hall decorated with German, Swiss, French, and American flags. The members addressed each other as "citizen" and used the familiar "*du.*" Bamberger presided, and Kriege kept a record of the proceedings. The debates were long and furious, the accomplishments almost nil. Kriege was accused by the extremists of coquetting with the *bourgeoisie* and betraying the proletariat, and he replied sharply that he was beginning to find the latter quite unreliable. Near the close of the sessions, Weitling made an address bemoaning the extreme factionalism of the Congress, a condition which his own position helped to perpetuate. He described the proceedings as "much talk and little action." As a matter of fact, he played a very minor role in this "Congress of Democrats," and when he suggested equal pay for all, his proposal was greeted with raucous laughter. When he insisted on proclaiming the communist state at once, he was rebuked by the presiding officer for "theoretical quarreling."[10] The congress ended by adopting various resolutions including the customary declaration about the rights of man, and issued an appeal for support of the Viennese revolutionists. A second meeting, called for Cologne, never took place. As a matter of fact, several members were arrested before the end of the deliberations in Berlin. One historian has described this strange gathering of varicolored reformers as "the most unreasonable, arrogant and uncouth assembly" in German history.[11]

By November, 1848, General Friedrich von Wrangel's forces moved into Berlin, and Weitling departed hurriedly for Hamburg. Early in January of 1849, he calmly reported to the Hamburg police, representing himself as a harmless writer who was living with a distant relative and working on a "scientific work." As a propagandist he was more successful in Hamburg and Altona than he had been in the Prussian capital. As the agent of the New York *Befreiungsbund*, he founded two lodges in these cities, and their membership, which probably reached 400, has been estimated as high as 1,000. Here Weitling expounded his principles to his followers. Sometimes he appeared in a red jacket as he presided over their meetings, though black was his usual costume. His lectures covered the whole range of his interests from a new kind of money to communism. The latter he continued to relate to "Christian love." Each initiate of the organization received a membership card, a fact of which the secret police were soon aware. Weitling published a pamphlet describing the propaganda techniques of his organization. It could be developed rapidly, he professed to believe, to the point where it could start the revolution and establish the provisional government, which would precede the complete acceptance of his communistic system, and the *Tauschbank* and *Kommerzbuch*, which were the heart of his proposals. A sec-

[10] See Max Quarck, *Die erste deutsche Arbeiterbewegung*, 157–59, 180–91.

[11] T. Klein, *1848: Der Vorkampf*, 364–67; see also Valentin, *Geschichte der deutschen Revolution*, II, 255–63; and *Rep. d. Arb.*, June 14, 1851.

ond edition of the *Nothruf* also was published in Hamburg, and a third edition of the *Garantieen,* the latter selling 1,000 copies. Meantime, its author also contributed a daily article to a local paper, for which he was paid ten marks a week. Among his devoted co-workers at this point in his career were a shoemaker, named Bögenitz of Hamburg; the paper hanger Starke, with whom he lived; and Conrad Schramm of Crefeld, who had deserted to the United States to escape military service and had returned with an American passport.[12]

In August, 1849, the Hamburg police decided to move against the harmless littérateur in their midst. A deputation of Hamburg workmen appealed to the Senate of the city to let this "quiet, peaceful, harmless man of learning" alone, and petitions to the same effect were presented by half a dozen German societies. Nevertheless, Weitling was given orders to move on. When the police arrived to search his room they found that their quarry had fled. It was on this occasion that they confiscated two trunks full of papers and books, including the manuscript for the *Gerechtigkeit* already referred to. Fortunately, a box containing 350 copies of the *Garantieen* which had been dispatched to Leipzig escaped confiscation. Weitling's address book showed that he was sending copies of his publications to Paris, Lübeck, Kiel, Breslau, Frankfurt, Leipzig, and other German and Swiss cities, and that his correspondents at the time included Bakunin, Kriege, Stephan Born, Edgar Bauer, Mathilda Anneke, Herwegh, and scores of otherwise unknown craftsmen, including several from Poughkeepsie, Cincinnati and St. Louis. Starke, the paper hanger who had harbored Weitling in his home, decided it would be best for him to go to London, where he continued to operate as a member of a communist group under the name of F. Geyer.

Weitling proceeded via London to the United States. He never saw his native land again. In New York, he made one last enthusi-

[12] Wermuth and Stieber, *Die Communisten-Verschwörung,* II, 137; and A. Vandermenien, *Enthüllungen aus der höheren Region der politischen Spionage* (Berlin, 1862), 92–100.

astic effort to put his ideas into practice on the friendly soil of America. Like so many of the Forty-eighters, however, he continued to be interested in the affairs of the Continent, and for years his heart was torn between the old and the new fatherland. Like scores of other refugees, including Schurz, Heinzen, and many other leaders of distinction, he expected the revolution to break out again in Germany at almost any moment. Finally, after many months of waiting and sober reflection, he concluded that the failure of 1848 was due primarily to the mistaken effort to unite the proletariat with the *bourgeoisie* in the name of democracy, and that two thirds of the leaders of 1848 "represented the old money bags." "We tried in '48 to emulate the French Revolution too much, and the birth turned out to be a bastard. . . ." As time went on, he made some unfortunate, uncomplimentary remarks about "the men of phrases" and especially about the Jews, who he claimed did nothing but talk in 1848, and constituted four fifths of the leftists of Berlin.

Weitling brought with him to the United States a number of copies of the revolutionary papers published during the glorious days of 1848-49, and these he preserved among his personal possessions as mementos of that chapter in his public career which now spanned two continents. Among them was a file of *Das Volk* ("The People"), edited by Born. It reported the two congresses in Berlin which Weitling had attended. Among them also was *Der Volksfreund* ("Friend of the People"), a labor paper edited by Gustav Adolph Schloeffel and Edmund Monecke, who advised their readers to be unafraid of "the spectre of communism"; the paper of the *Arbeiterverein* of Cologne; and *Der jüngste Tag, eine freie Zeitung aus Hesseland* ("The Judgment Day, a free journal from Hesse"), which espoused Weitling's theories about labor, money, and exchange.

When Louis Kossuth, the Hungarian patriot, arrived in the United States and received a tremendous ovation from the American people as one of the heroes of the suppressed nationalities of Europe, Weitling cautioned against the strong spirit of nationalism which such receptions seemed to condone. He reminded his readers that Kossuth had carefully refrained from committing himself on issues close to the heart of the workers, who do not need "your political frontiers." [13] Immediately, Weitling was attacked by papers such as the Baltimore *Wecker* and the Baltimore *Deutscher Correspondent* and represented as the enemy of Kossuth and Hungarian liberty. Samuel Ludvigh, a German-Hungarian who started so many German papers in the United States that he was known as "Fackel [Torch]-Ludvigh," charged that men of the type of Weitling were by nature "despots," despising everyone "who is not a crazy communist."

Presently, Gottfried Kinkel, the professor and poet who had turned revolutionary in 1848 and who had been liberated from prison with the help of Carl Schurz, arrived in the United States to float a national loan for a new German revolution. Mass meetings were held in many cities in response to Kinkel's appeal for funds, and many workers donated a day's wages to the cause. Weitling and Brisbane spoke at a large gathering in New York to commemorate the February revolution of 1848.[14] As late as 1852, as many as a thousand little revolutionary societies were engaged in raising money among the Germans of the United States in preparation for the new uprising in Europe which they were sure would come.[15]

Actually, the results of Kinkel's campaign were extremely meager, and as usual the German element in the United States divided sharply on the question, resorting to disgraceful recriminations. Weitling had little interest in this "foggy German Republic of the professors" or in their fine phrases about liberty and republicanism, and he did not hesitate to express his resentment against German republican intellectuals because of their bad treatment of the German working class and their indifference to its demands. With stubborn consistency, he would settle for nothing less than

[13] *Rep. d. Arb.*, February 14, May 1, 1852.
[14] *New Yorker Staatszeitung*, March 2, 1850.
[15] *Der deutsche Pionier* (Cincinnati), VIII (1876), 90–97, 155–59.

a revolutionary party of the workers, dedicated to communism. Weitling contrasted the financial failure of Kinkel's campaign with the sacrifices which working men make regularly for their fellow workers and added mournfully, "Kinkel has been received with loud rejoicing. . . . Not a soul inquired about me."

The *Republik der Arbeiter* for 1851 contained many excited comments about the European situation and continued to discuss the possibilities of a new revolution. Weitling was ready to accept Louis Napoleon as "the heir of Louis Blanc," and predicted that this noncommunist would do more in five years to provide a solid foundation for communism than Cabet could have accomplished in fifty years. Even when Napoleon was crowned emperor, he clung to the hope that the revived Napoleonic Empire would prepare the road for communism. Weitling persuaded himself that the emperor had the workers' interests at heart, really wished to abolish poverty, and had been forced by the aristocracy and the moneyed powers to accept a throne to make sure that he would not revert to his earlier sympathies for socialism. For months Weitling and his *Republik der Arbeiter* vacillated between fear of "the brainless adventurer," who was making France into a "penitentiary," and joy over Napoleon's dismissal of the "900 talkers" in parliament, which ended "the humbug of democracy." "It will be easier, by Revolution, to get rid of one tyrant than nine hundred," he reasoned. The communist editor could hardly claim Napoleon III as "one of us"; he was "not our Messiah"; yet Weitling never entirely abandoned hope that eventually he would woo the proletariat, conquer Europe, and issue the call to establish a German social republic.

As late as March, 1855, the editor of the *Republik der Arbeiter* still hoped for a new European revolution led by a dictator who would abolish private property and then, as the people became educated and converted to the new order, would gradually relinquish his powers and transform his regime into a popular government, along the lines indicated in the *Garantieen.*

The new revolution never came, because for one thing so many of the emissaries of revolution had left Germany for the United States. The year 1848 marked the end of a definite period in the history of socialism in Germany and the end of Weitling's prominence as a propagandist among the European proletariat.

Chapter IX

A RADICAL JOURNALIST IN AMERICA

WRITING in one of the last numbers of the *Republik der Arbeiter*, which he published in New York for five years after he had resolved to have done with Europe and to propagandize America, Weitling referred to the Forty-eighters, of whom he was one, in the following terms: "By the thousands, they migrated to America, the model republic, the last hope of their dreams. But here they discovered again what they had left behind in Europe: a general, wide-spread ill-humor, due to their disturbed dreams of liberty and the crushed flowers of revolution. . . . The enthusiasm which the European revolutions had kindled here, had evaporated with the defeat of the revolutionaries. They were humbled, disappointed and discouraged." [1]

Weitling was not easily discouraged. With a naïve optimism that sustained him through five years of heartbreaking defeat he made a final effort to carry his program of social reconstruction to fruition. He offered a triple-headed program of action to all Americans, though he addressed himself particularly to the large number of German craftsmen whom he found in the United States on his arrival. His program included the re-establishment of the *Befreiungsbund*, for which he had done spadework during his first visit to the United States, as an *Arbeiterbund* (Workingmen's League); the publication of a newspaper, to be known as

[1] *Rep. d. Arb.*, July 21, 1855.

Die Republik der Arbeiter and to serve as the official organ of the *Bund* and as the mouthpiece of its founder; and the founding of a communist colony where the theories of the *Garantieen* might be put into practice.

Weitling's decision to return to the United States after the failure of the Revolution of 1848 had attracted the attention not only of New York papers such as the *Schnellpost*, but also of German-language papers as far west as the Columbus (Ohio) *Westbote*,[2] for the name of the communist leader was widely known in German-American circles.

When Weitling immigrated to the United States, he found America in ferment. The slavery question was moving rapidly toward a final crisis. The Compromise of 1850 did not provide the solution which the politicians of both major parties desired, and the Fugitive Slave Law had rubbed new salt into the wounds of sectional controversy. The question of the expansion of slavery into the territories was an issue so acute that it presently shattered all old party alignments. The demand for free homesteads for actual settlers was gathering support rapidly and was especially strong among new arrivals eager to vote themselves a farm. The tide of immigration reached a new high in the early 1850's as Irishmen and Germans poured through the American ports of entry, and either settled in eastern cities or fanned out on the agricultural frontier of the Middle West and Northwest. Labor was in the process of organizing for better wages, better conditions of employment, and social reforms of many kinds. Though the popular interest in Fourierism probably had passed its zenith, many native and foreign-born Americans still were dreaming of ideal Utopias to be planted in the open spaces of the Mississippi Valley.

The New York City of the early 1850's, in which Weitling now established his home, had a large German section, extending along upper William Street and into the neighboring streets from Pearl to Beekman. Many refugees lived in the small two-story houses on William Street, and in this neighborhood Forty-eighters could

[2] Columbus *Westbote*, October 12, 1849.

be found in large numbers, in the taverns, stores and beer halls operated by their German countrymen. Eugen Liever's Shakespeare Hotel, at the corner of Duane and William Streets, was the meeting place for many German societies. Several German newspapers were published in the vicinity and to their number Weitling now added his *Die Republik der Arbeiter*. Third Avenue still was a country road marked with little hills, and to the east, in the area of Fortieth Street, there were small frame houses built and occupied by Germans in a section known as Squattertown. East of the present location of the New York Public Library on a little elevation stood a sizable and substantial farmhouse owned by a German which was frequently used by the Germans as a picnic place. Many streets of the growing metropolis were unpaved and muddy, and droves of cattle occasionally were driven along its main thoroughfares. Travel was largely by stage. Yorkville, a popular meeting place for German workers who came to picnic in its dense woods, could be reached by Dingeldein's Stage in an hour and a half.

About 1850 the Germans of New York lived in a fairly compact area which included City Hall Place, and Gold, William, Ann, Beekman, Chatham, Forsythe, Pearl, Bayard, Broom, and Hester Streets. Much of their social life centered along Bayard and Hester Streets. Here refugees—some of whom were men of education and distinction—eked out a meager existence in tailoring or other trades, gave music lessons, or performed ordinary manual labor. Joseph Fickler, who had been prominent in the revolution and at one time a creditor of Weitling, operated a restaurant at Duane and William Streets. Rösler von Oels, once a member of the German Parliament, conducted a German-American school at Oliver and Henry Streets. A tavern on William Street, operated by Friedrich Komberg, a refugee from Baden, was known as "Festung Rastatt," to commemorate the fortress which had figured so prominently in the revolution. On Gold Street, there were a number of tailor shops, some of them managed as co-operatives, where German workers sat on their tables and benches and listened to a *Vorleser* whom they employed to read to them and lead them in discussions. The *Turner*, a group dedicated to the cause of physical culture and conviviality, staged spectacular public exhibitions of their athletic skills and frequent parades, marching through the streets of New York with banners bearing the inscription, "Liberty, Welfare and Education."[3] May festivals featuring singing, speeches, and dancing were attended by large crowds from the German sections of the city.

Contemptuous of what many refugees regarded as the low cultural level of a new and raw country like the United States, some of the most tactless and opinionated among these newcomers manifested an intolerance toward their American neighbors which could only end in bitter controversy and antagonisms. The German Forty-eighters were divided into warring factions which quarreled violently over ridiculous and trivial differences of opinion and policy, lived in narrow cliques, and occasionally were so boorish in their intercourse with neighbors that native Americans were genuinely disturbed. Thus was provided a measure of justification for some of the nativist reactions of the Know-Nothing movement of the 1850's, one of whose aims was to protect the institutions and customs of the American Republic from further European immigration.

A New York saloonkeeper may be cited as an extreme example to illustrate the utter defiance of American customs manifested by some of the most intolerant newcomers among the radical Germans. To parody and ridicule the ceremonies of the church and to express his contempt for the clergy, the owner of the saloon had erected a pulpit at one end of his place of business from which he addressed his customers each Sunday morning on the tyranny and superstitions of organized religion. Such intolerable and tactless conduct was a rare exception and revealed a lunatic, extremist fringe among the German immigration which did great damage to the German-American group as a whole. Fortunately the forces of Americanization were so strong that even the radicals settled

[3] New York *Tribune*, August 19, 1851.

down after a short interval to a peaceful and contented existence as members of the prosperous American middle class. Engels wrote in 1851 to Weydemeyer, who had come to America as a Marxist propagandist, "Your greatest handicap will be that the available Germans who are worth anything become easily Americanized. . . ." [4]

The Irish also were present in great numbers in the New York of the 1850's, and on many an occasion German and Irish immigrants became involved in bloody feuds and pitched battles over incidents arising from the numerous outings of which both groups were fond. The Irish of New York lived east of the German sections and for the most part north of Eleventh and Fourteenth Streets between Broadway and the Bowery, in the area extending to the East River. The New York papers of the 1850's reported many cases of friction between them and their German neighbors, and the picnics of the German *Turner* seem to have been special targets for attacks by rowdies. New York also had a number of descendants of its old Dutch stock who though born in America spoke inadequate English. A small French quarter was located above Canal Street and west from Broadway.

This was the New York which Weitling knew during his early years in the United States. Fortunately for him and others of his kind, living costs were low. Room and board could be obtained at $1.50 a week, and as late as 1861 it was possible to rent a five-room dwelling on the ground floor for $9.00 a month. A pair of good shoes cost $1.25; cigars sold from one to three cents apiece; and a bottle of imported Bordeaux cost twelve and a half cents. As yet the city required no liquor licenses, and whisky and other drinks were sold in the back room of most groceries. *Lagerbier* did not become popular until the Civil War. Policemen, known as "watchmen," were not uniformed, and the fire departments consisted of volunteer companies that contributed more to the

[4] Quoted in Karl Obermann, *Joseph Weydemeyer, Pioneer of American Socialism* (New York, 1947), 28.

color and excitement of life in the city than to fire protection.[5]

To found a foreign-language newspaper in the compact immigrant communities just described, was a fairly simple matter. To keep it alive for any length of time was quite a different problem. Between May, 1850, and May, 1852, twenty-eight German papers appeared in New York and twenty-six suspended publication. Seven more were started before 1854. Most of these papers were weeklies, and only the more important dailies, such as the New York *Demokrat* and the *New Yorker Staatszeitung*, survived for any considerable period. The latter has managed to continue publication to this day.

It was relatively easy to find enthusiastic, like-minded readers and adherents to almost any cause among the members of the German community of New York and the larger cities. Almost any editorial program would find some support among the diverse radical factions that were part of the German element of the 1850's. But the enthusiasm of the radicals for causes was not matched by their resources, and consequently the casualties in the radical German press were very high. That Weitling could keep a paper alive for more than five years in New York is a tribute both to his radical constituency and to his remarkable energy and ability.

Die Republik der Arbeiter had numerous competitors in and outside New York. In the city itself, Heinzen published the *Schnellpost* and later the *Janus* and quickly became involved in a newspaper feud with the newly arrived communist. In addition, Fröbel's *Allegemeine Zeitung*, the *Demokrat*, and the *Abendzeitung* were published in New York, and the last named was a serious competitor for Weitling's paper. Other short-lived radical papers were the *Luzifer;* the *Hahnenruf*, edited by G. Scheibel and J. A. Försch; Gustav Struve's several papers; Weydemeyer's

[5] See "Erinnerungen und Erlebnisse eines Achtundvierzigers," *Pionier-Illustrierter Volks-Kalendar für 1900* (New York *Volkszeitung*), 35–42. The article probably was written by F. A. Sorge.

Die Revolution, which survived through two issues only; several German church papers, and a humor sheet planned in imitation of the *Kladderadatsch.* In the 1850's, outside New York, there were radical papers like the *Arbeiterzeitung* of New Orleans and Cincinnati; *Die Reform* of Baltimore, which was an organ of the workers' association of that city; the *Kommunist,* published by Leopold Stiger in Cleveland; the *Neu England Zeitung* of Boston; Wilhelm Rothacker's *Menschenrechte* of Cincinnati; Fritz Anneke's *Newarker Zeitung;* H. Rösch's *Proletarier,* the first socialist paper founded in Chicago in 1853; and Christian Essellen's brilliant *Atlantis,* from whose pages Weitling quoted extensively. Even so selective and incomplete a list indicates the vigor of radicalism among the German immigration and the large number of refugee Forty-eighters who turned to journalism in the United States.

The first number of *Die Republik der Arbeiter* appeared in New York in January, 1850. The editor and publisher offered it for sale at six and a fourth cents a copy, and announced that until it could be expanded into a daily the paper would appear each month on the fifteenth. The prospectus appealed to both workers and employers, for Weitling classified all but capitalists as workers. With a true but somewhat immodest reference to his long services for the working class in Europe, Weitling offered to become their champion in America, to "take up his cross" anew in his adopted fatherland, and to brave the opposition, ridicule, and mockery of friend and foe, of stupid and intelligent. He likened his steadfastness to the faith and devotion of a Columbus venturing out on unknown seas and boasted that he had never yet failed in any activity which he had undertaken.

In the opinion of the editor, the final objectives of the new paper were the establishment of a bank of exchange (Weitling's *Tauschbank*), to be considered more fully in a later chapter; co-operative stores and warehouses; a new kind of currency based entirely on the amount of labor expended; and the founding of a colony where communist theories could be practiced. Obviously such a program could not be achieved in its entirety immediately, and the first objective of the new paper was of necessity the building of a large circulation list among German-American workers so that they might be welded by propaganda into a homogeneous body devoted to specific common ends.

Weitling believed that 1,000 converts in any given locality would be sufficient to institute a *Gewerbetauschbank* for workers, employers, and farmers. He urged workers to pay part of their earnings in cash to a central bank, accept paper money in exchange, and permit the use of the available cash for the purchase in outside markets of what the members could not produce among themselves. By a weird financial legerdemain, Weitling estimated that savings of $3,000 a week would result from this bank of exchange. He rejected all other reforms as mere palliatives. Needless to add, he was completely dissatisfied with the existing major political parties and proposed a new party of the workers, to be led by himself, which would hold labor congresses annually, summon a "Social Parliament" based on occupational representation, and eventually supplant the existing Congress of the United States.

Thus the first issue of *Die Republik der Arbeiter* was a recapitulation in the main of theories expounded in the *Garantieen*, and the editor's statement ended with a challenge to his readers to produce "something better." Weitling launched his ambitious plan to proselyte America with total assets of $1.50. Without appealing directly to any German organization for aid, he went from house to house among the Germans of New York, rang doorbells on four streets, and in four days secured 400 subscribers.

To build circulation, the editor counted heavily on the help of agents in the larger cities who would solicit subscriptions and supervise the distribution of the paper. Franz Arnold, a mechanic from Frankfurt am Main who was a gifted speaker and at the moment an ardent supporter of Weitling's movement, traveled about and addressed groups in Pittsburgh, Philadelphia, and Cincinnati.[6] Weitling himself made several long trips into the interior, to be described in the next chapter, so that he might meet and recruit

[6] See Louisville *Beobachter am Ohio,* June 11, 1850.

the workers face to face. His enemies tried to block his new venture by circulating false tales that he was a spy—how else could he have escaped so often the clutches of the police in Europe? They charged also that he was not the editor of his paper but received payment from some mysterious unnamed source for the use of his name. According to Weitling's own account, he lost 200 subscribers after the first issue but gained 250 new readers immediately.

Die Republik der Arbeiter had a circulation during the first two months of less than 1,000. Most of the subscriptions had been solicited by the dauntless editor himself, in a house-to-house canvass. With the third issue the circulation jumped to 2,000, and by the end of the first year it reached 4,000. Copies were mailed to Germany, France, and Switzerland, and letters from abroad indicated that the paper was being read by some of Weitling's old followers. The first business office was located at 77 Chatham Street above the offices of the *Schnellpost* and the *Demokrat*, and in the same building the *Bund* maintained a co-operative boarding house. Weitling, however, seems to have received most of his personal mail at the Shakespeare Hotel.

The new paper got a mixed reception from the German press of the country. The New York *Demokrat* spoke favorably of Weitling's general objectives, but deplored the editor's indifference to other reforms, such as free homesteads, an issue which he had dismissed with the comment that it was merely a "stereotyped" slogan for politicians. Others referred to him as an unbalanced and impatient "zealot" who was unwilling to accept a more practical piecemeal program,[7] and a few pictured him as a paid propagandist and a selfish exploiter of the workers. The *Belleviller Zeitung*, which was the mouthpiece of the more conservative, older German immigration of the 1830's, commended the tone, style, honesty, and courage of *Die Republik der Arbeiter*,

[7] *Belleviller Zeitung*, October 24, 1850. See also Columbus *Der Westbote*, December 13, 1850, which cites the Buffalo *Weltbürger*, the *New Yorker Staatszeitung*, and the Cincinnati *Volksblatt*.

but repudiated communism and exchange banks as chimeras.[8] The Cleveland *Germania*, on the other hand, recommended the paper warmly and believed to have discovered evidence to show that its editor had "become more practical" since his arrival in the United States.[9] The *Illinois Staatszeitung* admired Weitling's "courage and fire" but was extremely doubtful about his methods. The New Orleans *Republikaner*, the St. Louis *Anzeiger des Westens*, the Philadelphia *Freie Presse*, the *Pittsburger Courier*, the Baltimore *Deutscher Correspondent*, the Milwaukee *Der tägliche Volksfreund*, and the *Michigan Tribune* recommended the new paper to the attention of their readers and with few exceptions wished Weitling success in his new undertaking.[10]

Weydemeyer, soon to lead a workers' movement in strict conformity with Marxian principles and in opposition to Weitling, in a letter to the *Neu England Zeitung* described the paper of his competitor as "a museum specimen and therefore . . . of some interest, albeit slight, to archeologists." [11] Catholic papers, such as *Die katolische Kirchenzeitung* and the *Wahrheitsfreund* of Cincinnati, and the St. Louis *Lutheraner* denounced the new paper because of its anticlericalism and its attacks on miracles and revelation. The Baltimore *Fackel*, though a radical paper, dismissed Weitling's proposal for a bank of exchange as nothing more than a "pious hope," and the otherwise sympathetic Buffalo *Demokrat* found it impossible to accept the editor's program in its entirety. Papers such as the Philadelphia *Demokrat*, the Philadelphia *Volksvertreter*, the Baltimore *Herold* and the Cincinnati *Volksfreund*, on the other hand, made short shrift of all such "world reformers" and their "pretty playthings." [12] The Columbus *Westbote* thanked God there were no refugees "with their damned socialism" in the Ohio capital, and the Baltimore *Wecker* commented sarcastically on the "vanity" and "selfishness" of "dictators" and

[8] *Belleviller Zeitung*, December 5, 1850; also January 19, 1854.
[9] Cleveland *Germania*, May 15, 1850.
[10] See *Rep. d. Arb.*, February, March, May, and June, 1850.
[11] Quoted in Obermann, *Weydemeyer*, 71; and *Rep. d. Arb.*, July 9, 1853.
[12] Cincinnati *Volksfreund*, May 18, 1854; Baltimore *Herold*, March 18, 1851.

"new Messiahs" of the workers.[13] A few American papers, notably Horace Greeley's New York *Tribune*, quoted occasionally from the new labor paper,[14] but Weitling was deeply hurt and disappointed because the *New Yorker Staatszeitung* paid so little attention to him and his program.

In view of the factionalism so characteristic among radical refugees, it is not strange to find that *Die Republik der Arbeiter* became involved in violent newspaper polemics with some of its competitors. Almost from the outset a serious threat to its future developed from the activities of a group of German editors, typesetters, and printers who decided to publish a paper in New York on a co-operative basis. Weitling agreed to serve as editor, provided the venture would follow his "specific school" of thought as a part of his movement instead of as a separate association. The Central Commission of the United German Crafts of New York to which Weitling belonged apparently approved a plan which would have made such a paper virtually an evening edition of *Die Republik der Arbeiter*, to be known as the New York *Arbeiterzeitung*. But presently a quarrel broke out between the two groups which became so violent that it finally was carried to the courts. The new paper kept up a running fight with its competitor, Weitling insisting on complete centralization of the workers' movement under his "spiritual guidance," and the *Abendzeitung* (the name finally agreed upon) favoring local autonomy and decentralization and accusing Weitling of fomenting dissension between manual and brain workers. The latter countered with the charge that his competitor had stolen hundreds of his subscribers by a deliberate policy of misrepresentation, called attention to "the worm at the heart of our beautiful movement," and accused his opponents of having learned the "art of destruction" from Marx and Engels.

Die Republik der Arbeiter also became involved in a feud with Friedrich Hassaurek and his Cincinnati *Hochwächter*. A veteran

[13] Baltimore *Wecker*, August 7, 1851.
[14] See New York *Tribune*, April 22, 1850.

of the Viennese revolution, in which he had participated as a mere lad of sixteen, Hassaurek considered his paper "an organ for intellectual enlightenment and social reform." An agnostic and an enemy of the church, he had become a leading spokesman for the *Freie Gemeinde* and the *Freimännervereine*, rationalist societies which wanted to substitute ethical culture for old-fashioned religion and organized churches. Weitling distrusted and opposed the movement, "lest it lead us back into the tutelage of the confused . . . German philosophers" and "the vague, dizzy craving for liberty which we have successfully combated for twenty years." [15] He was willing to credit these freethinkers' associations with rendering real service to science, knowledge, and culture, but he regarded religion "as something higher, which presupposes that man has the capacity to transcend himself, and with living emotion, reach across to that which is greater than he is." [16] The atheism of Hassaurek and the *Freimännervereine* represented nothing more to Weitling's mind than "simply another philosophical form . . . to bring the destruction and evil inclinations of the heart . . . under the control of decency. . . ." Hassaurek retaliated by attacking the "brain storms" of all the disciples of Saint-Simon, Fourier, and Weitling and by consigning the *Arbeiterbund* and its sponsor to Russia where all "czars" belong.[17] Quite unfairly he accused Weitling of being a "slave of the priesthood," though on one occasion the latter actually supported Wilhelm Nast, the founder of German Methodism, in an attack in his *Christliche Apologete* on Hassaurek's materialism. Karl Heinzen once referred to the editor of the *Hochwächter* as a mere "beer hall Demosthenes." As a matter of fact, Hassaurek developed into a successful orator in both the English and the German language. In due time he shed much of the anticlerical radicalism of his youth, and became a political appointee of Lincoln, who sent him to Ecuador as minister. In 1872, Hassaurek became a Liberal Republican, and in 1876 he voted for Tilden.

[15] *Rep. d. Arb.*, August 9, 1851. [16] *Ibid.*, December 3, 1853.
[17] Cincinnati *Hochwächter*, April 28, 1852.

Weitling's conflict with Heinzen, champion of materialism and radical democracy, began as soon as the two refugees reached the safe shores of America, and Weitling with his usual naïveté asked Heinzen to join his communist movement. The latter found it almost impossible to co-operate with anyone, and least of all with a communist. Though he always respected Weitling far more than most of the intellectuals in the communist group who accepted Marx as their high priest, Heinzen, in a curt reply to a courteous invitation, refused to join forces with the promoter of the *Arbeiterbund*.[18] The result was a long verbal battle in their respective papers, Weitling deploring the division in the forces of radical reform which deprived him of control of them, and Heinzen becoming more violent and personal in his attacks on the simple-minded tailor. The deep-seated distrust of the craftsman for a university man is apparent in Weitling's rejoinders. He finally finished with Heinzen by calling him a megalomaniac without "an original idea" or a "social system" in his head, utterly ignorant of the workers' problems, and lost in confused notions about parliamentary government, God, and women's rights. Heinzen, in turn, rejected Weitling's attacks on property and his theories about money and exchange *in toto;* sarcastically advised the tailor to stick to his trade, and shed "the mask of the Messiah"; accused him of reprinting libelous matter from other papers; and ridiculed his role in the Revolution of 1848–49. The controversy between Heinzen's *Schnellpost* and *Die Republik der Arbeiter* reached a new low, even for that era of violent personal journalism.[19]

Though the course of the radical journalist was neither smooth nor easy, Weitling claimed to have won 4,500 subscribers by November, 1850, and he listed assets of $450, liabilities of $190, and a cash profit of $260 which he thought would rise to $800 if all papers still on hand could be sold as propaganda leaflets. By

[18] Karl Heinzen, *Erlebtes* (Boston, 1874), II, 164–67.

[19] See *Rep. d. Arb.*, October 4, 1851; also, Wittke, *Against the Current: The Life of Karl Heinzen*, for references to Weitling, and chap. x, on "Social Reform Without Communism."

February, 1851, however, 10,000 copies were stored in his room as "dead capital." He requested a contribution of six cents a month from each member of his *Arbeiterbund* to enable him to start an effective propaganda in England and France, and for several years he considered the possibility of publishing an English edition of his paper. It was clear almost from the outset that lack of funds would make such a project impractical.

By the summer of 1851, *Die Republik der Arbeiter* had encountered new difficulties and its editor was in serious financial straits. He wrote to his friend J. Kriege to describe his "Herculean" patience and suffering and explained that editorial costs had been reduced to as low as $4.00 a week, and that two agents who had promised to provide $25 and $12 respectively had failed to deliver the money. Of the 350 copies dispatched regularly to St. Louis less than a fourth had been sold, and subscribers in that city owed him $125. Though postage amounted to only $2.00 a week, his helpers received $9.00 a week, and total operating costs amounted to no more than $21 a week, Weitling was in arrears for five weeks' rent, amounting to $45. The harassed editor minced no words about subscribers who did not pay their debts, but he had no intention of abandoning the venture.[20] The charge was frequently made, even by fellow radicals like Struve, that Weitling was in debt primarily because he lived beyond his means and did not work as hard as he should. Such accusations drove him into a rage and always brought forth the same answer, namely, that what he owed were "honest debts, incurred for the cause"; that he lived with his workers and drew less pay than his typesetter; and that besides carrying the editorial burdens, he performed much of the heavy manual labor connected with a printing establishment.

Weitling decided that his troubles would diminish substantially if he could find more reliable carriers for his paper, convert it into a weekly at four cents an issue, deliver it each Saturday evening, and print half of it in English and half in German. With his weak-

[20] Weitling to Kriege, June 25, 1851. MS letter in Library of Congress.

ness for figures, he calculated that it would cost $67 to produce an edition of 3,000 a week, provided $350 could be obtained for new printing and typesetting equipment. From an edition of 2,000, he anticipated a surplus of $15 a week, provided the paper were printed solely in German. He estimated the potential circulation at 1,000 in New York, 200 in Baltimore, 250 each in St. Louis and Philadelphia, 150 in Cincinnati, 100 each in Louisville and New Orleans, 70 in Williamsburg, 50 each in Newark and Pittsburgh, and 30 in Buffalo. The rest were scattered through many smaller towns.[21]

The issue of April 18, 1851, summarized the circulation for cities outside New York and indicated that Baltimore received 500 copies, Philadelphia 400, St. Louis 300, New Orleans 200, Cincinnati 150, and Pittsburgh 100. The remaining subscriptions ranged from one each in isolated parts of Texas, Alabama, Michigan, and Iowa, to larger totals in cities as widely scattered as Bridgeport, Buffalo, Chicago, Cleveland, Detroit, Columbus, Dubuque, Elgin, Galena, Indianapolis, Louisville, Rochester, Troy, and Washington. Three copies were mailed regularly to Communia, Iowa, and ninety to Europe. Always there were more papers sent than paid for. In June, 1851, Weitling estimated the circulation outside New York at 2,100.

It was at this point that the editor decided upon a propaganda tour through the eastern half of the United States, to be described in the next chapter. He offered the editorship during his absence to Gustav Struve, another Forty-eighter of radical persuasion who had curious interests in phrenology and vegetarianism, but the latter declined the responsibility and presently issued his own *Der deutsche Zuschauer* ("The German Observer"). Leon Rymarkiewicz, a Pole, finally accepted the editorship but was forced to give it up only two months later for health reasons, though he continued to serve as a correspondent. During the closing months of 1852, Weitling was seriously ill with typhoid

[21] Wilhelm Weitling, "Kreisschreiben an die Tauschkommissionen und Centraltauschkommissionen der Verbrüderung." MS in Library of Congress.

and could not resume his editorial functions until the very end of the year. For a part of 1853, Leopold Alberti acted as editor, thus enabling the founder to devote more time to the *Bund* and the colony in Iowa. In addition to other duties, Weitling wrote an average of eighteen letters a day. To add to his mounting difficulties, his early disciple and agent, Franz Arnold, broke with his organization, organized co-operatives of his own, and founded a paper in Baltimore, which expired after three weeks.

Weitling tried the familiar devices of circulation managers to boost circulation. Copies of the *Garantieen* and of Andreas Dietsch's *Das tausendjährige Reich* were offered as a bonus for new subscribers. From time to time he sold copies of his major works to raise badly needed funds. In August, 1851, he was forced to move the office of *Die Republik der Arbeiter* to 107 Cliff Street. A year later, it was back at *Arbeiterbund* headquarters at 73 Beekman Street. April 8, 1854, the paper moved again to 6 Center Market Place, the next month to 27 James Street, six months later, to 75 Bowery and in April, 1855, to 126 Allen Street. No doubt inability to pay the rent and desperate efforts to retrench were the main reasons for these many migrations. Yet rumors continued to circulate that Weitling was getting rich from the profits of *Die Republik der Arbeiter.* Beginning January 1, 1852, the paper was sent only to subscribers who paid for a year in advance. By November, 1854, the paper became a monthly again, and the editor announced that he might find it necessary to omit issues occasionally because of other demands on his time and energy, and that the substance of his message was available in "The Library for the Workers," small pocket-size, paperback editions, which he sold for from ten to eighty cents a volume. The series consisted almost entirely of reprints of his earlier publications.

By the end of 1854, the publisher no longer could afford to employ carriers, and advertising, because of the sharp decline in circulation, reached the vanishing point. The last number of *Die Republik der Arbeiter* appeared July 21, 1855. In it Weitling thanked his exchanges and expressed his intention of sending them his treatise on a universal language soon as a token of his appreciation for their co-operation. He explained that his duties at *Bund* headquarters and in the colony in Iowa made it impossible for him to continue his newspaper. He pointed to his accomplishments in the American labor movement and, for the benefit of his hostile critics, reiterated that his own compensation had amounted to $7.00 a week plus a small allowance to meet his frugal expenses for room and board. In due time, Struve took over the printing plant of *Die Republik der Arbeiter* for his *Soziale Republik, Organ der freien Arbeiter*.

It is clear that Weitling derived no substantial financial rewards for his efforts on behalf of labor. His satisfactions had to come from quite a different source. Perhaps in that unhappy summer of 1855 when he was depressed by the many failures that were bringing his public career in America to a close, he recalled letters such as the one from a worker in Saginaw City, Michigan, to whom *Die Republik der Arbeiter* had brought "a ray of hope" that "pierced his soul"; or the letter from Watertown, Wisconsin, which reported "the spread of socialism like wildfire," thanks to four copies of Weitling's paper which were delivered regularly to the Germans in that community; or the letter from another frontier community, where the settlers "now feel the breath of this blessed spirit . . . even in the densest forests"; or similar notes of appreciation from correspondents in larger cities. Perhaps also he may have found pleasure in recalling a letter written by Heinrich Huhn of St. Louis upon returning to the United States after sixteen months abroad. Greeted on his arrival in New York by the familiar labor paper, he compared it with "the beautiful snowdrop that delights and refreshes the friend of nature, as it raises its head above the icy plain." "Carry on, restless warrior," he concluded, "even though the road be rough and full of thorns; at its end you will find the most beautiful palm which a victor has ever received—you will live on in the grateful hearts of millions of workers."

Die Republik der Arbeiter was a vehicle for the dissemination of Weitling's theories, not a newspaper in the modern sense of the term. Its advertising was so limited that little revenue was derived from this source, especially since the charge was but five cents a line. Weitling refused to accept money from clairvoyants, astrologers, "embryo killers," quacks and patent-medicine fakers, who advertised extensively in other papers. In its earlier numbers the paper carried a small amount of paid, classified advertising by German pharmacists, doctors, lawyers, bookdealers, watchmakers, bookbinders, and hotelkeepers. It also carried announcements of the meetings and activities of workers' and trade associations and provided a sounding board for their many factional quarrels. Occasionally, Weitling announced the birth of a new paper, like the *Skandinaven i Amerika*, or the New York version of the *Kladderadatsch*, edited by Max Conheim. More often he advertised free of charge the appearance of new liberal journals like Mathilda Anneke's *Die deutsche Frauenzeitung*.

Though Weitling usually wrote a clear, forceful, and even eloquent German, it is interesting to note the slow infiltration of "German-Americanisms" into his newspaper style. The rapidity with which the German spoken by immigrants deteriorates into a strange jargon that is neither grammatical German nor English is notorious in the United States. In the later issues of *Die Republik der Arbeiter*, one can discover such borrowings and corruptions as "setteln," "recorden," "Expensen," "Verrenten," "Settlung" and "geentert."

The bulk of each issue of Weitling's paper was devoted to discussions of such topics as "Value," "Speculation," "Capital and Interest," "Property," "Inheritance," "Law," and the progress of the labor movement here and abroad. Contributions came from workers, or were extracted from papers of a similar viewpoint, like Essellen's *Atlantis* or Fritz Anneke's *Volksfreund*. Occasionally the editor translated from the New York *Tribune*, especially on the progress and experiences of the co-operative movement in Great Britain. Communist activities in Europe were covered by correspondents such as August Willich, and there were numerous special articles devoted to such topics as the misery and poverty of New York's "five points" district, the progress of the labor movement in England, and the argument for a tax on the unearned increment of land.

Much space was devoted to the history of existing communist colonies. Some of these descriptions were written after personal visits to them by the editor, or by one of his correspondents; others were copied from exchanges. In the course of several years, *Die Republik der Arbeiter* carried interesting accounts of life at Oleana, the unsuccessful colony of Ole Bull, the noted Norwegian violinist; of Oneida, the community of the Shakers and Perfectionists; of Ebenezer, a settlement of German Pietists near Buffalo; of the North American Phalanx at Red Bank, New Jersey, copied from Madam Anneke's *Frauenzeitung;* of the colony of Trappist monks in Iowa; of the New Buda of the Hungarian refugees in the same state; of Friedrich Rapp's Economy in Pennsylvania; and of Joseph Bäumler's Zoar in Ohio.

Foreign affairs always received considerable emphasis in Weitling's paper, and the first article of each issue usually was entitled "What is going on in the world." *Die Republik der Arbeiter* carried interesting reports from former colleagues in Europe addressed to "dear brother Weitling," which chronicled the progress of the movement which he had helped to found in Paris, Bern, Geneva, London, and the German cities and gave details about old comrades or about factional quarrels among the communists. The paper circulated to some extent in parts of Switzerland, Germany and France, and occasionally was quoted by European papers, such as the *Deutsche Arbeiterhalle* of Hanover. Quite often it published appeals for funds for the relief of European comrades.

Material of this kind illustrates Weitling's continuing connections with the communist movement abroad. In addition the paper carried many other articles on foreign affairs. H. B. Oppenheim reported regularly on British politics from London, and there were other contributions on conditions in England and the prospects for a social revolution. Weitling personally believed that the national pride of the British was so great, and their infatuation with freedom of speech and of the press so deep-rooted, that a resort to revolutionary methods was extremely unlikely. *Die Republik der Arbeiter* pledged support to the Hungarian revolutionists, and Willich and Carl Schurz reported in 1852 and 1853 on French affairs and on Louis Napoleon's *coup d'état.* Weitling's opinion of Russia was extremely unfavorable, and he pictured the country of the czars as a colossus that threatened all Europe with strangulation and despotism. The paper also carried notable articles on China, Japan, and Australia, and on the progress of communism in the Orient. As far as American policy was concerned, it advocated the annexation of the Hawaiian Islands and chided President Fillmore for his timidity and indecision; favored acquiring Mexico to rescue that country from the intrigues of Europeans and priests; and referred to Cuba as the "outpost of European absolutism in the western hemisphere."

The editor also printed an amazing number of miscellaneous contributions. In 1852, for example, a professor from the University of Giessen contributed a series of articles on agriculture. In 1854, Weitling published a two-act play dedicated to the *Arbeiterbund, Der Sylvesterschmaus* by Friedrich Röpenack. Poems by such liberals and radicals as Freiligrath, August Becker, Madam Anneke, Leopold Alberti, and H. Lauten appeared frequently, with occasional extracts from Weitling's own *Kerkerpoesien.* Harro Harring's "Der Menschheit Auferstehung" was reprinted because it advocated Christian love and a Kingdom of God on earth. Finally, the paper carried a curious assortment of parables and little essays couched in the symbolic language of religion. Such material was repeatedly used as filler. These items were intermingled with articles on inventions, the adulteration of milk, the mortality rate on immigrant ships, the Mormons in Utah, and the relative merits of homeopathy and allopathic medicine, a debate that waxed so violent among his excited readers that the editor had to refuse to accept further contributions on the subject.

Perhaps the most striking feature of this labor paper was the relatively little space devoted to current American issues other than labor. In this respect, Weitling's policy was in sharp contrast with that of many other German-language publications, and their editors frequently commented on their colleague's total ignorance of practical politics. In 1850, Weitling denounced both Whigs and Democrats as "humbugs" and mere seekers of political spoils. Two years later, he endorsed Horatio Seymour for governor of New York, solely because the Democratic state ticket was pledged to fight nativism, temperance legislation, and Sunday-closing laws, issues on which the German element was easily aroused and completely united.

American presidential campaigns impressed Weitling as "comedy" and "shadow-boxing" in which workers should take no part. He favored elections in which men voted for principles and issues; but voting for individual candidates by merely counting noses, and equating the vote of an intelligent and honest man with that of the most "ignorant rowdy," he dismissed as "stupid nonsense." He was not interested in nations as "cultural entities," and agreed with Marx that "the proletarian knows no fatherland."

Karl Heinzen's *Pionier* stands out as a notable exception among German-language newspapers of the last hundred years because of its courageous championing of equal rights for women. The vast majority of German-American editors were confirmed opponents of woman's suffrage and believed that the prime concerns of the females of the race should be *Kinder* and *Küche,* if not always *Kirche.* Weitling accepted a completely masculine interpretation of history, but as an advocate of equal rights for all he felt it necessary to make his position clear. *Die Republik der Arbeiter* adhered to the doctrine that all workers who were not completely free should be emancipated, but added: "If the whole human being is emancipated," then "the wife, and the Jew will be free also. A reformer who knows his business will not concentrate on the emancipation of any particular group."

Weitling's most extensive contribution on the subject of women's rights appeared in the issue of August 28, 1852, and was entitled "Concerning the emancipation of women." Reviewing the problem, with many references to literature from Solomon to Proudhon and Heinzen and to the comments of medical experts on the physical deterioration of women, he expressed a willingness to give women all rights "to which they are entitled, and capable, by nature" of exercising. But he made it clear that he would not have his over-all program of reform modified or restrained by the desires and views of women, for he believed that they were more individualistic than men and not likely by nature to espouse communism. Therefore he tried merely to demonstrate that they would benefit, especially in matters of marriage and parenthood, from a communist regime, and argued that the state of the future must provide equal treatment for men and women as far as wages, social legislation, education, and other rights and responsibilities were concerned. The demand for the vote he dismissed as nonsensical, largely because he considered the whole existing democratic process as "political frippery." In the truly communist state women would have the honor and respect and equal opportunity which was due all human beings, and he agreed with Fourier that "*l'extension des privileges des femmes est le principe général de tous les progrès sociaux.*" Weitling saw his first woman in bloomers in Cleveland in 1851 and ever after wrote sympathetically about dress reform.

Weitling's position on abolitionism fitted logically into his general pattern of reform. He disapproved of slavery. He had made that clear, with some very uncomplimentary references to the "model republic" across the sea, in the *Garantieen*. In 1850, he specifically denounced the new Fugitive Slave Law. A year later, in a strong editorial "On the Slave Question," he denounced slave auctions, the horrors and indecencies of the master-slave relationship, and the intolerable position of the freed Negro in the South and tried to arouse his fellow German immigrants so that they might view the slavery question in its true light. In 1853, *Die Republik der Arbeiter* carried a long article exposing the nonsense underlying theories of racial superiority.

Nevertheless, Weitling had no special interest or part in the agitation of the abolitionists. Unlike Heinzen, he did not make his paper an instrument of the great crusade for freedom of the Negro. Weitling knew very little about the economics of slavery. His editorial guns were trained on the whole system of wage slavery and he was afraid that concentration on Negro slavery alone would divert attention from his more basic program. Thus abolitionism became a side issue. Moreover, Weitling did not relate the problems of free labor in the North to the existence of a slave system in the South, as a few of his contemporaries did. In the first German workers' congress held in America in 1850, sponsored by Weitling, there was not a single reference to slavery.

It is well to remember that German immigrants as a class were slow to take up the antislavery issue. Kriege in 1846 actually argued that the slave system was essentially a question of property and that if the abolitionist crusade should succeed, it would only increase competition among free workers, depressing the white worker without elevating the black.[22] Though he took no part in the abolitionist movement as such, Weitling predicted that eventually there would be a political realignment around an antislavery party which would attract other reformers who championed such issues as land and labor reforms and equal suffrage. He himself continued to support the Democratic party, not because of its attitude toward the sectional controversy, but because of its greater friendliness toward the immigrant, and because he believed the Whig party was full of nativists and antilabor men. By the time of the Civil War, Weitling no longer had an organ for the expression of his views on public issues, and he had virtually retired from the arena of public debate. He followed the course of the war with great interest and accumulated quite a file of

[22] New York *Volkstribun*, quoted in Hermann Schlüter, *Die Anfänge der deutschen Arbeiterbewegung in Amerika* (Stuttgart, 1907), 189.

clippings on the subject, but we have no knowledge of what attitude he took on the specific controversies of the war and reconstruction.

The issues of land reform, free soil, and free homesteads attracted considerable support among immigrant groups during Weitling's public career. Kriege, as pointed out in an earlier chapter, was closely associated with the German land reformers in the 1840's, and voiced their demands in the *Volkstribun*. Weitling believed that the state should own the public domain, and he opposed individual ownership no matter how it might be acquired. Despite great pressure to induce him to support free homesteads, he advocated a system by which tillers of the soil would pay a "use price" into the public treasury. On several occasions he was challenged to public debates with the "land reformers," and once he signed one of their petitions, but he continued to regard their proposals as totally inadequate. His difficulties in maintaining his position in the face of the growing desire of his German compatriots to "vote themselves a farm" perhaps are illustrated best by pointing out that in 1852, *Die Republik der Arbeiter* requested the Germans to petition Congress for homestead legislation; a year later, it sharply criticized a system which would perpetuate individual ownership, and in 1854, it reversed itself again and endorsed the homestead bill. In the meantime, in 1851, Weitling had outlined his own plans for a "rural credit bank."

As far as reforms of special interest to labor are concerned, *Die Republik der Arbeiter* gave much space to the activities of labor groups in the 1850's and to descriptions of the miserable conditions under which many laborers were compelled to work. Weitling deplored the lack of a federal employment service and proposed that his *Arbeiterbund* perform that function for German craftsmen. In his *Nothruf an die Männer der Arbeit und Sorge*, reprinted in his paper on July 29, 1854, he denounced the United States as a "babylon of capitalists, merchants, lawyers and preachers" who live "by thievery, fraud, misrepresentation and hypocrisy," and he produced figures to show what it cost the American people to support such a flock of parasites. He reviewed his theories about the unequal burden of the law upon rich and poor and the frequent miscarriages of justice. In his *Der Katechismus der Arbeiter*, he predicted the decline and fall of the American Republic because of the prevailing caste systems, the Southern slavocracy, the white slavery of the immigrant workers, and the universal decline in public morality. Most of his contributions along these lines were primarily destructive criticism. For all existing evils he had but one remedy: a complete revolution ending with the establishment of the Utopia described in the *Garantieen.*

Die Republik der Arbeiter printed the news about strikes but did not regard them as a means to progress. Weitling had no interest in mere wage increases, and thought they resulted only in spiraling costs and prices. He understood and emphasized the difference between real wages and take-home pay; he deplored the selfish competition for wages between various crafts and the callous unconcern which the organized trades manifested toward the unskilled and the unemployed; and he frankly admitted that in this respect the working class was "as egotistic, selfish, unintelligent and avaricious" as other groups.[23] In short, Weitling was not interested in strikes until *all* workers could be included and the demonstration of labor solidarity carried out under a unified leadership, for the attainment of the basic reforms which he had outlined.

Finally, though *Die Republik der Arbeiter* was more of a propaganda sheet than a newspaper, it felt a certain responsibility to the German-American element, as interpreter, defender and preserver of German culture in a new and strange land. Weitling loved the singing and the comfortable social intercourse of his German fellow countrymen as it found expression in singing societies, *Turner* Halls, taverns, and beer evenings. He frequently attended German *Sängerfeste* and *Volksfeste* and thought some of them equal to the best he had seen in Europe. Such festivities

[23] Wilhelm Weitling, *Der Katechisimus der Arbeiter* (New York, 1854), 11.

provided a cultural nourishment and camaraderie which German immigrants sorely missed in puritanical America, and Weitling believed that such organizations could serve to bridge the gap and end the misunderstandings between Germans and Anglo-Saxons.

But the editor of *Die Republik der Arbeiter* never forgot that he proposed to live "by and for a principle." He agreed with the comments of another German refugee in the *New Yorker Sonntagsblätter*, that "the beer-drinking, song-singing German *Gemüthlichkeit*, as soon as a job and lager beer are available, wants [from its press] only entertaining daily news which it can take in without reflection or exacting cerebration. . . ." Weitling knew that German-language papers could not exist without advertising and that therefore a journalist might be forced to sacrifice some of his independence, but he himself refused to make the slightest concessions of principle. He was particularly irritated by the great interest of the Germans in lodges organized purely for social purposes, and he was among the first to expose this "Logen-Humbug" with its "colored rosettes and ribbons and secret follies," its silly aprons and "stupid faces." Yet these lodges furnished much of the advertising and provided most of the job printing for the German-language press. Weitling exposed their ridiculous antics and demonstrated how they wasted men's time and robbed them of money which could be put to better use. He spoke his mind with laudable courage, but thereby he alienated the financial support of the only group with the resources to keep a German-language press alive.

Weitling was equally disillusioned about the *Turner* movement. Theoretically, it was devoted to the cultivation of the body and to the development of the mind. Many *Turnvereine*, at least during their earlier years, were centers of radical and liberal thought, counting among their members some of the best intellectuals of the German immigration. However, the transition to societies emphasizing the social and the convivial to the gradual exclusion of more serious intellectual interests was easy to make, and it was not long until many *Turnvereine* developed a far greater interest in the bar where good beer was served than in the bar on which they were supposed to practice their giant swings. Weitling regarded Father Jahn, the founder of the *Turner* movement, as "a man who may have been unable to comprehend a sound social idea because he was so preoccupied with physical exercises." He approved of physical exercise, but he could not comprehend the need for special societies for that purpose in a land where there was still so much to be done with ax, spade, and hammer. Though the *Turnvereine* provided an outlet for man's desire for recreation and exercise, they did not produce either more or better socialists than might be recruited among "nightwatchmen, ropewalkers, musicians and trick riders." Weitling could discover no logical relationship between radical politics and somersaults.

Always a friend of the theater, Weitling urged his readers to support German theater companies wherever they existed. He pleaded with parents to teach their children the German language, but he made it clear that his purpose was to develop a bilingual second generation and that he did not intend to use the language as a means of isolating the German group from their fellow Americans.

Weitling enjoyed his social glass of beer or wine as much as anyone. But his paper frequently discoursed on the "national vice" of the German people, too much beer drinking. He seriously maintained that this national weakness had proved a real handicap to the political progress of the German people, who regarded a drunkard almost "as something of a saint," and he pointed out that Germany had produced few, if any, statesmen comparable in stature with those of other nations. More specifically, he attributed the failure of 1848-49 in large measure to too much wine and beer. Occasionally he printed material to illustrate the evil effects of alcohol and tobacco on the nervous system. He ridiculed his fellow countrymen for their failure to unite on any American issue save the beer glass, their "holy of holies." According to his estimate, the German-American group alone spent $20,000,000 annually for beer, an amount sufficient to build a great national university and finance many desirable reforms. Yet, when "Puritanical fanatics" tried to legislate on the personal habits of the people and interfered with the German's desire to observe the Sunday holiday in his own Continental way, Weitling became a rabid defender of "personal liberty"; and when the New York legislature seemed about to pass a prohibition statute, he wrote defiantly: "We will keep on drinking, come what may!"

Die Republik der Arbeiter, like other papers which were the mouthpiece for immigrant groups, was deeply concerned with the problem of protecting the newcomers to America, both on the overcrowded immigrant ships and from the swindlers and "immigrant runners" who infested the port towns and swindled and robbed their innocent prey as soon as they docked in the promised land. Weitling proposed using funds of the *Arbeiterbund* for the erection of a home for immigrants. Occasionally, during periods of disillusionment, Weitling reminded prospective emigrants in Germany that "all was not gold that glitters [*sic*]" in these United States, and that materialism and egotism were as powerful here as elsewhere in crushing "the buds of hope for reform." In such articles he described the dirty streets of America's crowded cities, predicting that soon men would be building skyscrapers and "will be born and die without having seen a cornfield." The sectarian spirit which he found rampant in the United States irritated him also, and he regarded puritanism as a blight which hung over the land and unnecessarily restricted individual liberty. He believed that Germans had a special mission in America, to initiate a labor movement and nurture it to power and influence. However, like many other leaders of immigrants, he quickly discovered that they were becoming Americanized, and that the more they prospered, the more they lost interest in anything save what Engels once called the beau ideal of the *bourgeoisie.*

CHAPTER X

ON TOUR FOR THE CAUSE

AS A JOURNEYMAN Weitling had traveled widely in France, Switzerland, Austria, and the German states, much of the road on foot, after the custom of itinerant craftsmen. In the United States, in the half-dozen years that mark his activity on behalf of an American labor movement, he made no less than seven journeys into the interior. In fact, he was traveling so much of the time that his newspaper and the *Arbeiterbund* suffered because of his long absences from New York. His last five trips were concerned either directly or indirectly with the colony in Iowa, where he struggled to apply his principles of communal organization. The first two were undertaken primarily as propaganda for the Workingmen's League which he proposed to create as a national organization as soon as an adequate number of local *Gemeinde* had been organized, and as an attempt to obtain subscribers for *Die Republik der Arbeiter*. Weitling made detailed reports on these journeys, and although they were concerned chiefly with the progress of his organization, much that he wrote throws light on other aspects of American life in the 1850's, and particularly on the nature of the German immigrant communities.

When Weitling began his propaganda tour he expected that his name, his European reputation, and the importance of his message to the Germans in the United States would ensure adequate publicity in the German-language press. He was bitterly disappointed to find that the competition for space—with better-known figures such as Gottfried Kinkel and Louis Kossuth, fellow refugees who were touring America at the same time, and with the many foreign and domestic crises of the 1850's—was so great that his own activities attracted relatively little notice.

Weitling was accused repeatedly of wasting the funds of his followers in useless and expensive travel. He replied that his first two trips had not cost the propaganda chest of the *Arbeiterbund* a penny, and that statement is substantially correct. The payments for subscriptions to *Die Republik der Arbeiter* were dispatched promptly to the central committee in New York or were used to buy supplies for co-operative stores which Weitling helped to establish in several cities. He was extremely sensitive to the charge that he was engaged in a money-raising campaign and insisted that organization, not finance, was his major purpose. He supported himself largely from the sale of his own books or lived on the hospitality of his friends. In midsummer of 1851 the remainder of his books had arrived from Germany. He sold the *Garantieen* for a dollar a copy, and the *Menschheit* for ten cents. Early in his American career he had received one of those "free tickets" by which people of some public importance were able to deadhead on the railroads, and this railroad pass accounts for the relatively small amounts listed in his account books for travel fare. In July, 1855, Weitling reported that his total expenses for this purpose during all of his seven journeys amounted to $472.65. His first trip cost $125. Friends and followers not only offered him the hospitality of their homes but frequently contributed to his travel fund as well. A Polish barber of Trenton, New Jersey, for example, a veteran of the uprising in Cracow, sent regular contributions of two dollars a week throughout 1851 and 1852, and there are other evidences of the complete confidence which members of the working class had in this champion of their cause.

In the early spring of 1851, Weitling journeyed to Baltimore to address a great fraternal festival of the workers, which also was attended by members of singing societies, a teachers' association, the "Society for Enlightenment and Social Reform," and other German groups. Before a crowd estimated as high as 1,400, he made one of his most charming addresses, a speech which had little to do with propaganda, and which was devoted largely to the subject of immigration and what contributions the Germans could make to the development of true republicanism in America. The speaker was honest enough to report that not all of the 1,400 were interested in the intellectual menu offered them. Apparently only about 400 listened to the address, while the others eagerly turned to the food and drink to which the fifty-cent admission charge entitled them, and Weitling complained that he had to yell himself hoarse to be heard above the resulting tumult.

In July, 1851, *Die Republik der Arbeiter* reported that the founder was ready to begin an official propaganda tour to build circulation for the paper and to enroll members for an *Arbeiterbund*. Weitling announced that he would issue a complete constitution in English, French, and German for the Workingmen's League as soon as enough members had enrolled, and that monthly payments to a pension fund would begin soon. When the membership reached 3,000, he would call a congress of delegates which would represent all local groups.

Interested wherever he went in reporting on prices, rents, wages, and conditions of employment, Weitling found that wages were higher and rents lower in Connecticut than in New York. A day laborer received $1.00 a day, and skilled workers as much as $10 a week, and in the factories, he found employees working a thirteen-hour day for $14 a week. Board and lodging were obtainable for $2.75 a week. Weitling was surprised to find a German community of about 300 in Bridgeport, and he learned that Eduard Schroeter, a prominent figure among German-American liberals and radicals, had been there before him to organize a congregation of freethinkers; apparently the Germans of Bridgeport had no church as yet. Fifteen joined the *Arbeiterbund* and subscribed for *Die Republik der Arbeiter*. Weitling seized this opportunity to visit the home of P. T. Barnum, a name which German editors used frequently as a synonym for American humbug.

He was greatly depressed when he found it necessary to spend Sunday in Bridgeport, a town "as still as the grave."

In New Haven, Hartford, and Springfield, he found that half of the Germans were Jews engaged either in business or in operating inns, and with that trace of anti-Semitism which the champion of equality never overcame altogether, he reported that they did not constitute "a favorable factor for enobling the German element." The beer was poor, the wine adulterated, and the whisky plentiful in these New England citadels of "temperance." He found the Irish addicted to drink and the Germans to playing cards. He visited a number of factories where he saw the daughters of New England farmers tending machines for $20 to $25 a month, with board and lodging for $1.50 a week, and he concluded that they were well treated. In New Haven he attended a lecture by the "speaker" of the *Freie Gemeinde* which Schroeter had organized, and found a small group of twenty-five who were eager to co-operate in the workers' movement. Weitling expounded his own system so dogmatically that he frequently made enemies rather than friends. In Hartford, he found thirty Germans who were ready to sponsor a *Freie Gemeinde*, but few who had money left for the *Arbeiterbund*. Everywhere in New England he noted the "hypocricy" bred by prohibition, and he came to the conclusion that the section would benefit greatly from an immigration of German gardeners and brewers. He also urged a German doctor and a German butcher to move at once to Hartford.

When Weitling reached Troy, New York, he learned that the town had seventeen German innkeepers and so many German lodges that the community could not be interested in any new organizations. Nevertheless, he stayed longer than he had planned and apparently had a thoroughly enjoyable time. As in New England, he visited the textile mills and again could find no "misery" among the girls who were tending the machines at wages of $3.00 to $5.00 a week. He reported that he had seen "no ragged, dirty people" in New England, and that conditions in general were far better than in New York. A few miles from Troy, he addressed an assembly of German picnickers and presided at a public ceremony where several children were baptized according to the principles and ritual of the workers' fraternity without a minister or the formalities of the church. In solemn words, Weitling gave the babies their names and admonished his hearers to accept full "moral responsibility" for the support of the parents as well as the children, in case of accident or misfortune. He was disappointed because he was unable to visit the Shaker colony near by. He succeeded in interesting a little nucleus of Germans in Poughkeepsie in his propaganda, but the German colony of Albany proved to be very apathetic, with its interest divided among *Turnvereine*, singing societies, and lodges.

Weitling moved westward across the state, stopping, among other places, in Rochester and Buffalo. In Rochester he learned of an American shoemakers' co-operative with a capital of $7,000 which had failed, and he decided that the cause of the failure was that "every one wants to rule." In Buffalo he addressed a meeting of workers, and then went on to visit Niagara Falls with his friend Josef Stiger. He found the view of the falls from the Canadian side particularly rewarding and fell asleep on the bank of the river. He ended his account of his visit to America's greatest natural wonder by contrasting this bucolic idyl with the lot of the workers in New York. He could not understand why anyone should care to live in the big congested cities.

Six miles from Buffalo lay the villages of Ebenezer, the first of a number of experiments in communal living which Weitling visited during his journeys across the country. He referred to his stop at Ebenezer as "the most interesting" experience of his life. He was delighted with the four villages that constituted the colony, stretching out over a distance of eight and a half miles. The houses were spotlessly clean and the vegetable gardens neat and well-ordered. A thousand people lived from the products of 8,000 acres, bought originally for $20 an acre and in the 1850's worth more than a million for the whole. Weitling visited the meeting house of these pietists who lived by "inspiration," without the services of preachers, and described the believers as "more noble than the *Freie Gemeinde*." Apparently he took no offense at the religious spirit that pervaded the colony. He merely commented that here the principles of Marx and Engels were realized, not through atheism, but by faith in a divine law of communism.

Weitling enjoyed the food set before him, saw his first poppy field in America, and studied with great satisfaction the prosperous economy which not only satisfied the wants and desires of the members of the colony, but produced a surplus for a lively trade with near-by Buffalo, as well. He learned that men worked twelve hours a day in the mills without supervision and were content to satisfy all their wants from a common store. His only unfavorable criticism was prompted by the lack of interest in the arts and letters: although Weitling was forced to rate the colonists as men and women of average intelligence, the colony had no newspaper, no theater, no library, no musical organizations, and no dancing. The secret of their success as a community lay not only in the character and piety of the members, but in their cautious policy with reference to the admission of new members; their approval of marriage and parenthood; and the fact that the whole group avoided dissension and disunity by accepting the authority of an aged prophet who acted by divine inspiration. While men were rioting in near-by Buffalo over a fugitive slave, here men and women were living in "a Christian communist community," separated from, and at peace, with the world.[1]

Returning from this pleasant Utopian interlude to the stern reality of trying to enlist a badly divided German element, a hostile press, and a skeptical "aristocracy of intelligence" in his high cause, Weitling began to consider some day establishing a colony of his own. This interest grew rapidly into a determination to put his communist system into practice somewhere in America. Apparently he already knew of the region in Iowa which was to be

[1] For a complete history of this society, see Bertha M. H. Shambaugh, *Amana That Was and Amana That Is* (Iowa City, 1932).

the seat of his ill-fated experiment in colonization, for he wrote from upper New York that he must hurry on to Cincinnati and Iowa, and he urged his friends to raise funds, even before his arrival, which might be added to the resources of the *Arbeiterbund* to buy land, build model farms, and "create a model state in the old, decaying commercial state." He requested that his mail be forwarded to him at "Kolonie Kommunia, Elkader Postoffice, Clayton County, Iowa."

At Cleveland, Weitling was delighted to find a co-operative tailor shop operated by the German women tailors of the city, and he reported that the venture seemed to be successful, though a similar attempt by the men had failed. The experiment in cooperation was the result of a bitter fight with employers over wage and price cuts. The "social tailor" addressed about a hundred listeners in Cleveland, but his audience was materially reduced by a picnic which German singing societies and the *Turner* were having a half-dozen miles away. Fourteen of the hundred listeners joined the *Bund* and made their initial payments. Weitling was impressed with Cleveland's wide streets and avenues of beautiful trees, but he was disappointed that the people of the city had failed to sense the possibilities offered by Lake Erie and had not reserved the lake front for a public park. In the store of a German bookdealer he saw "silk trimmings" which he claimed to have invented years before in Vienna and perfected in London, and which were just now coming in vogue in America.

Weitling did not visit Zoar, another communistic venture sponsored by a German religious sect near the modern town of New Philadelphia, Ohio, but he received a detailed report on the settlement from the nephew of its leader, Joseph Bäumler. For two years the young man had acted as bookkeeper for his uncle's venture and now he lived in Cleveland. He estimated the holdings of the colony at approximately 9,000 acres valued at $2,000,000, under the absolute control of Bäumler. Weitling regretted that such colonies could not be integrated with his *Arbeiterbund*, for he was convinced that three successful demonstrations in communal living would be sufficient to affect profoundly the government of the entire United States.

A visit to Sandusky, then and for many years afterward an important center of German settlement on Lake Erie, yielded fifteen recruits for the *Bund*. Lest they become discouraged, Weitling reminded his followers that the Odd Fellows lodge was started with only five members and predicted that the *Arbeiterbund* would be launched with an initial membership of 1,000. Using his fantastic method of prediction by geometrical progression, he pointed out that if 100 members could be enrolled at the outset and each member would bring in one new member at fixed intervals, the *Arbeiterbund* would have over 50,000 adherents in ten years, and a pension fund of $2,000,000 to be invested in stores and shops. From this investment he believed a profit of $500,000 could be derived, although $25,000 a year would probably be sufficient to meet all legitimate claims! "We shall come to power along this road," he predicted, "if only the leaders will remain steadfast, and the members will accept that leadership and not dissipate their strength through internal factional controversies." In passing on from Sandusky to Toledo, Weitling stopped at a little settlement of former German students and army officers, led by a Graf Degenfeld, and was much interested to find a community which lived by hunting, sold wood for powder and brandy, and seemed to work as little as possible.

In Detroit, the members of an existing *Arbeiterverein* and the association of German cabinetmakers voted unanimously to join Weitling's *Bund*. That unexpected success so stimulated the sponsor that he immediately revised his earlier estimates and predicted 25,000 members in two years. He described the state of Michigan as very beautiful, but Detroit proved a disappointment, for it was without paved streets, except for the main thoroughfare, and it was full of churches and lodges. In Chicago, working conditions were bad and Weitling enrolled but one member, a brewer. At

Kalamazoo, he discovered his old collaborator in Switzerland, Simon Schmidt, now working as a tanner. The little settlement at the time had only thirteen Germans, but a number of Hollanders lived near by.

By September, Weitling reached Milwaukee, where a colony of interesting and intellectual Germans gave him a warm welcome, echoed by a friendly Milwaukee press. He was invited to stay at the home of G. F. Becker, a colleague from Paris days. The singing society of the *Arbeiter und Bildungsverein* gave a reception for its distinguished visitor, and here Weitling met its director of four-part singing who was another of his old friends, a communist tailor from Switzerland.

In this "German Athens," the rising empire of the German brewery barons, Weitling found that wages and working conditions were bad, but that beer gardens and music were plentiful. Various German dialects were spoken on the streets, and there were many excellent bakeries. Milwaukee, at the time, supported three German papers and a German school with a staff of three teachers. Its *Freie Gemeinde* met in its own building and was able to pay Eduard Schroeter, its "speaker," a salary of $300 a year. The cost of living was low, butter selling at eleven cents a pound, eggs at seven cents a dozen, and beer for five cents a large glass. "We live here as in a German city," Weitling wrote sentimentally, "hear singing in the streets in the evening, see German signs and churches, read German papers, and go to German entertainments."

On the other hand, Weitling pointed out, real-estate values had gone up sharply, so that lots on which hunters had shot wild ducks only six years earlier now sold for $1,010, the unearned increment lining the pockets of speculators. He did not like the large number of Catholic churches in Milwaukee, the wretched bridges in the German sections of the the city, the large number of Democrats, and the numerous lodges to which so many of the population belonged.

His stay in Milwaukee proved very pleasant, despite a heat

wave, swarms of mosquitoes, and a cholera epidemic. The results for the *Arbeiterbund*, however, were meager.

Weitling moved on to Waukesha, Watertown, and Madison, where he stayed with Fritz Anneke and the feminist leader who was his wife. He noted with satisfaction that Wisconsin permitted immigrants to vote after one year's residence in the state. Madison, at that time a beautiful, lake-rimmed village of 2,000 souls, proved very attractive. The fishing was good, and the itinerant propagandist forgot his mission long enough to go hunting in the surrounding woods. His friends the Annekes were counted among the intellectual leaders of the community. They had organized a reading club, and Anneke was employed as cataloguer of the law books in the state library. Weitling was reluctant to leave his generous and interesting hosts.

In Watertown he found that most of the Germans seldom had more than a dollar in cash except after harvest time, and as he went from village to village, bouncing along in a stagecoach over the rough roads of frontier Wisconsin, he was more and more impressed with the prevailing scarcity of circulating money, and with the system of "store pay," which had been developed as a substitute. In the stagecoach which carried him through the state there were nine adults and three children, a veritable melting pot of English, German, Irish, Norwegian, and American travelers. Several times the stage was mired in the bottomless roads and had to be pulled out by ox teams.

The fare from Milwaukee to Galena, Illinois, was $10, including food. En route, the travelers passed a number of lead mines. By October, Weitling was in Communia, Iowa. "For the first time in my life," he wrote exuberantly, "I stand on the sacred soil of a communal brotherhood." He added, quite truthfully, "This land, as far as the eye can see, belongs to us," for on the preceding day he had taken the fateful step of amalgamating the colony with the *Arbeiterbund*. That transaction will be described in detail in a later chapter. It had unhappy consequences for Weitling personally and for his entire movement, but at the moment he could think only of the "holy cause" for which he had fought so long in Europe and which now at last was coming to fruition on the prairie of Iowa.

Weitling's first visit to Communia was very pleasant. The fall weather was marvelous and invigorating. He inspected the neighboring country and tramped four miles across the prairie to the colony of "Liberty," founded by a group of Mecklenburgers. Though the settlement was then in the midst of difficulties that eventually caused its collapse, Weitling was delighted with what he saw and especially pleased to meet again a man and his wife whom he had known in Hamburg. On October 6, 1851, he moved on, confident that his colony was on a sound footing and absolutely convinced that "animals and men now feel at home there."

In Dubuque a well-attended meeting netted fifteen members for the *Bund* and contributions amounting to $33. At Galena, twelve more were enrolled. In this beautifully situated town Weitling encountered many French Canadians who were employed in the lead mines or in the lumber camps as modern *coureurs-de-bois*. While in Davenport he might have visited the Bishop Hill Colony of the Swedes, but he did not learn of the location of this religious community until too late to turn back. Fourteen of the citizens of Davenport signed membership cards, most of them North Germans from Holstein. The city already had two German lodges, one of them the Odd Fellows; a Democratic Club; and a German school.

From Davenport, the traveler proceeded by boat to Nauvoo, the home of the Icarians. Here he saw the ruins of the old Mormon temple and visited the followers of Cabet who now resided in the ghost town which the Mormons had evacuated. For Weitling, Nauvoo was a place of peculiar interest. He had been introduced to Cabet's theories in France, and now he found the latter's followers trying to put them into practice in America. It was not long before the two prophets of Utopia began to correspond, but a plan to combine their forces was never realized.

The Icarians had developed their town around the ruins of the old Romanesque temple built by followers of Joseph Smith. An imposing structure with emblems of the sun, moon, and stars on its pillars, it had running springs inside. Behind this central structure they had erected a two-story house, some 150 feet long, with a kitchen built into an ell. Upstairs there were rooms for twenty couples, ten on each side of a long gallery. Downstairs was a large hall where the French presented their theatrical entertainments, concerts, and dances and transformed the American Sabbath into "the Parisian Sunday." Weitling welcomed such evidences of the Continental spirit in Puritan America. Some of the members of the colony were living in houses recently abandoned by the Mormons. The children of the colony, at the age of two, were taken from their parents to be given a communal education, but were permitted to visit their homes on Sunday afternoon. They seemed to be entirely happy with that arrangement.

Weitling was delighted with the high intelligence, the moral tone, and the self-sacrificing spirit which he found among the Icarians, but he was greatly disappointed by their slow economic progress. Though the community of 300 was nearly three years old, only half the required number of houses had been finished, and many colonists worked on a rented farm and lived in rented houses. The main community farm of 700 acres was five miles away from the settlement and was leased, not owned by the colony. The workshops were widely scattered, and the colony lacked skilled artisans. Sickness, unfriendly neighbors, and frequent floods added to the colony's difficulties and helped keep the standard of living low. No beer or wine was available, but the distillery was in full operation to supply the men with their regular allotment of whisky. The colony had little sugar; butter and eggs were scarce; milk was available only for women and children; the coffee was poor; the meat supply, however, was adequate. Nurseries and vineyards had been planted, and the livestock was increasing. Weitling noted that the women of Nauvoo were not expected to work in the fields, as in the German colonies of Ebenezer and Zoar. The Icarians held regular weekly meetings and published a paper known as the *Popular Tribune*, but tolerated no religious services of any kind. Weitling enjoyed his visit with his fellow communists, whose language he was able to speak fluently, but he reluctantly concluded that amalgamation with his *Arbeiterbund* was impractical.

The next important stop was made in St. Louis, then an ugly river town with muddy streets, where good beer was sold two glasses for a nickel, and a dog tax of thirty-five cents was levied. Weitling addressed three meetings, including an assembly of English Socialists. He enrolled forty members for the *Arbeiterbund* and collected $70 in dues. He noted that the *Freimännerverein* of St. Louis already had begun to decline, though it maintained a good school, and he concluded that little support for a workers' movement could be expected from such "university people." He advised his followers to build workers' halls to serve as schoolrooms for the children during the day and to meet the needs of adults in the evening.

Early in November, Weitling reached Cincinnati, a city which was to become one of the bulwarks of his movement. The German element there was of great importance, and Weitling enrolled more members than in all the cities he had visited previously. About $2,500 in cash and property were pledged to the *Bund*, and another $2,000 was promised by the following spring for colonization purposes. The workers of Cincinnati already had a hall and a co-operative grocery, which did a business of $4,500 in nine months, at a profit of $600. This group of sixty-five members, an *Arbeiterverein*, a tailors' co-operative association, and a German mutual benefit insurance society joined the *Bund*. The *Turner* and the freethinker's society, however, refused to affiliate with Weitling's organization. Cincinnati at the time had four German newspapers, and one, a labor paper under Catholic influence, proved especially hostile, repeatedly attacking Weitling's "pleasure trips at the expense of the workers." In Cincinnati, the philosophical tailor met Kinkel, the university professor, and found him to be such a "lovable and friendly" person that *Die Republik der Arbeiter* promptly endorsed his cause. One mishap marred this otherwise happy experience in the Ohio River metropolis: Weitling's trunk failed to arrive. In it were his overcoat and 300 copies of the books which he expected to sell to defray a large part of his traveling expenses.

From Cincinnati, the itinerary was upstream to Pittsburgh, where the outlook seemed favorable. The German tailors and cabinetmakers of the city had abundant orders for their co-operative stores and shops and promptly joined the *Bund*. At the time, the Germans of Pittsburgh were supporting three singing societies, three *Turnvereine*, a theater company, a reading club, and many churches. Here Weitling met a street-corner preacher who denounced all religions and advocated a socialist "Jesusville." Weitling did not complain of the smoke and dirt for which Pittsburgh already was noted, for he believed they served as antidotes for diseases.

Not far away from this expanding industrial center was the German communist colony of Economy. Weitling interviewed its governing elders and visited their clean, prosperous village of brick and frame houses. "Ah, if the *Arbeiterbund* only had this place," he sighed, as he inspected hotel, stores, meeting house, communal laundry, vineyards, mills, and the great house and garden of Rapp, the leader of the community. The visitor drank good wine and enjoyed an excellent meal for which he paid twenty-five cents at the hotel. The prosperous little community consisted of some three hundred people, who lived in a hundred houses, and whose property was appraised at $12,000,000 or $14,000,000! Much of their prosperity, however, came from outside the colony, for the community had invested its revenues in several private enterprises. Weitling was honest enough to point out that "their stocks yield more than their labors." He felt happy and at home among these kindly, pious, simple German folk, who reminded him of the people he had seen in Württemberg. He would have been glad to tarry longer. Apparently he was not disturbed by their lack of interest in the social revolution and their faith in the Second Coming! Weitling marveled that the leaders of the community were able to enforce celibacy although most of the members lived in individual houses. He advised the restoration of marriage to ensure the future of the colony but did not succeed in convincing the governing elders.

From Pittsburgh, Weitling moved down the river, via Wheeling, to Cincinnati. The boat fare was expensive, and in Wheeling he detected the evil influence of "preachers, Jews and Democrats." In Cincinnati, he found that the cabinetmakers were on strike and that rioting had occurred near one of the factories because of a ten per cent wage reduction; as a result twenty-one workers were under arrest. He was invited to address a mass meeting of the strikers and their sympathizers; and he seized the occasion to explain his views on the inadequacy of ordinary trade-union methods and the futility of isolated local strikes, as he pleaded for affiliation with his *Arbeiterbund*. Hassaurek spoke at the same meeting, and on this occasion, at least, the two men refrained from attacking each other.

Before the middle of December, 1851, Weitling was in Louisville, one of several important river towns which had been acquiring a sizable and influential German group during the immigration of the 1840's and 1850's. Many Forty-eighters had settled there, and the city already supported two German papers, a German theater, and other German organizations. About one third of the total Louisville population was German, and the number was being augmented almost daily by new arrivals from the fatherland. A local historian, writing in 1852, referred to the Germans as "one of the best classes of our population . . . careful, painstaking industrious people, of quiet, unobtrusive and inoffensive manners; and . . . in a majority of instances, men of education and ability." [2]

Weitling felt quite at home in this vital, growing German community. Seventy-two joined his league, and others contributed

[2] Ben Cassaday, *The History of Louisville* (Louisville, 1852), 247–48; see also *Der deutsche Pionier*, I (1869), 46–50.

a total of $540 for the co-operative movement and other "League purposes." He was honor guest at a great "fraternal banquet and ball," and he engaged in a public debate with a "Mr. X" on the subject of land reform. He found working conditions and wages better than in the North and East, and the cost of living lower. At his boardinghouse, known as "Wolf's Tavern," he paid two dollars a week for a good bed, and the board included meat three times a day and fowl three times a week. Geese were selling in Kentucky for twenty-five to forty cents apiece. The prevailing minimum wage for workers was a dollar a day except for tailors, who, according to Weitling, had fallen almost "wholly under the slavery of Jews." He was surprised to find that the people tolerated the wild speculation in land and city lots. The weather turned out to be the most disagreeable feature of Louisville. In two days it changed "from Siberia to Italy," and on that account Weitling was forced to remain longer than he had anticipated and to abandon his plans for a journey to Texas.

By the first of January, 1852, he was on his way from Louisville to New Orleans, another port town that managed to hold a large number of the German immigrants who landed there. The journey required sixteen days by boat, and on the way down, the traveler witnessed one of the many steamboat explosions and fires so common on the Mississippi at that time. The indifferent attitude of the river men toward the loss of a few Irish and "damned Dutch" made him furious, and he charged that the captain and most of the crew belonged to "God's chosen people."

In New Orleans, Weitling stayed at the home of a carpenter named Heer. A workers' movement already was in existence in the city, a result of the organizing activity of W. Grosser, a German shoemaker who later became an agent for Weitling's *Arbeiterbund*. In 1850, Grosser had founded a "shoemaker's association" to establish a bank of exchange in New Orleans. Tailors and carpenters had supported the venture, and together the three groups had managed to raise a capital stock of more than $1,100. From the proceeds of a ball, the members had acquired a hall for their meetings, but their ambitious plan to print a labor paper had ended in failure. Weitling was greatly impressed by this evidence of workers' solidarity, but bad news also awaited him in New Orleans. A German from Baden who was the agent of *Die Republik der Arbeiter* not only had defaulted on his payments but had failed to deliver papers to subscribers for as long as three or four months. Even after 3,000 undistributed copies had been retrieved, the agent still owed $51 to the New York office. As a result of this experience, Weitling decided to publish hereafter all receipts for the paper and the *Bund*, with membership lists and individual contributions.

More than sixty persons joined the *Arbeiterbund* in New Orleans, but despite such signs of enthusiasm, Weitling concluded that the German element was far more interested in singing societies and *Turnvereine* than in the labor movement. The tailors' association was in financial straits, but the carpenters, more affluent at the moment, blithely pledged to the *Bund* three building lots, on which they had made down payments of $465. By way of contrast, the Germans of New Orleans had raised $2,000 for Kinkel's "national loan" and had supported a *Deutsche Zeitung* with 800 subscribers. Before starting north again, Weitling bought 4,000 cigars and five kegs of wine for $105 in the Crescent City, to fill orders from workers' co-operative stores in Louisville and Cincinnati.

In Baton Rouge, the homeward-bound traveler discovered a Hungarian society led by a former member of one of his communist societies in Switzerland, and learned that the group was operating a co-operative boardinghouse at a profit. In Natchez, the German population consisted of a little more than two hundred, who supported a society for the payment of sick benefits but as yet had no German church. Weitling found the location of the town ideal, and working and living conditions satisfactory. Vicksburg he considered far less attractive. It contained few Germans and offered little prospect for recruiting for the *Arbeiterbund*.

In 1852, Weitling made a special trip into Missouri to visit the colony known as Bethel, founded by Wilhelm Keil. Keil had been a ladies' tailor in Darmstadt. He came to the United States in 1838, worked at his trade in Pittsburgh, and then became a Methodist preacher of the shouting revivalist type, in Kentucky. Bethel was located about forty miles from Hannibal, and the eager Weitling made the journey to the settlement on foot. Again he hoped to annex the colony to the *Arbeiterbund*. He found a group of four villages about six years old, Bethel, Elim, Hebron, and Nineveh. They were inhabited by some 600 people, who lived in 150 brick houses. The first blockhouse, a reminder of the hardships encountered by the pioneers, was preserved as a memorial. With typical German thrift and practicality, it was used as a barn. The colony owned 3,000 acres, operated small mills and factories and a distillery, and sold its surplus products to St. Louis. Life followed a strict communal pattern, and houses, herds, food, and clothing were held in common. The colony supported a band of thirty musicians directed by a former music dealer from Cincinnati, and occasionally staged great feasts, such as a Pentecostal celebration at which they entertained and fed several thousand invited guests from the neighborhood.[3]

Weitling had great difficulty "fathoming the mysteries of Keil and Company." He learned that Keil had sent out agents in 1844 to find this garden spot and finally had made the selection because of his acquaintance with a Swiss widow who lived near Hannibal. He had undertaken the venture in 1845 with a capital of $40,000 and a membership of 1,100, but his followers now had dwindled to about half that number. Every member who withdrew had had his original investment returned to him in full. The colony seemed prosperous enough. Among other things, it produced $8,000 worth of kid gloves a year, operated several steam-driven plants and sawmills, and had an abundance of livestock.

That "equality" for which the colony had been established

[3] For other accounts, see W. G. Bek, "The Community at Bethel, Missouri, and Its Offspring at Aurora, Oregon," *German-American Annals*, New Series (Philadelphia, 1909 and 1910), VII, 257–76, 306–28; VIII, 15–44, 76–81; "A German Communistic Society in Missouri," *Missouri Historical Review* (Columbia), III (1908), 51–74, 99–125.

seemed to elude even so favorable an observer from the outside world as Weitling. Keil and two others apparently managed everything. A "company" held title to the property, but Weitling could not discover who constituted the "company." Keil acted as preacher and physician for the colony. His wife and his most ardent disciples called him "Saviour" and treated him like a second son of God. There could be no doubt that the new Messiah was a dictator. He called no meetings, counseled with no one, and gave no accounting of his activities. Weitling found that he read neither books nor newspapers, could not write a decent letter, and was "not a speaker, but a practiced shouter." At one of the colony's services, Weitling heard its leader shout himself hoarse, pound the pulpit and leap around like a "hyena in a cage," all the time discoursing ungrammatically, and without any semblance of unity, on Thirteenth Corinthians. The burden of the sermon seemed to be a condemnation of all books and rational thinking and a demand for absolute obedience to the leader, the "man of will" in whom earth's fire really burned. In a later sermon, however, Weitling heard a moving appeal for help for the poor of Germany, and he found the exhorter far more attractive and sensible in private conversation than in his public appearances.

Keil was a strong, broad-shouldered man, with regular features and thin lips. He lived in a fine country house on a wooded hill in Elim. It had a beautiful garden and an ample supply of good wine. Keil was a passionate hunter. Every Saturday afternoon he decreed free time for hunting, and in deviation from strict communist principles, each hunter was allowed to keep what he shot. The colony consisted largely of Swiss, Pennsylvania Germans, and former Rappists. One of the most affluent members was the storekeeper, who belonged to the church, but not to the "company."

Weitling was completely confused about the economic structure of the colony. "Vorsteher" divided up and assigned the work and supervised the distribution of food and clothing. An apothecary was supported by the colony, although he was not a member of the "company." At certain seasons of the year, laborers were hired outside the community for $6 to $10 a month, and board and lodging. The colony bought its supplies in Hannibal and St. Louis, and its members drove to the city markets, camping in the streets and sleeping in their wagons. Alongside its noisy revivals, public confessionals, and numerous fast days, the colony supported a singing society, but dancing had been prohibited after several attempts to legalize it had ended in tumult and disorder. Every man received his glass of whisky each morning, and workers in the fields a more generous allotment. The sexes were segregated carefully, even in church, and a nightwatch saw to it that the younger members did not violate this regulation.

Returning to Pittsburgh, Weitling went by steamer, stage, and railroad to Baltimore, covering the distance in twenty-four hours. After many months in the field, he was eager to return to his headquarters in New York. He was completely satisfied with his work, and confident that he now had sufficient members to justify the formal launching of the *Arbeiterbund.*

When Weitling reached Baltimore, however, the city in which he had experienced one of his most notable triumphs the previous year, he found that his movement was falling apart into warring factions, and that the co-operative groceries, bakeries, and tailor shops which he had helped to organize were in virtual bankruptcy because of wasteful business methods and exorbitant salaries for the managers. In an effort to restore harmony, he addressed a meeting of his erstwhile followers but had little success, enrolling only eleven new members. Discouraged by this experience, he moved on to Philadelphia, where he learned to his dismay that the tailors' association had been liquidated, and that a co-operative grocery in New York had failed, with a loss of $2,500.

Weitling launched a bitter personal attack on those who had opposed centralizing the movement by giving him control, and who had insisted on the autonomy of local groups. He exposed abuses in the administration of the sick-benefit funds of local groups and showed how in Philadelphia members had falsely reported illnesses to collect their insurance. The entire experience strengthened his determination to fight local autonomy with all the resources at his command and to resist all proposals to settle controversial issues by mere majority vote. He concluded that it was his solemn duty to hold all authority in his own hands and to provide unity through a constitution which would cover every last detail.

Early in September, 1852, Weitling was seriously ill with typhoid fever, and he did not recover fully for several months. By November, he was able to go to the farm of a friend at Forklanding, in New York State, to recuperate. Three weeks later, he moved to Philadelphia to live in the Workers' Hall and to be near his doctor, a homeopath. He became an ardent advocate of homeopathy, remarking on one occasion that it could do less harm than other types of medical treatment, and that nature would have to do the healing after all. He learned "how much a mere change of scene can do for one suffering from his nerves" and presently reported to his friends that he was able to write again for two hours a day, but that he could not yet walk any distance without becoming completely exhausted. His health was not fully restored until the end of December. Meantime, his movement was seriously handicapped at a critical period in its history by his long illness.

Weitling made five additional trips into the West, mostly on colony business. Part of the way he traveled on emigrant trains filled with newly arrived Europeans on their way into the interior, and thus he became interested in advocating better treatment for emigrants. Without food and washrooms, this "homeless, traveling proletariat" was packed into dirty cars and subjected en route to all kinds of shameful treatment.

In the spring of 1853, Weitling addressed a labor rally in Louisville; in Cincinnati, he visited the *Turner* Hall and the rooms of the *Freimännerverein* and baptized several children at Pentecost. He sampled New Orleans claret in St. Louis and urged local societies to stock it for their bars. Back in Philadelphia, he was honored by a serenade from a chorus of fifty recruited from the

Arbeiterbund, who sang special songs written for the workers' movement. From such experiences the impractical champion of the proletariat, who often was attacked most viciously by the very people whom he was trying to help, managed to renew the courage he needed to continue his fight for social justice.

CHAPTER XI

THE WORKINGMEN'S LEAGUE

THE decade preceding the panic of 1857, which acted as a sharp, although temporary, setback for the labor movement in the United States, also marks a transitional period in the history of socialism. From the purely communistic Utopian type it was developing into a type which would aim at political power by the use of political weapons. In this development Weitling was an important figure.[1]

The period from 1838 to 1857 has been described as "the period of humanitarianism," or the "star-gazing period," in the history of American labor. During these years labor leaders, like other Americans, were genuinely concerned with the growing inequalities which were coming to light in this young and powerful nation dedicated to the principle of equality for all. Robert Owen's panaceas for a brave new world were well known in the United States, where Orestes A. Brownson was wrestling with some of the same problems. Albert Brisbane had introduced Americans to the doctrines of Fourier, had rejected both political action and the class struggle, and had sought to reorganize society into units whose economic and social relationships would be in perfect adjustment.

Brisbane converted to Fourierism Horace Greeley, the poor New Hampshire boy who may have derived his deep sense of "universal justice" from the New England Transcendentalists;

[1] See Frederic Heath, *Social Democracy Red Book* (Terre Haute, 1900), *passim.*

and the New York *Tribune* published contributions by Brisbane on this and similar themes, beginning in 1842. William Ellery Channing, George W. Curtis, Thomas W. Higginson, Charles A. Dana, the poet Whittier, and the novelist Henry James also were involved in various noble schemes which would reconstruct the world more in accord with their hearts' desire, affording the principles of freedom and equal opportunity for all.

Proposals dealing with profit sharing, co-operatives, and new systems of currency, banking, and exchange were widely current. As early as 1827, Josiah Warren, the Bostonian who is known as the first American anarchist, opened a "time store" where labor could be exchanged for labor in the purchase of goods and services, and in 1846, he published his *Equitable Commerce,* a treatise on how to eliminate profit. Weitling was familiar with Warren's theories, and his own objectives were strikingly similar to those of some of these early American reformers.[2] Many of his followers among the German immigrants, however, were far more radical than the average American craftsman of the 1850's, who was turning away from the vague humanitarianism of the prophets of Utopia to a more practical trade-unionism. Among the adherents of Weitling's *Arbeiterbund* were former members of the European League of the Just, the Young Germany movement, the Communist Club of London, and Kriege's Social Reform Association.[3]

There were local labor societies in the United States before 1837. From 1834 to 1837, the cost of living for the average worker had risen sixty-six per cent, and laborers resorted to sporadic strikes to improve the standard of living and to combat the evils that seemed to stem from the factory system. Mathew Carey, a Philadelphia publisher, issued his "Appeal to the Wealthy of the

[2] See Henry E. Hoagland, "Humanitarianism, 1840–1860," *Documentary History of Labor in the United States* (New York, 1918), I, Part IV.

[3] See also F. A. Sorge, "Die Arbeiterbewegung in den Vereinigten Staaten," *Die Neue Zeit,* I (1890–1891), 497–502, 542–47; II, 193–202, 232–40; C. F. Huch, "Die Anfänge der Arbeiterbewegung unter den Deutschamerikanern," *Mitteilungen des Deutschen Pionier-Vereins von Philadelphia,* XVII (1910), 39–52.

Land, Ladies as Well as Gentlemen," in 1833, and four years earlier Thomas Skidmore in his "The Right of Man to Property" had advocated the equal division of property. In 1840, a Working Men's Protective Union of Boston announced that "The Money-Power must be superseded by the Man-Power" and "Universal Monopoly must give place to Societary ownership, occupancy and use. . . . Our Lowells must be owned by the artizans who build them. . . . Lynns must give the fortunes made by the dealer and employer to those who use the awl and work the material. . . ." Industrial congresses were held annually in the United States from 1845 to 1856, and were attended by such prominent figures in the history of social reform as Brisbane, George Ripley, Wendell Phillips, William Lloyd Garrison, Charles A. Dana, Gerritt Smith, Cassius M. Clay, Horace Greeley, and Hermann Kriege. Although the agenda of these gatherings covered a multitude of proposals, from the ten-hour day to free homesteads, they provide abundant evidence of an America in ferment which was seeking progress in many different directions.

Working conditions in the 1840's and 1850's account for the rise of labor organizations and the resort to strikes and boycotts. The census of 1850 revealed that the average wage for factory labor in the United States was sixty-five cents a day. In the 1840's, bricklayers in Cincinnati were receiving $7.00 a week; the bakers of Boston were working eighteen to twenty hours a day; and the carpenters of Philadelphia were being paid $1.25 a day. Despite President Van Buren's effort to establish the ten-hour day as a standard, many American men and women still worked from sunrise to sunset. During the first half of the 1850's, the demand of the organized crafts of New York was for shorter hours and a base pay of $7.00 a week. Unskilled Irishmen were receiving sixty-five cents a day and lived in hastily constructed shanties because they could not afford to pay rent in the tenements. Strikebreakers were readily available, and on one occasion when Irishmen laid down pick and shovel and demanded better treatment, their jobs were filled with newly arrived German immigrants, and the police had to be called to stop the rioting which resulted. In May, 1850, the Laborers' Union of New York City, which included only the unskilled, demanded a rate of $1.12½ a day.

Among all the workers who complained of the economic and social maladjustments from which they were suffering, the lot of the seamstresses was perhaps the most pitiful. A tailoress in New York received eighteen cents apiece for making summer vests, twenty cents for pantaloons, eighteen cents for light coats, and from four to eight cents for shirts. For the finest shirts, which required two days to make, they were paid but fifty cents. Parasol stitchers, who covered the ribs of umbrellas with silk, received four cents per umbrella. It is apparent from such figures that a seamstress might earn a maximum of twenty-four cents a day by working twelve hours and producing three shirts a day. The number of seamstresses employed under such pitiful conditions was estimated at 40,000 in New York alone. Many worked in hot, miserable quarters in the worst tenement areas of the city. When the shirt sewers finally organized in 1851, they had little difficulty in enlisting the support of many public-spirited citizens, and Horace Greeley and Henry Ward Beecher pledged one hundred dollars each to their union funds.[4] In 1855, a committee of workers petitioned the City Council of New York to appropriate $500,000 for the erection of tenements on lots belonging to the city, partly to make work for the unemployed and partly to provide cheaper housing.

Such conditions produced an epidemic of strikes which reached a climax just at the time Weitling landed in New York. The New York papers for 1850 contain many notices of labor meetings and in addition to the more common trades, list organizations of hat finishers, porters, "baggage smashers," milliners, marble polishers, sculptors, paper hangers, jewelers, brushmakers, "segar makers," and members of other trades. Because of the newly established Croton water system the plumbers of New York for the first time became important enough to justify a separate organization. Some

[4] New York *Tribune,* June 8, 1853.

of these unions maintained separate offices for their German- and English-speaking members. The city fathers permitted the City Industrial Congress, representing more than forty labor organizations, to hold its sessions in New York's City Hall. In Pittsburgh and St. Louis, the iron molders were on strike, and the movement for better working conditions involved most of the larger cities in the whole northeastern quarter of the United States. Weitling's *Die Republik der Arbeiter* pointed out that in New York City alone twenty trades had organized in 1850 in the short space of two months and had forced wage increases up to twenty-five per cent. He proudly called attention to the fact that German workers had set the example in many of these trades for their English-speaking colleagues.

A number of the strikes of the early 1850's were temporarily successful. Others resulted in months of bitter controversy, and some ended in bloodshed. The New York tailors' strike of 1850 was one of the worst. Weitling claimed much of the credit for the organization of the craftsmen in his old trade. Because of the propaganda of *Die Republik der Arbeiter*, 2,000 German tailors joined the organization in one day and voted to endorse the "complete social reform" advocated by its editor. The German tailors met regularly in Hillebrandt's Hall on Hester Street. They sent literature to tailors in other cities in the hope of creating "one, unified, great labor army." Weitling was ready to propose a constitution containing his familiar ideas about administrative committees, associations, and paper money. He actually suggested an organization made up of three degrees and with a membership, who were subject to strict military discipline, who wore uniforms consisting of blue shirts, black belts, and oilcloth caps and carried a red flag with a white and silver triangle at its tip.

The strike of the New York tailors began in the summer of 1850 with a walkout of the Irish. The German tailors were drawn into the controversy almost immediately and walked out to support their English-speaking fellow craftsmen. Weitling drafted a formal appeal of the German strikers, entitled "The Rights of Labor *versus* the Rights of Thieves and Drones." Rioting broke out on 38th Street when windows were broken in several tailor shops. Strikebreakers were driven into their houses, and a mob of German workers tore up unfinished garments in shops on upper Broadway and, armed with sticks and stones, engaged in a battle with the police. The latter reported that a mob of several hundred, "apparently all Germans," were responsible for the disturbance and thirty-eight Germans were arrested. The tailors insisted that they had been provoked and attacked by the police while peacefully engaged in trying to win new members for their union.[5]

Late in July, a mass meeting was held in front of the New York City Hall to protest against the conduct of the police. Weitling addressed the German group, and Brisbane spoke in English. After the oratory, the crowd marched through the Bowery and down Hester Street to the headquarters of the German tailors, where a rousing reception awaited them.

On August 19, Weitling again addressed the German tailors at Hillebrandt's and announced that although he disapproved of strikes, favoring co-operatives and banks of exchange instead, the strike must be carried to a successful conclusion. Two thousand workers promptly authorized the formation of an executive committee of thirteen and chose Weitling as one of the group. This committee sat almost continuously but, from the outset, was hopelessly divided on principle and tactics. Thoroughly disgusted, Weitling denounced the "tower of Babel of counselors and leaders" and argued that in times of crisis a temporary dictatorship was absolutely necessary. Though he regretted and disapproved of rioting, he wished for the Parisian proletariat, which would neither have been inhibited by the Anglo-Saxon's regrettable innate respect for law nor divided as the workers were in America "because of differences in language, nationality, and religion." The divisions in the committee were not serious enough, however,

[5] New York *Tribune*, August 6, 1850.

to prevent plans for a co-operative clothing store, for which Greeley consented to act as treasurer.

Weitling represented the German Central Committee of the United Trades in the city's Industrial Congress. Occasionally he acted as secretary of this larger body. He helped frame the resolutions of the German group, hailing the tailors' demands as "moral, moderate and just," and protesting the violence of the police in a country where "we did not expect to find . . . a Russian police." [6] His proposal to establish an association clothing establishment, where clothes would be exchanged for loans, and wages would be limited to just enough to meet the cost of living until all such loans were repaid, was "received with applause" [7] and was approved by "industrials of all branches." On the occasion of Weitling's address to the German journeymen bakers at Concert Hall on Grand Street, the New York *Herald* was sufficiently impressed to refer to the speaker as "a sincere convert and disciple of the system of Icarian socialism." The account referred to the agitator's "ardent oration" which opened to "the astonished vision and imagination of the German journeymen bakers a prospect of wealth, ease and independence and abundance, without much work, by merely joining the Socialist Union. . . ."

Meantime, the thirty-eight German tailors were packed into twelve small cells. Their bail had been fixed at such an excessive figure that it proved impossible to effect their release. The men turned out to be such model prisoners that their lot aroused sympathy both in labor and nonlabor circles. Though the New York *Tribune* reported that the Industrial Congress of the city had failed to raise a penny for their defense, other efforts were made to raise funds in New York and elsewhere for their relief. The case was described as another example of the law's delay whenever a minority group engaged in an unpopular agitation was involved. By the end of November, 1850, the tailors were still in

[6] New York *Tribune*, July 25, 1850; see also *New Yorker Staatszeitung*, May 11, 1850.

[7] New York *Tribune*, August 8, 1850; and John R. Commons *et al.* (eds.), *Documentary History of American Industrial Society*, VIII, 296–309.

prison. They were tried finally on December 3, and the controversy was ended when they accepted pleas of guilty to assault and rioting.

The labor demonstrations of the 1850's and the prominent role played by immigrants in the growing demands for higher pay and shorter hours startled conservative Americans. The sudden rise of organizations like the *Sozial Reformer*, the *Freie Gemeinde*, the *Arbeiterbund*, the *Ouvrier Cercle*, and the "Polish Democrats" seemed to foreshadow an organized assault upon property by recent arrivals whose poisonous propaganda was hidden under a foreign tongue. Brisbane addressed the German tailors and advocated putting an end to "the servitude of capital," and there was much talk of a general strike and "revolution" at the meetings of certain foreign-language groups. In 1853 a new French paper, *Le Republicain*, dedicated to the programs of Brisbane and Considérant made its appearance in New York.

To conservatives who regarded the demand for homesteads as communistic, the situation was most alarming. James Gordon Bennett's New York *Herald* predicted that bands of the discontented soon would be marching on Wall Street to plunder the banks; and he lumped socialism, Fourierism, and infidelity into one great mass of iniquity. Bennett described Brisbane as "a genuine, red republican and dyed-in-the-wool Fourierite of the French class" and warned good native Americans to avoid all such foreign "theoretical nonsense." To the *Herald*, socialism was "all nonsense, humbug, cant, hypocricy, rascality and visionary," and men like Weitling were ridiculed for their inadequate command of the English language and accused of "playing and working upon the feelings of the brave, noble, simple, honest-hearted Germans." [8] Other New York papers, such as the *Courier* and the *Enquirer*, ranted in much the same terms against a labor movement which they viewed as a communist assault on the pillars of society.

The one notable exception to such newspaper attacks was Greeley's *Tribune*. Horace Greeley had reached his position of

[8] New York *Herald*, April 19, 27, 1850.

influence after a long hard journey which had started with his indenture as a boy apprentice to a master printer. As a young man, he had worked twelve hours a day and had lived in a boarding-house with a group of shoemakers. Mindful of these early hardships and of his association with many honest craftsmen, he courageously presided in 1850 over the first meeting of the Printers' Union in New York and in due time established a plan of profit sharing and employee participation in the ownership of his paper.[9] Greeley was a friend of George Ripley, and he had read Brisbane's *Social Destiny of Man*, the best exposition of Fourierism in America. Such questions had been discussed in the *Tribune* as early as 1842. Charles A. Dana covered the Revolution of 1848 for Greeley's paper and engaged Karl Marx as a regular contributor, paying him five dollars an article until the panic of 1857, when his honorarium was cut in half. Of all the important New York papers, the *Tribune* alone dealt sympathetically with the rising labor movement and endeavored to report it accurately. Its columns were open to discussions of the theories of Marx, Brisbane, and Proudhon, and its editor personally contributed time and money to the early labor movement. Not until the arrival of Jenny Lind did the labor news disappear from the front page of the *Tribune*. Then even Greeley surrendered to the glamour of the Swedish nightingale.

Weitling became deeply involved in the labor troubles of the 1850's because his fellow craftsmen and fellow countrymen played such an important role in them. Yet he distrusted all sporadic strikes, and was suspicious of leaders who did not have complete blueprints for the future. Moreover, he was dubious about the amalgamation of the working class and *petite bourgeoisie* which he saw developing steadily under American conditions. The piecemeal methods of the American reformers lacked that "common unity" which he desired. From his standpoint, it was essen-

[9] See Henry Luther Stoddard, *Horace Greeley, Printer, Editor, Crusader* (New York, 1946), *passim;* Don Seitz, *Horace Greeley* (Indianapolis, 1926), *passim.*

tial to "emancipate the workers from the wage system and the employer" altogether and to relate all labor politics to that ultimate objective. Though his experiences since the publication of the *Garantieen* had modified his views in some details, he still regarded his magnum opus as the platform for a genuine social revolution, a new kind of exchange, and the right kind of workers' associations.

The German Central Committee of the United Trades, of New York, and its representation in a permanent industrial congress which presumably spoke for all workers, regardless of nationality, seemed to Weitling to be at best only a small beginning. It is true that the movement spread into other cities, and that the New York Germans at first contributed rather generously to a common treasury. Before the end of 1850, Weitling was in correspondence with persons as far away as Michigan, Kentucky, and Wisconsin who wrote to seek advice as to the proper kind of labor organization to be established. In reply, he proposed his *Arbeiterbund*, with membership books like those used in Europe; he described a program which should include old-age pensions, sick benefits, a new medium of exchange, and a plan of social organization to end the existing employer-employee relationship. Weitling knew that months of preparation with local groups and a substantial accumulation of dues and contributions would be required to launch such a program on a national scale. The propaganda tours described in the preceding chapter were planned to carry his gospel to the Germans in all parts of the United States, but his inadequate English made it impossible for him to make a more general appeal, a fact which Weitling deeply regretted. He tried in vain to enlist the formal co-operation of leaders like Brisbane and Cabet, but the *Arbeiterbund*, started "officially" in 1852, was almost wholly his own work.

Meantime, Weitling's *Die Republik der Arbeiter* published encouraging accounts of the spread of its founder's principles into Philadelphia, Pittsburgh, Cincinnati, Louisville and other cities. Franz Arnold initiated the movement in Pittsburgh, Baltimore, and

Philadelphia, and for a time, it was vigorously supported by the Philadelphia *Freie Presse*. The *Arbeiterverein* of Newark adopted a constitution which was reprinted in *Die Republik der Arbeiter*, and its 122 signers, representing a number of different crafts, joined Weitling's movement. A farewell banquet for Arnold in Baltimore was attended by more than 600 persons. George Lippard, a youthful exponent of Weitling's principles, founder of a labor league, and publisher of an English-language paper, worked untiringly for the *Bund* in his City of Brotherly Love, and in Boston some American radicals found Weitling's theories not unlike those of Josiah Warren. In April, 1850, at the Shakespeare Hotel, Weitling addressed meetings of German bookbinders, portfolio makers, shoemakers, cigar makers and cabinetmakers and sought their support for his association.[10]

By the fall of 1850, the optimistic promoter of the *Arbeiterbund* expected to have 100,000 followers of all nationalities, enough "to control the presidential election." He called upon the "new apostles" to carry his gospel from city to city and from house to house. In St. Louis, long extracts from *Die Republik der Arbeiter* were read aloud at mass meetings of enthusiastic workers. In Pittsburgh, a workingmen's congress launched a *Volks Tribun* with 500 subscribers. In New York, a weekly addressed special appeals to French workers. German tailors paraded with a band through the streets of Buffalo, to the great disgust of more conservative citizens. Weitling announced that he was busy with plans for a German workers' congress to be held in October. Though all such activities were merely preliminary to the formation of the *Arbeiterbund*, the leader of the proposed organization was completely satisfied with his achievements during his first year of activity in the United States. He was especially pleased by the attention he was receiving from some of the German-language press and pointed out that he would have been treated far less generously in Germany.[11]

[10] New York *Tribune*, April 29, 1850.

[11] See Schlüter, *Anfänge der deutschen Arbeiterbewegung*, 128–60. Among

The chief opposition to Weitling's program came from such papers as the Washington *Zuschauer*, which accepted political advertising from the Whigs; from Catholic papers; from conservative Democratic papers like the Columbus *Westbote;* and from the *New Yorker Staatszeitung*, which regularly referred to socialism as a "rhinoceros." The *Westbote* ridiculed Weitling as "the dictator and saviour of these latest world reformers" who talk about a "blood red republic"; it suggested that if Americans could read propaganda of this sort in English translation, they would be forced to conclude that Germany had emptied her insane asylums in the United States.[12]

There is some evidence to show that Weitling would have preferred postponing his call for a workers' congress to found a workers' party until more preliminary spadework had been done. Nevertheless he found it desirable to take the initiative in inviting the German workers of the United States to send delegates to Philadelphia, and he scheduled October 21, 1850, as the date for the beginning of their deliberations. Officially, the call was issued in the name of the German Central Committee of United Trades and the German-American Workingmen's Society of Philadelphia. Representation was fixed at the ratio of one delegate per hundred members, and each worker was asked to contribute twenty-five cents to cover the expenses of the congress. At the request of *Die Republik der Arbeiter*, other German-language papers joined in the call.

The debates in the various *Arbeitervereine* concerning the purpose of the congress, and the contests for election of delegates proved spirited and exciting.[13] The New York *Abendzeitung*

Weitling's papers there is a letter to Brisbane in which he suggested, "I may be and am inclined to be of use to you. Your paper can break its course at any time, so long not another paper such course has taken." See also *Rep. d. Arb.*, September 30, 1854, and Redelia Brisbane, *Albert Brisbane: A Mental Biography* (Boston, 1893).

[12] Columbus (Ohio) *Westbote*, November 29, 1850. For a list of papers fairly sympathetic with Weitling's program, see *Rep. d. Arb.*, December, 1850, and *Belleviller Zeitung*, August 22, 1850.

[13] See St. Louis *Anzeiger des Westens*, September 24, 1850.

opposed the movement because it objected to any "centralization" of the labor movement under Weitling. Papers like the Lancaster (Ohio) *Volksblatt* had little sympathy for the "Utopian ideas of refugees," and the Columbus *Westbote* remained consistently hostile to Weitling.[14] On the other hand, the *Beobachter am Ohio* argued that the labor movement needed unification badly and that the founder of *Die Republik der Arbeiter* was the natural leader to weld the scattered forces of the workers into one powerful organization.

Weitling's German Labor Congress was the first ever held in the United States, and in some respects it marked the climax of Weitling's influence in America. The delegates, representing between 4,360 and 4,400 workers, came from *Arbeitervereine* of varying strength in many parts of the nation. In St. Louis, for example, a membership of 310 was represented, in Buffalo 260, in Louisville 150, in Pittsburgh 160. The Philadelphia delegation represented 153 tailors, another group of 60 from the same trade who called themselves a "Social Tailors' Society," and an *Arbeiterverein* of 300.[15] Other sizable delegations came from Baltimore and Cincinnati. The New York group represented 946 organized carpenters, 500 tailors, 120 shoemakers, 80 sculptors, 30 printers, 25 cigar makers, 35 bakers, and other smaller constituencies and included, besides Weitling, such prominent leaders in German labor circles as H. Seeman, F. Steffen, J. Frankony, and J. Triebswetter. The cash resources of the organizations represented at Philadelphia totaled over $19,000. The expenses of the congress were estimated at $600; contributions amounted to $1,000.[16]

The congress was in session from October 22 to October 28. Most of the delegates were adherents of the Weitling program, for it was almost wholly due to his propaganda that this novel assembly in German-American labor history had been called. In a week

[14] Columbus *Westbote,* November 29, 1850.
[15] For the complete roster, see *Rep. d. Arb.*, October and November, 1850.
[16] Schlüter, *Anfänge der deutschen Arbeiterbewegung,* 83–84.

of arduous committee work and lively plenary sessions, the congress hammered out a set of resolutions covering a wide range of subjects. Indicative of Weitling's dominant role, first place in the platform was given to his views about banks of exchange, and co-operative associations. The special committee which reaffirmed his familiar theories on these matters consisted of Weitling, Franz Arnold, at that time still his ardent disciple, and C. Jüngrig of Buffalo. Resolutions were adopted which called on local organizations to deposit their funds with a central bank of exchange and to accept paper money in return; raw and finished products deposited in central storehouses were to serve as security. To implement such a fundamental revolution in the economic system, labor groups were urged to form local co-operatives, to acquire warehouses for purposes of storage and display, and to create central organizations in the larger cities which might eventually co-ordinate their activities into a single unified system. It was proposed also to have the *Arbeiterbund* act as an employment bureau to which all vacancies would be reported.

Only after banks of exchange, currency, and co-operatives had been thoroughly discussed did the platform deal with problems of political organization. Among reforms in this field, the congress favored the selling of public lands to actual settlers only, protection of homesteads against forced sale, limitation of the amount of land held by any individual, high taxes on land privately owned and withheld from use, better protection for immigrants and the granting of citizenship on grounds other than mere residence, direct election and recall of all officeholders, the administration of public works by the banks of exchange (*Tauschassoziation*), and the repeal of all restrictive legislation dealing with Sabbath observance.

Indicative of the genuine interest in education and learning which Weitling and many of his fellow Germans had, the congress advocated a system of free public schools from kindergarten through the university, for the "harmonious education of the whole man according to all his powers and capacities"; better pay for teachers, who were to be elected by the people; the complete divorce of church and school; public libraries; special institutions for the blind, orphans, and the deaf and dumb; adult education for workers in evening and Sunday schools which emphasized technical and general education, and instruction in English; and the development of reading clubs, bookstores, *Turnvereine*, and other organizations for the improvement of the mind.

Another set of resolutions dealt with ways and means to raise the funds necessary to carry out the proposed program. Every member of the *Arbeiterbund* was expected to contribute six cents a month to a propaganda chest, to seek new converts by personal solicitation, and to support *Die Republik der Arbeiter*, the official organ of the movement in New York. Plans to finance an occasional supplement in French and English for non-German readers also were considered. Lastly, there were resolutions on colonization, looking toward the creation of "workers' republics" from the surpluses to be derived from the co-operatives and the banks of exchange.

The congress adjourned with the expectation that further meetings would be held. A final manifesto signed by twenty members, including W. Rosenthal of Philadelphia, who had served as presiding officer, Weitling, Franz Arnold, and other representatives from New York, St. Louis, Louisville, Baltimore, Buffalo, Cincinnati, Pittsburgh, Williamsburg, and Newark expressed complete satisfaction with what had been accomplished and predicted great things for the future.

News of the congress reverberated through the radical German-language press for some time. Some of the local organizations solemnly ratified the congressional resolutions, and for a brief period, the *Arbeiterbund* seemed to boom. Co-operatives multiplied and small sums were raised for a bank of exchange, an aspect of the movement to be treated more fully in the following chapter.

In Weitling's own words the purpose of his *Bund* was to spread, by word of mouth, printed matter, and example, information about a "republic of the workers." By that term he meant a state organized solely in the interest of those who toil for their living. His ultimate goal was one great league of workingmen which would exercise a powerful influence on questions of wages and working hours and would unite all existing workers' insurance and benevolent activities under a central treasury strong enough to pay sick benefits and old-age pensions to all its members. Weitling's immediate objective was social insurance; his ultimate goal, a complete social revolution.

With his usual disregard for actualities, the founder of the *Bund* forecast the enrollment of 1,000 dues-paying members the first year, 3,000 the second year, 7,000 the third, and 125,000 by the end of the seventh year. He solicited contributions to the social-insurance fund, ranging from $1.00 to $10, and assured prospective members that their investments would yield a substantial interest rate and would be safer in the treasury of the *Bund* than in fraternal lodges or private banks. To prove his point, he demonstrated how coal worth $100, bought at wholesale at a saving of twenty-five per cent to forty-five per cent, could be resold at retail to members for $125 to $145. The profit of at least twenty-five per cent then would be used immediately to buy and sell flour and other products, and these profits would be reinvested until the total yield reached a figure adequate for use as the capital stock of a workers' bank.

Recognizing that homogeneity and unity were the *sine qua non* of success, Weitling advised extreme caution in admitting new members; because of his distrust of the democratic process, he urged as few meetings and as little debate as possible. After all, he saw little to debate about a "mutual insurance company," and he was convinced that to ensure success all authority must be vested in the leadership of the Central Committee. That committee, meeting weekly, was expected to administer all the affairs of the *Bund*, to provide pleasant and profitable social gatherings for its members, and to leave "the parliamentary apple of discord" to others. Weitling regarded *Die Republik der Arbeiter* and the *Garantieen* as the Bible of the new movement, and he wanted all questions of principle and procedure settled by an appeal to these basic sources.

The founder and chief promoter of the *Arbeiterbund* promptly provided himself with an account book, in which he planned to keep an exact record of the receipts from each member of the organization, with such additional data as the date and place of admission to the *Bund*, a record of the individual's initial deposit of $10, and of his monthly dues of $1.00, and other notations about the member's travels and personal experiences. At various points in his career, Weitling was charged with profiteering at the expense of the workers. The evidence is to the contrary. His account book was preserved when, late in life, he destroyed a large part of his personal papers, and it reveals a man of scrupulous honesty and simple living habits. His own name appears in the book as the first member of the *Bund*. He paid his initial deposit of $10 and his monthly dues like everyone else. These payments totalled $180.80. His expenses for his various activities were held to a surprisingly low figure. Each member had a membership book in which his dues were receipted, and Weitling carried a book like all the rest. The accounts which have been preserved for 1851, 1852, and 1853 include the names of some 500 members, arranged in columns, and also a list of the "withdrawals."

Throughout 1851, largely because of his own activities in the field, various local groups and many individuals joined the *Bund* and sent their payments to headquarters in New York. These revenues came from many cities, and they are not to be confused with the larger sums which local bodies raised for the establishment of co-operative stores and workshops or for workers' meeting halls in their own localities. These Workers' Halls (*Arbeiter Hallen*) were social and cultural centers for the German element as well as meeting places for labor groups or mutual-insurance societies. Weitling personally visited a number of these halls and addressed the brethren during the five years of his leadership and periodically printed model constitutions for such workers' benefit societies. The receipt of the first issue of *Die Republik der Arbeiter* in San Antonio was responsible for the formation of an

Arbeiterverein in that city. Twenty members of a newly organized group in Nashville hailed the "dawn of a new era" for the worker in America, and Cabet, replying in French to a letter from Weitling, promised to call on him in New York to discuss the pooling of their resources.

The size of the *Arbeiterbund* may be estimated variously from 1,000 to 5,000. In the first burst of enthusiasm, many societies announced affiliation *in corpore*, but the real test was the number of members who actually paid dues. By this criterion, it seems unlikely that the *Bund* exceeded 4,000 members at its highest point of success. Additions and withdrawals occurred so constantly that accurate estimates are exceedingly difficult to make. Weitling's own figures indicate that after four years of activity the net membership had dropped to 967. He once announced that he would not call another congress until he had 3,000 members. No such congress was ever held.

Before the close of the first year, dissension broke out in the ranks. The causes were many. Weitling objected to a proposal to summon other German organizations, such as the *Freie Gemeinde*, to future labor congresses. A group in Philadelphia charged that he was seeing the country at the expense of the workers and accused him of regarding the *Bund* as but another fraternal insurance society. In Detroit, the *Arbeitervereine* were attacked from Catholic pulpits and were forced to publish rejoinders in the *Michigan Tribune*. In Cincinnati, a band of secessionists demanded "a complete break with Weitling." Before the end of another year, Rosenthal of Philadelphia, who had presided over the congress of 1850, and A. Minsky, an erstwhile Polish supporter, were read out of the *Arbeiterbund* as traitors. Weitling insisted that "Whoever has created a cause is its natural leader. . . . Every effort to upset this principle stems from selfish ambition." Harassed and depressed by such unhappy developments, he unburdened himself in a letter to his old friend, Simon Schmidt, with whom he had worked in Switzerland. Schmidt replied with a complete endorsement of his old comrade's course of action and sent him thirty calfskins from his tannery in Kalamazoo, one half to be sold to the associated shoemakers of New York, the other half to be accepted as a donation to *Die Republik der Arbeiter*.

Despite increasing evidence of internal friction, the official organ of the *Arbeiterbund* reported early in 1852 that additional groups had been organized in many cities and listed substantial financial receipts from these new sources. Weitling himself tried to infuse new life by a prodigious correspondence which he carried on with his followers everywhere. In Cincinnati, 89 members paid $477 into the central treasury, and they owned and operated a hall and a co-operative grocery which seemed to be quite successful. In Sandusky, a nucleus of four members grew to fifty. Detroit sent in contributions from eighty members, and the news from Milwaukee and Buffalo was equally encouraging. Buoyed up by such reports, Weitling decided that the time had come to put the whole movement on a sound constitutional basis. In the issue of *Die Republik der Arbeiter* of April 3, 1852, he published his new constitution.

Weitling was the sole author of this constitution, which officially proclaimed the *Arbeiterbund* in existence after May 1, 1852. Later, when he was criticized for having ignored democratic procedures, he replied that such complaints were "the voice of ambition and conceit," and he urged the dissatisfied to withdraw. He promised, however, to submit the constitution to a congress for revision as soon as the membership should reach 3,000. Though the number of bona fide members still was small, the founder's mastery of the multiplication table convinced him that as a result of the new constitution, the *Bund* would grow by leaps and bounds.

The constitution itself described a workers' league with the following main purposes: to establish a mutual-insurance society which would pay death, sickness, old age, fire, and, eventually, unemployment insurance; to found economic associations to make goods and services available as cheaply as possible; to create a savings bank, a building and loan association, and a colonization society; and to carry on propaganda for the realization of these objectives. Dues were fixed at $1.00 a month. An initial contribution of $10, payable also in goods, was required of all members. Weitling considered this initiation fee a mere loan, for he was certain that the benefits of the organization would quickly repay the initial investment. To complaints that dues were too high the founder replied that workers could be expected to devote one thirtieth of their pay to "the cause of the future" and demonstrated that they spent much more money in one evening in their lodges or churches.

The new constitution consisted of 270 paragraphs, neatly subdivided. Part I described the insurance and pension funds in detail. A yearly pension of $150 or free admission to the colonies of the organization was promised every member when he should reach the age of fifty, provided he had belonged to the *Bund* for ten years. Plans were announced to provide homes for injured and maimed workers and for admission of their families to the colonies. Sick benefits were fixed at $3.00 a week, death benefits at $20. A fire-insurance fund was contemplated when the membership reached 3,000. In the meantime, the *Bund* guaranteed to pay up to $100 in each case of fire damage. Of the monthly dues of $1.00, 25 cents was assigned to propaganda and fire-insurance purposes, 25 cents for sick benefits, and 50 cents for the pension fund. Members also were encouraged to invest their surplus cash with the central treasury, their deposits to be used for the good of the cause and to be returnable on demand. Administration of these various funds was to be carried on practically without cost to the members, or would be financed by voluntary gifts and by the sale of publications. The pension fund was to be invested in real estate and primarily in the property of such colonies as the *Arbeiterbund* might establish. The fund accumulated for the payment of sick benefits would be used to finance co-operatives, and Weitling expected a return of twenty five per cent from that investment and stipulated that all profits above that figure should be paid into the common treasury of the *Bund*. The constitution made members subject to assessments, however, if the return from their local co-operatives should fall below ten per cent. The fantastic suggestion was made that profits might reach 520 per cent. In that event, they would be credited to members' dues.

Part IV of the document dealt with colonization and provided, in elaborate detail, for colonies to be established with the funds of the *Arbeiterbund*, whose permanent congress would act as trustee for all colony property. A considerable amount of local autonomy was guaranteed to such settlements as long as the mode of life in the colonies did not conflict with the basic principles of the *Arbeiterbund*. The constitution described minutely the process of gaining admission to a colony. A period of probation was provided; and members were required to make an initial deposit of $100 for each adult and $50 for each child, to finance their own travel expenses, and to provide sufficient clothing and bedding for one year. The constitution stipulated that all colony property be held in common and that members who withdrew could never claim more than their original investment.

Another section of this extraordinary document described the procedures for establishing and operating local co-operatives, workers' halls, and building and loan associations; the Central Committee of the *Bund* was authorized to initiate such undertakings on its own responsibility, if necessary. Section VII dealt with various methods of propaganda and again designated *Die Republik der Arbeiter* as "the compass" and "heart" of the movement.

Of even greater importance were the provisions for the administration of this vast dream empire of the workers. At the base of the pyramid were the local *Gemeinde*, above them a *Kreis*, and at the top a congress of from 25 to 100 members. The *Gemeinde* were to elect the members of the congress by a complicated nominating process which was expected to rate candidates according to fitness and devotion to the cause. The organization, of course, reflected the plan described in Weitling's earlier writings. Those members of the congress who lived at headquarters constituted a central executive committee and were the real governing body of the organization. This committee kept the records, administered the pension fund, directed the propaganda, levied assessments, conducted elections, and kept in touch with the local *Gemeinde*. A Commission on Admissions (*Aufnahmekommission*) consisting of the president, secretary, and leader of the propaganda held office on indefinite tenure; it was expected to meet weekly to pass on applications for membership. Women were eligible but were expected to maintain a separate health-insurance fund. The constitution closed with admonitions to the members to attend meetings regularly and to observe a dignified procedure. Significantly, it also described a method for expelling undesirables.

The constitution represented an incredible mixture of minute regulations and eloquent propaganda and was intended to deal with every conceivable detail. Its grandiose proposal for a pension fund was expected to yield the fantastic total of nearly $2,500,000 in ten years. Weitling readily admitted that his whole structure rested on faith and high moral principles and was designed to ennoble the human species. Though he had failed utterly to provide sound means for implementing his ambitious program, he seemed completely satisfied with his handiwork. He convinced himself that the movement was progressing as a practical program, for it combined all the useful precepts of all the reformers. And though the masses might lack faith and the "sophists" oppose his plans, he was proud and confident of his achievement: he had founded an *Arbeiterbund* open to "communist, socialist, Democrat, Republican, Catholic, Jew, Protestant, and Atheist" alike, provided they subscribed to its general insurance program and paid their dues promptly. With such an organization, he expected to revolutionize America within a few years.

Beginning in April, 1852, *Die Republik der Arbeiter* reported regularly on the membership lists and the funds that were received from a surprisingly wide area, from New England to Texas, and from New York to Iowa. These lists continued to be impressive well into 1854. In addition, the paper carried reports of organizations which had resolved to join in a body and of special balls and entertainments to raise money for the pension fund. New locals of the *Arbeiterbund* appeared in various parts of the country in 1852 and 1853. A report selected at random from the May 8, 1852, issue of *Die Republik der Arbeiter* listed total receipts of $1,536 since the last issue of the paper. These contributions varied from larger amounts, such as $175 from Cincinnati and $330 from New York, to $1.00 from Madison, Wisconsin. In addition to such payments, a number of individuals made deposits for membership in whatever colonies might be established. The issue of September 11, 1852, reported $462 in deposits and $154 in dues collected by the New York *Gemeinde* alone. Of this total, $577.50 was paid into the central treasury. Cincinnati, at the same time, collected $296.71 in deposits and $124 in monthly dues and turned over $356.94 to the treasury. Figures for eight cities revealed contributions to the treasury of the *Arbeiterbund* ranging from $106 to $476.50.

The first annual report of the treasurer reported receipts comprising deposits, dues, and loans, made either with or without interest, of $14,629.87 and total expenditures of somewhat over $12,000. The figure for expenditures included more than $7,000 for the colony in Iowa and $2,000 for "propaganda." Under the latter category were included $274.28 "for editorial services," $690.88 for typesetting and printing, $111.08 for the printing of membership books and the new constitution, and $24.15 for printing a new kind of paper currency. Two months later, Weitling estimated the membership at 500 and the capital stock at $17,000, including the assets of the colony. Loans in varying amounts, beginning with $100 and totaling $6,000, had been made for ten-year periods without interest by a number of members who thereby automatically acquired the status of trustees of the *Bund* and its property.

Weitling's personal membership book bore the number 1,025, and he carried it with pride. He was even prouder of the many workers' halls that were opened as the result of his movement, thus providing social, intellectual, and cultural activity for his fellow craftsmen. In October, 1852, the New York *Gemeinde* dedicated its *Arbeiter Halle* at 73 Beekman Street with a program of music, singing, dancing, and speaking, and the workers' chorus sang a new song which had been written especially for the occasion and was sold thereafter as a four-part composition for eight cents a copy. The hall was used three times a week by women and children for all kinds of entertainments. F. A. Sorge, one of the most prominent figures in the early history of the socialist movement in the United States, worked at the New York hall in the winter of 1852–53 for $3.00 a week. Weitling himself continued to act as the man of all work for the *Gemeinde*, a service for which he received $6.00 a week and room and board until the final collapse of the movement.

The New York group supported an excellent singing society, and its theatrical company presented a play each Sunday. Sunday afternoons were reserved for the admission of new members; Monday evening was dedicated to singing and dancing; and for the rest of the week, the hall was available as a social room for reading, smoking, and drinking beer. Lectures and debates were arranged only rarely. In April, 1853, the ladies' auxiliary presented the men with a new mural decoration representing a beehive embroidered on a red background, with the inscription "*Heil dem Arbeiterbund*," and on that festive occasion, a lad of seven recited Weitling's poem "Ich bin ein kleiner Kommunist."

St. Louis, Philadelphia, Detroit, and New Orleans had similar halls and staged many celebrations. In Philadelphia, the picture of "our master Weitling" hung on the wall alongside the insignia of the *Bund*. The group owned a good piano and maintained a grocery in the basement of the building. Its facilities were available for dances, weddings, and singing societies five nights each week. In New Orleans, the workers' hall was decorated with a red banner and on the wall were inscriptions with Weitling's name in the middle, the German word *Tauschbank* to the right, and "Emancipation of the Worker," in English, on the left.

Weitling believed that his little band made up in quality what it lacked in quantity. In his "New Year's Reflections," an editorial of January, 1853, he compared himself and his loyal followers with Leonidas and the 300 Spartans who had held the pass at Thermopylae. Though he had great faith in his work, Weitling was extremely sensitive to the criticism of his enemies, and he pleaded again and again for more understanding and sympathy. Like a great father in the conservative tradition, he lectured the young men and women on sex and marriage, temperance, continence, and the preservation of a "sacred sense of shame"; as a liberal, however, he was concurrently advocating greater rights for women, and appealing for "strong bodies, enlightened minds and noble hearts" for the "sacred cause." The symbolism of the martyr and of the Messiah traveling a thorny road to save the working classes appeared more and more frequently in his pleas to the faithful, which were always a curious mixture of paternalism, preaching, Bible quotations, and lectures by a loving father who knows what is best for his children. Yet Weitling insisted that he had not the least desire to become a dictator and referred constantly to himself as the first servant of the people.

The *Arbeiterbund* already had entered upon a serious decline when "New Year's Reflections" was written in 1853. Letters from Cleveland and Philadelphia reported that interest was rapidly waning. In Cincinnati, a hundred seceders had formed a new organization late in 1852, and a group in Louisville had followed their example. Unfortunately, the factional strife of the Cincinnatians was thoroughly aired in the Cincinnati *Volksblatt*. The charges centered on the founder's "stubborness and grandfatherly manner," and he was accused of substituting his dictatorial "will" for "principle." In December, the Cincinnati group actually advertised a debate on the subject "Is dictatorship necessary in order to carry out our reform program?" Weitling pointed out that some of his most violent critics had paid the least into the treasury. The storm blew over and in the end some rebels rejoined the *Bund*, but similar complaints continued to come from other cities. One reason for the trouble, apparently, was that many members had expected the movement to produce jobs and financial prosperity for them and were bitterly disappointed to find that the constitution specialized not in jobs but in principles.

Early in March, 1853, the German workers of New York tried to capitalize on the arrival of August Willich to infuse new life into their radical movement. Weitling had known Willich in Europe. He was a Forty-eighter, a fellow refugee, and an ardent radical who like himself had become an opponent of Marx. At a huge banquet in Shakespeare Hall, where at least 350 people were seated at tables in a hall decorated with red flags and the triangle that symbolized Weitling's movement, Willich addressed his fellow radicals in an eloquent and revolutionary speech on the theme that bread was more essential than liberty. Weitling, in the main address of the evening, declared that "Communism alone is the alpha and omega for the redemption of a suffering humanity," "the gospel of the poor and the oppressed, for whom a prophet, deserted by his people, had been crucified on Golgotha." Turning to Willich, who wore a bright red scarf across his breast, Weitling presented him with an enormous secondhand sword in the name of the workers of New York, reminded him that Christ had come to bring not peace but a sword and urged the newly arrived comrade to make good use of this new symbol of power and leadership "in the holy battle for the finest treasures of mankind."

The celebration was a very successful and happy occasion. A collection was raised for the relief of fellow communists in the jails of Cologne and Paris, and a youngster recited Weitling's poem about the "little communist." When the formal program ended shortly after midnight, the celebrators adjourned to the hall of the *Arbeiterbund*, where they danced until dawn. The occasion, however, did not give the *Arbeiterbund* the stimulus which had been expected. The New York *Demokrat* ignored the event altogether, and the *Abendzeitung* gave it only four lines. The *New Yorker Staatszeitung* ridiculed "Brother Weitling's speech about Jesus Christ, the first proletarian" in its account of the comic-opera presentation of the sword to Willich, who looked "like King

Solomon arrayed in all his glory," and the *New Yorker Allgemeine Zeitung*, always critical of the founder of the *Arbeiterbund*, referred to the latter's "rhetorical manner which suggests that of a Methodist preacher."

More serious than such unfriendly references to this bizarre celebration was the response of about 800 German workers in March, 1853, to a summons in the *New Yorker Staatszeitung* to meet in Mechanics Hall, 160 Hester Street, to discuss plans for a rival *Allgemeiner Arbeiterbund*. The new movement emanated primarily from Joseph Weydemeyer, an ardent young disciple of Marx who had come to New York to become the leading propagandist for the Marx-Engels group. For a time, Weydemeyer had considered taking over *Die Republik der Arbeiter*, but Marx had advised him to have no traffic with its owner and publisher.[17] The Marxists had neither an organ nor an official representative among the German-Americans until Weydemeyer assumed the leadership of their group in New York and undertook to defend Marx from the relentless attacks by former associates such as Heinzen, Willich, and Weitling, all of whom were now in America. Weydemeyer, the official spokesman for the Marxists, organized a club known as the Proletarian League shortly after his arrival in the United States and in 1852 founded the short-lived *Die Revolution*, remembered only because Marx contributed his famous essay on "The Eighteenth Brumaire of Louis Bonaparte" to this little radical sheet. Though attacked immediately by Weitling for advocating a piecemeal program of mere political patchwork, Weydemeyer persisted in his efforts to recruit a following among the Germans, and his *Allgemeiner Arbeiterbund* soon became a dangerous rival to the older organization.

Weydemeyer's *Bund* was content, at least for the present, with a program of essentially bourgeois reforms. All of them could be achieved by political action, including the ten-hour day, land re-

[17] See Franz Mehring, "Neue Beiträge Zur Biographie von Karl Marx und Friedrich Engels," *Die Neue Zeit*, XXV (1907), 99.

form, child-labor laws, quicker naturalization, cheaper judicial remedies, mechanics lien, and similar proposals. The new organization enlisted the support of men like Dr. G. Kellner, former editor of a paper in Kassel who was then in charge of the New York *Die Reform,* and of Dr. Abraham Jacobi, a prominent young Forty-eighter who is best known today as America's first great pediatrician. Weydemeyer organized the workers by wards and constantly stressed "working class reform" by political action. He rejected Weitling's "one big union" idea, with his religious Utopianism, bank reforms, colonization plans and other panaceas. Thus the battle of Brussels between Marx and Weitling was renewed on American soil.

Many of Weitling's followers joined the new *Bund,* and nothing he could say in denunciation of the plagiarism and competition of the recently arrived "Marxian Sophists" could hold them in line. One reason for the success of the new organization was that its methods were more in accord with conditions in America, where political change was frequent but social revolution impossible.[18]

Papers like the Cleveland *Wächter am Erie* published Weydemeyer's platform and urged their readers to join the new organization to escape from the "fog of fantasy."[19] The Louisville *Anzeiger* accused Weitling of sabotaging this genuine workers' movement. The Columbus *Westbote,* consistently conservative, continued to thunder against all reformers who "hang out the red rag and blow full blast into their trumpets" and pointed out that the world was full of uplifters "who sought to make all mankind happy from behind their beer glass."[20] Actually neither Weydemeyer nor Weitling's organizations could possibly have survived the panic of 1857, the slavery crisis, and the Civil War, when issues far greater than theirs divided the nation. Years later other *Arbeiterbunde,* such as Gustav Struve's *Soziale Republik,*

[18] See Obermann, *Weydemeyer,* 65–70; and F. A. Sorge, "Joseph Weydemeyer," *Pionier-Illustrierter Volks-Kalendar für 1897* (New York), 54–60.

[19] Cleveland *Wächter am Erie,* April 13, September 29, 1853.

[20] Columbus *Westbote,* April 22, 1853.

were organized among the Germans, but the socialist movement as such virtually had to make a fresh start in America after the Civil War.[21]

By 1854, ugly charges were circulating about financial irregularities in Weitling's declining *Arbeiterbund*. The New Orleans *Gemeinde* reported that its accounts did not tally with those printed in *Die Republik der Arbeiter*, and Weitling accused the treasurer of the central committee of failing to report several contributions, whereupon the latter filed his accounts in the presence of witnesses. As of February 26, 1854, they showed an income for twenty-one months, including subscriptions to the paper and payments for the colony, of $18,240.48, the bulk of which had been paid out to Communia, Iowa. Two thousand dollars had been spent on *Die Republik der Arbeiter*. The treasurer's cash balance amounted to only $865 for the various insurance projects of the organization, though the pension fund was carried on the books at $7,195 and the fire-insurance fund at $482. Weitling believed that a movement was on foot to force him to sell the colony and appealed to local treasurers to send their funds more promptly to New York headquarters.

In April, 1854, a number of the *Gemeinde* refused to give Weitling the power of attorney he had requested for the *Bund* and the colony to facilitate clearing up the tangled relations which were forcing both enterprises into bankruptcy. Further secessions followed his admission that the property of the colony was now the only remaining security for pensions. Thereupon, certain *Gemeinde* stopped payments altogether, demanded the return of their deposits, and became more and more abusive in their attacks on Weitling's personal character. The New York group split into two factions because Weitling postponed the election of a new central committee, and presently the *Arbeiterbund* was involved in a

[21] See Hermann Schlüter, *Die Internationale in Amerika* (Chicago, 1918), 6–7; Heath, *Social Democracy Red Book*, 29; Heinzen's *Pionier*, September 5, 1858; C. F. Huch, "Geschichte der freien Sonntagsschule des Arbeiterbundes bis zum Jahre 1884," *Mitteilungen des Deutschen Pionier-Vereins von Philadelphia*, XIV (1910), 28–40.

nationwide controversy over the feasibility of calling another labor congress. There were many original members, however, who continued to defend the "spotless character" of their leader and to assure him of their unqualified allegiance.

As matters grew steadily and rapidly worse, Weitling became more violent and more emotional in his defense against the charges of dictatorship. He accepted full responsibility for assuming the office of treasurer of the *Bund* and announced that he would not surrender his mandate until and unless the congress proposed for 1855 ordered him to do so. He protested his inability to find reliable and competent helpers and insisted on obedience from the disgruntled minority. In a dramatic rejoinder to his critics, full of metaphors and similes, ranging from the old Napoleonic guard that never surrendered, to the helmsman standing fast at the wheel through a roaring storm, Weitling announced that he would remain firm in the face of adversity. "Our propaganda is going backward instead of forward," he wrote in October, 1854; "the membership of the *Bund* is decreasing instead of increasing. The circulation lists of the paper are shrinking and our resources are drying up. . . . We shall begin all over again with what is left. We have our honor, we shall benefit from our experiences and we shall build for the future." Two months later, he called the new congress, which never met. In May, 1855, he announced that he would try to extricate himself from the colonization fiasco so that he might, like Wallenstein, recruit a new army for the *Arbeiterbund*.

After March 1, 1854, when he assumed responsibility for the administration of all funds, Weitling kept the daybook of the *Bund*. It continued to show small receipts from individuals from many states, but the entries were diminishing rapidly and stopped completely in March, 1856. In July of 1856, a few additional contributions were recorded, and as late as July, 1857, two loyal members continued to pay their dues. The same account book contained a carefully itemized statement of expenditures including even such minutiae as five cents for a stamp and a few pennies for a lead pencil. It revealed the cost of operating *Die Republik der Arbeiter*, the New York *Arbeiter Halle*, and the colony. A balance in the treasury of $1,905.18 in May, 1854, had shrunk to $274.63 by December, 1857, although total receipts for the period had amounted to nearly $6,000. Assets of the *Arbeiterbund* in July, 1855, consisted of the thousands that had been hopelessly sunk in the colony, $1,100 in cash, and an inventory for the printing establishment estimated at $1,800. Few local organizations any longer paid dues into the central treasury. Some, like the *Gemeinde* in Cincinnati, not only had stopped payments but had circulated round-robin letters urging other groups to do likewise, and as a result, many local groups clamored for the return of their investments.

Weitling's wages had been $7.00 a week, plus the carefully recorded expenditures for rent, food, and medicine. From July, 1851, to July, 1855, the founder of the *Bund* had accepted $478.65 to pay for travel on colony and *Bund* business, and wages for 204 weeks at $7.00 a week, totaling $1,906.65. In addition, he had charged his simple living expenses at the New York headquarters, $30 to pay the doctor during his long illness, and a few gifts in the form of goods, amounting in all to $565.40. He insisted that the organization still owed him $512.72. He paid his own dues to the end of 1855. The last issue of his paper appeared on July 21 of the same year. There is nothing in Weitling's manner of living, either before or after 1855, to indicate that he profited financially to the slightest degree from his activities on behalf of the workingman.

As the end of the *Bund* drew near, Weitling reviewed his five years of activity. Blamed for the disintegration of the *Bund* and victimized by scurrilous attacks which pictured him as a common swindler, he could only reiterate that he had never profited in any personal way from the movement and restate his conviction that too much local autonomy and too little centralization were the main causes of failure. He believed he had dealt too leniently with the colonists in Iowa and that he should have forced them to sell out to the *Bund* at the very begining of his contacts with the colony. He admitted sorrowfully having learned too late that men whom he trusted had betrayed him, but he insisted that he had never been a dictator nor ever desired to be one.

The *Arbeiterbund* really had no official end. Its funds had been dissipated in several directions; and when the last shreds of control by a central body were torn away, the organization broke up into local groups, of which some endured for a time, others were dissolved at once, and others lived on in another form as purely social organizations. The *Bund* simply evaporated into thin air, but many local *Gemeinde* survived as active social and fraternal centers for the German-American element. The New York *Gemeinde* staged its most successful social occasions when the *Bund* was virtually bankrupt. Its Christmas and New Year's festivities in 1854 were unusually joyful, well-attended affairs, which featured the distribution of gifts, singing, dancing, and amateur theatricals. The society sponsored a huge picnic on Staten Island in the summer of 1854, with athletic games and plenty of beer, and it continued to operate its hall at a cost of $2,200 a year, one half of this amount coming from Americans who paid to use its bowling alleys. The Baltimore *Gemeinde* dedicated a new hall in August, 1854, which it rented for $500 a year; with beer selling at four cents a glass, this obligation was defrayed by the sale of drinks in one month. At Philadelphia, the *Arbeiter Halle* was so profitable that the *Gemeinde* was able to reduce the monthly dues of its members and to pay six dollars a week in sick benefits. The *Bundeshallen* in New Orleans and St. Louis were equally successful.

CHAPTER XII

BANKS, CO-OPERATIVES, AND RAILROADS

ON MANY occasions, Weitling emphasized that the heart of all his reforms was the *Tauschbank* (Bank of Exchange), or the *Arbeiterbank*, as he sometimes called it. He regarded the *Arbeiterbund* as a means of organizing labor for this ultimate objective; and though *Die Republik der Arbeiter* discussed many things, it never failed to stress that a new method of exchange was the center of its entire propaganda. Essentially, Weitling's plan involved substituting a new ticket system of accounting between creditors and debtors for existing currency and methods of exchange. Without abolishing the existing system of production, he would abolish the monopoly power of the capitalists by means of a bank of exchange. The plan in itself involved a striking deviation from pure communism.

Weitling's program proposed the establishment of workers' warehouses in which all raw materials and finished products would be deposited. In return for their deposits, the workers would receive a new kind of paper money based solely on the labor value of the products involved. Henceforth this would serve as their medium of exchange in all transactions. Obviously, if workers and farmers would deposit all their products in exchange for paper certificates of this kind, the middleman would be eliminated and the profit motive would disappear from the capitalist system. Furthermore, by this device, producers who were members of the bank of exchange could fix prices and control markets, avoid violent fluctuations in employment, and bring supply and demand into perfect balance. A centralized administration would reduce the expense of operation to a minimum. Speaking again for the skilled craftsman, Weitling proposed to give to guilds of journeymen and master workmen the function of deciding what goods should be produced and the responsibility for guaranteeing their quality. An expert commission would determine the amount of paper money to be issued in exchange. Part of the proposal was a requirement that the price of the products of the guilds be fixed at a figure sufficiently above the actual cost of production to ensure a surplus. Thus ordinary taxes would be unnecessary; and the funds required to pay management and to finance hospitals, the educational system, and other social objectives would be provided.

Weitling was enough of an economist to know that many factors, such as raw materials, machinery, capacity and demand, are involved in producing a finished, salable product, yet he insisted that the time consumed in its production was the only constant which could be accurately computed to represent its true value. Thus, a gold chain might be worth from 50 to 100 hours of work and a bottle of champagne from 12 to 18 hours, for their value for purposes of exchange depended solely on the work hours required to produce them.

To set his new plan in motion, Weitling expected the workers to buy stock in the bank of exchange with ordinary existing currency, but for the cash thus deposited they would receive the new paper money in exchange. It was assumed that they would be as well off after the transaction as they would be if they had kept the old-fashioned circulating medium. The ultimate goal of this financial legerdemain was a system in which society would really own all existing property, but actual possession and use would be in the hands of individuals because of the new processes of exchanging labor for labor. Weitling pointed out that under his scheme organizations of all kinds could preserve their peculiar interests and objectives and yet participate in the bank of exchange.

Thus personal liberty would be assured or, better still, redistributed to ensure all men an equal amount, though perhaps somewhat less than they had enjoyed under existing inequitable conditions. He was sure that the new paper money (*Tauschmittel*) would be an important step forward toward "the realization of Christian principles."

Weitling regarded the *Tauschbank* as a panacea for all the economic ills of society. He expected it to revolutionize the social order so completely as to make political campaigns and elections superfluous, and he was sure that his plan could be inaugurated by a relatively small group and once begun could attract the support of millions. "We Germans can do more for social reform in one year and with a thousand members, by means of the bank of exchange," he wrote enthusiastically in 1851, "than we could accomplish in a thousand years with a million votes."

This "time theory" of value was, of course, not an invention of Weitling. As already suggested, Josiah Warren's "time store" in Cincinnati operated on the basis of selling at labor cost, plus four per cent for shrinkage, freight, rent, and the service of waiting on customers. In Robert Owen's model settlement of New Harmony, Indiana, such a store was in operation for a short time, and Weitling's proposals were similar to Owen's Equitable Bank of Labor Exchange. Proudhon, to cite still another experimenter with exchange, advocated the organization of industry for the exchange of commodities on the basis of voluntary, self-governing associations of producers; free competition was allowed among the various associations under the general supervision of two national federations of consumers and producers. The connection of all these proposals with modern syndicalism, which seeks to replace the centralized sovereign state by a "cluster of sovereignties" based on units of production, is obvious.

Proudhon, like Weitling, regarded democracy as the most unstable of governments, an absurd and impossible way of governing, a "worn out childishness" that could only impede progress. Both men believed significant advances could come only from *des ésprits d'élite* and preferably from a dictator, not from the masses. There were significant differences between Weitling's *Tauschbank* and Proudhon's People's Bank, but these need not be developed in detail here, except to say that Proudhon's plan to establish free credit embraced all classes, including capitalists and owners who could borrow *crédit gratuit* from his bank, whereas Weitling's plan limited participation strictly to workers engaged in useful, productive labor and service to society. Incidentally, when Proudhon presented his proposal to the French National Assembly, to which he had been elected after the Revolution of 1848, his plan to supersede the Bank of France with a system of free credit through a Peoples' Bank received just two votes.[1]

Weitling believed he had evolved something greatly superior to the schemes of Proudhon, Fourier, Owen, and Cabet. Louis Blanc's national workshops, he felt, were mere "regulators" of the social system, whereas the national storehouses which he advocated would be the real "spring," and his new paper currency "the pivot," of a completely revolutionary economic system. He argued also that under his plan only land, houses, machines, and a few other kinds of property which were absolutely indispensable to society need become common property. The *Tauschbank* would permit every individual to buy and work very much as he was moved to do; yet at the same time each individual would help to pay all individuals, and all individuals would help to pay each individual.

Weitling was not deterred by some of the obvious criticisms that could be made of his plan for banks of exchange. For example, if the bank paid in terms of the full time value of labor, what would happen to products deposited by farmers, millers, butchers, and bakers which were perishable and might not be sold immediately? What would be the rate of compensation for a printer of books who might be unemployed a large part of the time because creative work was not produced as rapidly as expected or did not

[1] See also J. Salwyn Schapiro, "Pierre-Joseph Proudhon, Harbinger of Fascism," *American Historical Review*, L (1945), No. 4, pp. 714–37.

meet a fixed schedule? His answer, no doubt, would have been that his central regulatory body would wrestle with such problems; but it is difficult to see how a satisfactory, workable solution could have been found, for in the end, the *Tauschbank* merely "destroyed money through new money" and substituted one form of currency for another.

Weitling's criticism of the existing monetary and banking system of the United States was picturesque and eloquent in its revelation of abuses. In one issue of *Die Republik der Arbeiter*, he actually alleged that banks kept the deposits of all who died intestate. Though his diatribes recognized many of the shortcomings of modern capitalism, they revealed little scientific knowledge of its intricate operations. While Weitling indicted the economic system, he failed to see that money was not the sole cause of its evils but only a natural and necessary by-product of the system. It must be remembered, however, that he wrote at a time when banking and currency in the United States still were in a very unstable condition and the losses to the public very large.[2]

Every new proposal has some devoted supporters and Weitling's *Tauschbank* was no exception, though the plan never got further than the printing of a few sheets of new currency with funds from the *Arbeiterbund*. Franz Arnold in 1850 carried the new gospel to a number of American cities and debated furiously in Pittsburgh and Philadelphia with those who opposed the plan. Indeed, Arnold may have begun the agitation even before Weitling became its leading champion. A correspondent from Stuttgart writing about the coming proletarian revolution maintained that "there will be no golden age until money has been eliminated." A St. Louis paper endorsed both land reform and Weitling's bank of exchange and deplored the rivalry between the advocates of these two panaceas. The Cincinnati *Volksblatt*, edited in 1850 by Stefan Molitor and K. Resch, repeatedly supported the proposal

[2] See also F. P. Schiller, "Georg Weber, ein Mitarbeiter des Pariser Vorwärts," *Marx-Engels Archiv*, II (1927), 469. Weitling preserved among his effects a copy of *Thompson's Bank Note Reporter* which had to be consulted to follow the fluctuations in the value of bank notes.

for a new system of exchange, primarily because it would serve as a "protective measure" against existing bank notes. On the other hand, the Columbus *Westbote* labeled the plan "communist humbug," and Samuel Ludvigh's *Fackel* described it as a "pious wish," like so many of Weitling's impractical dreams. Some correspondents also wrote directly to the founder to complain that all his proposals failed to look beyond the interests of the skilled craftsmen and did nothing for the empty stomachs of people who most needed an increase in wages. In short, banks of exchange were but another example of offering labor "golden apples in silver shells."

Beginning in 1850, small groups organized associations for the purpose of establishing banks of exchange and began to accumulate small reserves of cash for that purpose. In March, 1850, *Die Republik der Arbeiter* announced that carpenters and shoemakers in New York already had organized such a bank; and the following month the New York *Herald* reported that an assembly of New York Negroes, who met to discuss how they were being exploited, had ended by selecting a committee of three to collect $10 membership fees for the establishment of a bank of exchange according to Weitling's plan. By July, it was alleged that 2,500 New York craftsmen with a combined treasury of $4,500 were ready to open a bank. As a preliminary, they had circulated a questionnaire to gather data as to what the members produced and bought regularly, what raw materials were required, and what their needs for the next year might be. In a letter from Michigan in November, 1850, a group of Swiss and German workmen, familiar with the "once so prosperous Swiss organizations," wrote to Weitling for advice about various plans, including a *Tauschbank*; and the Cincinnati *Volksblatt*, before the end of the year, reported great progress for the movement in the East and urged a more active propaganda in the western states.

In 1851, Weitling advised his friends in Paris that he was about to launch his favorite project on quite a pretentious scale and boasted that the contributions already received amounted to $341.

With his usual enthusiasm, he had listed promises from several hundred sympathizers who he believed were ready to make payments and loans to his central bank. In a memorandum which he prepared he announced that the new notes would be ready in a week but would not be put into circulation until the co-operative movement had made more progress and had been properly unified. He promised, however, to distribute specimens of the new currency among the "dear brethren" and explained how each city could have "a special plate," to print its own notes as needed.[3]

In April, 1851, *Die Republik der Arbeiter* reported that a convention of American workers in Philadelphia had by unanimous vote approved the Exchange Bank. In May, a "farmers' and workers' protective association" was organized in Weedport, New York, with a subscribed capital of $10,000 and a paid-in capital of $1,000. Their ambitious plan was to organize at least 100 other communities of the state into co-operatives, to build a common storehouse, operate a fleet of canal boats, and establish a bank of exchange so that "farmers will no longer be milked by merchants and speculators." From Louisville came reports of "fiery debates" about the issue, and in Cincinnati, 65 members began to contribute regularly to a *Tauschassoziation.* An American, Charles Sully, published an *Association-Manual* in English which included the "Constitution of the Mutual Provident Exchange Society, by William Weitling." The author paid his membership dues to the latter's organization. There were intimations also that the head of the New York Labor League, which was composed entirely of non-Germans, was friendly to the movement.

As a matter of fact, the undertaking was never realized; it was never even started, except for a few contributions from a few widely scattered individuals. Weitling carefully recorded these receipts on a few loose sheets preserved in the back of what he called his Little Note Book. The reasons for the complete failure of the plan need hardly be discussed seriously. It was apparent at

[3] See memorandum of February 11, 1851, MS in Library of Congress; also Eduard Bernstein (ed.), *Dokumente des Sozialismus* (Berlin, 1905), V, 180.

the outset that a number of radical leaders who were sympathetic with the *Arbeiterbund* rejected Weitling's proposals for a new system of currency. Josef L. Stiger, editor of the Cleveland *Kommunist* and founder of a reading room in that city which charged an admission fee of one cent a day, conducted a voluminous correspondence with Weitling in which he deplored the latter's undue emphasis on the *Tauschbank*. On the other hand, in a letter from Poughkeepsie, where eighteen members had contributed their dollars to the bank, the writer advised Weitling to pay less attention to communism, "for it frightens people" and was at best a very distant goal, and to concentrate on a campaign in *Die Republik der Arbeiter* gradually to win people's confidence for a bank of exchange.

Money actually saved from the dues of members of the local *Gemeinde* for purposes of a bank was generally diverted to more social and convivial objectives and was quickly spent. In the summer of 1851, for example, the New York association lent over half its accumulations for a bank to a group in Newark, New Jersey, who were building a workers' hall. By 1851, many members of the *Arbeiterbund* refused to contribute additional dollars for a bank until their co-operatives produced an adequate cash surplus. People generally were loath to part with lodge funds or the savings of their local mutual-benefit society for a nebulous investment in a central bank of exchange.

The main obstacle to currency reform, however, was the widespread interest in co-operatives. Weitling had favored workers' co-operative associations for a long time and had helped to develop them in France and Switzerland, but he knew that if they succeeded they were likely to prove a disruptive force and result in decentralization of his movement and emphasis on local achievements, instead of on the closely knit unity which he regarded as essential in the labor movement. Weitling wanted banks first and co-operatives second. The workers ignored his advice, preferring to put their hard-earned cash into the more tangible assets of stores and shops in their own localities. The more the co-operatives succeeded, the less the interest in a centralized bank of exchange became. Weitling sensed what was happening but had to yield to the trend.

The co-operative movement, obviously, was not invented by Weitling. It existed in the United States before he came, and it has passed through several cycles of rise and decline in the course of a century. The rise in the cost of living in the 1850's, caused in part by the boom resulting from the gold rush to California, was largely responsible both for the epidemic of strikes and for the rise of co-operatives. Moreover, the co-operative movement was but one manifestation of that wave of humanitarianism that characterized the two decades prior to the Civil War. Though some co-operatives which were established in the 1850's among the workers survived to the 1880's, labor, in general, turned back to ordinary trade-unionism after 1853.

As early as 1845, shoemakers in Lynn, Massachusetts, founded a producers' co-operative. The Boston Tailors' Associative Union followed their example in 1849, and the paper-mill workers of Hardwick, in 1850. Consumers' co-operatives began in Boston in 1845 with the Workingmen's Protective Union, and before the decline began in the 1850's as many as four hundred had sprung into existence, in many instances the result of unsuccessful strikes.[4] An editorial entitled "Labor Reform—The Cloud No Bigger Than a Man's Hand," in the New York *Tribune* of May 6, 1850, described the establishment of a "Union Bakery on Protective and Republican Principles" in 1847, with a capital of $400; it supplied its members with bread at "naked cost," increasing or shrinking the size of the loaf as the price of flour fluctuated, and paid sick and death benefits of $4.00 a week and $30, respectively. Its receipts rose from $86 a week in 1848 to $698 a week in 1850; the organization owned its own horses and wagons and employed fourteen persons at wages from $3.50 to $13.50 a week. Total receipts to May 1, 1850, amounted to $49,010.48 and expenditures

[4] See Norman Ware, *The Industrial Worker, 1840–60* (Boston, 1924), chap. xiii. See also chaps. xiv–xv.

to $48,655.53. Horace Greeley advised the printers to emulate the bakers and establish a co-operative printing plant, and he also accepted subscriptions at the *Tribune* office for stock issued at $25 a share for a boot and shoemakers' co-operative.

The Boston Tailors' Associative Union resulted from a disastrous strike of three months' duration. At the end of four months' operation, some seventy workers were able to show a profit of $510 on an initial investment of $700. *The Protective Union,* organ of the Labor Reformers of New England, had a weekly circulation of 3,300 in April, 1850. Brisbane, while on a lecture tour in Cincinnati, discovered a Journeymen Iron Moulders' Association, whose workers melted from 9,000 to 10,500 pounds of metal a day, manufactured and sold stoves, and earned from $12 to $15 a week. Their example stimulated the iron workers of Pittsburgh to organize a puddlers' association. A printers' co-operative in Cincinnati published the daily *Nonpareil.*

Late in the summer of 1850, the Coopers' Protective Union of New York City completed a new shop in three weeks, a two-story frame building fifty-six feet by twenty-two feet in which it began business with a number of cash orders. Other workers in New York formed an Industrial Home Association; by making small weekly payments they acquired a tract of land near the city, which they proposed to divide and sell to their members in quarter-acre lots. The New York Hat Finishers' Union, composed of a hundred hatters, started a co-operative shop with an initial capital of $7,000. Boston seamstresses operated a shop, the Beehive, at 50 Court Street and were reported to be doing a good business. Cleveland had a Female Co-operative Union Clothing Store, and in New York the Shirt Sewers' Union received donations of $100 each from P. T. Barnum, Henry C. Carey, and Horace Greeley, and $20 from John A. Roebling, a German immigrant who became America's earliest and greatest builder of suspension bridges. The co-operative movement spread rapidly through the larger industrial and commercial centers. It had the unqualified endorsement of the New York *Tribune,* which found in the co-operatives not only the answer to strikes and violence but also the proper method to teach workers "forecast, calculation, frugality and self-denial."

As already suggested, Weitling was fearful lest too many co-operative shops and stores and eating halls divide the resources and decentralize the leadership of the workers' movement and prevent the establishment of his favorite project, the banks of exchange. He regarded his colonization projects as subordinate to a bank of exchange also, for he believed that colonies would require such a central bank to survive the pressures of outside competition. His admonitions fell on deaf ears. Co-operation was in the air among the Germans as well as among other American workmen, and co-operatives were tangible, local projects in which workers were ready to invest. They promised employment and an end to over-production, and from their profits the workers expected to derive no end of enjoyment. Plans already had been worked out by several groups to employ musicians and artists with the surplus from co-operatives to perform for the workers and teach their children. In the face of such widespread enthusiasm, Weitling's only hope was to try to utilize the craze for co-operatives, in whose soundness he had believed for a long time, for the larger purposes of the *Bund*.

The German workers proved to be promoters as enthusiastic as their native American colleagues. In February, 1850, the German carpenters of New York planned a co-operative shop, and before the end of September, successful co-operatives had been started by German workmen in other crafts. Some promised to affiliate with Weitling's bank of exchange. In April, 1850, the German button and fringe makers met at Shakespeare Hall to discuss the movement; a New York co-operative grocery operated at twelve per cent profit, and the German confectioners had a "self-employing shop." German cabinetmakers, 2,000 strong, launched a plan to raise $5,000 for a shop which would guarantee employment during the dull season; and the members of the German Joiners' Association pledged one week's labor to a fund to erect a workshop seventy-five feet by thirty feet, equipped with a steam saw, and to build workers' apartments which would rent at $3.00 a month. Twenty-five houses actually were built by methods which suggest the procedures of modern building and loan associations. A single day's subscriptions in New York produced $3,000 for a German Innkeepers Joint Stock Brewery. In the same city, a German tailors' association employed two cutters and forty tailors in the fall of 1850, and the co-operating bakers were patronized heavily because of the excellence of their products.[5]

In Philadelphia, the German craftsmen were equally enthusiastic, and several shops were opened in a relatively short time. The tailors and shoemakers began operating their own stores in May, 1850. Pittsburgh had a coach factory, and a German cabinetmakers' shop which opened with a capital of $1,000. In Buffalo a carpenters' shop employed ten men; in Cincinnati a co-operative grocery operated successfully with a substantial profit, and the German cabinetmakers opened a shop in the same city in 1852. In St. Louis, representatives of the various trades met at Washington Garden in the summer of 1850 to plan a co-operative dining hall, and the German carpenters of St. Louis lent money to the bakers to enable the latter to open a co-operative bakery which would specialize in German baked goods. In New Orleans in June, 1851, a carpenters' association, composed of 156 members with $436 in their treasury, invested $335 in partial payment of a lot on which they planned to build a shop. "The people themselves," wrote one of the prominent members of the New Orleans group, "must do business with themselves, and determine their own prices. . . ." Another group, writing to Weitling from Davenport, Iowa, in April, 1852, requested a shipment of groceries to enable them to open a co-operative store; and in February, 1853, a society in Covington, Kentucky, asked him to help them operate a co-operative boarding house and beer hall.

[5] See *Rep. d. Arb.*, November, 1850, for a list of German co-operative stores and shops in New York City and their street addresses.

Unfortunately, the evidences of decay began to appear even as these encouraging notices were printed in papers like the Cincinnati *Volksblatt*, *Die Republik der Arbeiter*, and Greeley's *Tribune*. In the summer of 1851 a co-operative grocery collapsed in New York, with a loss of $2,400 to its German members, including funds supposedly reserved to pay sick benefits. Weitling blamed the disaster, as usual, on the lack of centralization and competent leadership, but apparently there had been private peculation also, for goods valued at $600 were unaccounted for. In November, 1851, the Philadelphia Tailors' Associated sold its store and supplies. In Louisville, after doing business for three months with a rising profit, the German grocery and the workers' hall were destroyed by fire. Other groups in Louisville and in Cincinnati became involved in a secession from Weitling's movement, and when the Louisville projects were revived under new auspices, they promptly failed a second time. In the course of the liquidation, one administrator managed to acquire the grocery, another the boarding house. In Baltimore, the tailors finally surrendered their shop and store to trustees and managers, who assumed the debts of the organization. The investments of the members proved a total loss. An association of German bakers in Baltimore met the same fate. In the course of a few years most German co-operatives went into bankruptcy, became private property, or were gradually transformed into lodges, *Turnvereine*, and other social organizations. Many were the victims of poor management and almost all lacked capital and had borrowed too heavily on the false assumption that, after all, the members were borrowing from each other.

One more plan for the new economy must be described in this record of Weitling's failures. In many ways, it was the most fantastic of all his proposals. Early in 1850, the American people were greatly interested in building a transcontinental road to the Pacific. Shortly after his arrival in the United States, when Weitling still believed he would have the resources to begin a social revolution in a few years and predicted that the receipts from his bank of exchange would amount to $50,000 a week, he proposed a plan to have the *Arbeiterbund* build the Pacific railroad. Ludvigh's *Fackel* sarcastically pointed out that "the raw materials necessary to lay the rails were still buried in the mountains of the Cape of Good Hope" and that such "socialistic fanaticism" failed to take cognizance of all the practical difficulties involved, but *Die Republik der Arbeiter* published the details for the plan in May, 1850.

Weitling called upon the workers to act as a unit and to demand of Congress the same Federal aid which that body was ready to grant to capitalists to build the road as a private enterprise for private profit. He proposed that 38,400,000 acres from the public domain be given to "the Republic of the Workers," with a financial subsidy of $50,000,000; and he urged the workers, irrespective of language or nationality, to bombard their Congressmen with petitions for this unique chance to build "a reform road" by a "union of workers." He thought the undertaking could be completed in two years at a total cost of $27,000,000, provided the government furnished the necessary engineers, allowed free use of the raw materials that lay along the proposed route, appropriated $10,000 a day to feed the workers, and donated a thirty-mile strip for a distance of 2,000 miles through the public domain. Weitling proposed that the actual construction of the road be supervised by a board of directors, to be chosen by delegates selected by an English and a German workers' congress. He stipulated that the directors must be able to speak English, German, and French, a requirement which he, for one, could meet.

The road would be built by a work force of from 20,000 to 100,000 men and upon completion would belong to the nation. The land grants would be preserved intact and undivided, as the common property of the "workers' republic," to be developed into farms by the men who built the railroad. Co-operative stores would spring into existence along the route, and they would do business with a paper money that would produce the profits expected of the *Tauschbank* system. Thus, finally, all who had participated in the enterprise would be able to acquire homes for themselves. By the time Weitling finished his calculations he found that the cost would be $73,000,000 less than if the railroad were built by private enterprise and that a profit of $13,000,000 would accrue from the transaction for the *Arbeiterbund*.

On December 25, 1858, Struve's *Organ der freien Arbeiter* referred to Weitling as "one who pointed the way" and "shook the worker out of his lethargy," even though he failed to lead him along the right path to happiness. As a result, according to the judgment of this fellow reformer, he actually though unintentionally had helped to destroy labor's confidence by the fantasies of a mind "unrestrained by . . . sober, disciplined reason."

In his *Der Katechismus der Arbeiter*, a 126-page brochure published in New York in 1854 which represents Weitling's final contribution to the literature of communism and reform, the disappointed author made the observation that "the working class is as egotistic, selfish, unintelligent and avaricious" as any other group. Though bitterly disillusioned, he still defended the "system" expounded in his earlier publications, although he was through with the "Garden of Eden" and weary of planning for a new society which would give each individual the freedom to work, consume, and enjoy what he wanted. At the same time Weitling concluded that a system of equal pay was unnecessary and undesirable. He admitted that he had learned from experience that voluntary associations usually failed, and that selfish instincts were deeply rooted in the human heart. Thus he found the explanation for his failures not in the defects of his own system but in the "vices of mankind"; and he could not resist a final comment, "If all had followed me as the children of Israel followed Moses out of Egypt, I would have succeeded."

Weitling, like many another ambitious radical reformer, learned at last that his German brethren were far more interested in lodges and beer halls than banks of exchange or co-operatives and were more likely to support the singing societies, *Turnvereine*, and bowling and shooting clubs of the *bourgeoisie* than a radical propaganda for a proletarian revolution. But the reason for the failures of the Weitlings in America is deeper; the swift decline of the influence of the radical wing of the German immigrants in the United States must be explained by more fundamental factors than the mistakes and failures of Wilhelm Weitling's personal leadership.

The bulk of the German immigrants to this country were primarily concerned with establishing a firm and secure economic foundation for themselves and their families. In the caste society of Europe, where a proletarian might properly feel that it was almost a hopeless task to try to raise his status by individual effort, it was not too difficult to interest the underprivileged and the poor in a scheme that promised a collectivist, revolutionary upheaval. In the United States, on the other hand, the very absence of a caste structure made such visionary plans seem utterly impractical and unnecessary. Here the most radical theorist could become a property owner under the prevailing system of cheap land and relatively high wages, and the most doctrinaire radical thus quickly acquired a comfortable middle-class psychology.

Weitling's prestige in the European labor movement, and his vigorous leadership explain the initial popularity of the *Arbeiterbund* and his other proposals, especially during those first difficult years when the newly-arrived immigrant was struggling with the complex problems of adjusting to a new environment and learning how to make a living in a new country. Weitling remained consistent in his radical theories but his constituency changed. His revolutionary proposals could not thrive under the altered circumstances provided by the United States, where equality of opportunity and a vigorous climate of rugged individualism prevailed. The sudden eclipse of Weitling's career as a radical leader in America can be explained by several factors, but the most important was the fact that his own erstwhile followers and disciples ultimately preferred American democratic methods to an authoritarian, revolutionary program and prospered under a system of free enterprise.

Weitling's experience is but another example of the fate of most alien radical systems imported into this country. Though they may have had brief popularity, to date their demise has been equally sudden. Even Friedrich Engels, in 1890, came to the conclusion that Americans "won't let theory be shoved down their throats" and must be allowed to "go their own way," following "their own experience and their own blunders and the results of them." [6]

[6] Quoted in Gilbert and Helen Highet (trans.), Gustav Mayer's *Friedrich Engels* (New York, 1935), 276.

CHAPTER XIII

COMMUNIA, IOWA [1]

THE hospitable soil of the young America before the Civil War nurtured many immigrant Utopias. Among the thousands who had resolved to try their fortunes in the New World there were many who hoped to establish an entirely new social order. There was room in the United States for almost any kind of experiment in group living; if neighbors were not always hospitable, they at least could afford to be tolerant, for in the broad Mississippi Valley there was land enough for practically every kind of experimenter with social reform.[2]

Though Weitling's Communia had its own unique history, it was but one of many colonies that are part of the general pattern

[1] The existing monographs on Weitling's activities deal almost wholly with the European aspect of his career. Very little has been written about Communia, and many details of its history probably will remain obscure. Clark, in his monograph on "A Neglected Socialist," locates the colony in Wisconsin and says it came to an end in 1853; Friedrich Muckle, in *Die grossen Sozialisten,* refers to it as "Kolumbia." Iowa historians have done almost nothing on the subject. Communia is mentioned in W. J. Petersen's "History of Northeastern Iowa," *Iowa Journal of History and Politics* (Iowa City), XXXI (1933), 80, and in Ralph Albertson, "A Survey of Mutualistic Communities in America," *ibid.* (1936), XXXIV, 406. *The History of Clayton County, Iowa* (Chicago, 1882) devotes two pages to the colony. The account contains numerous inaccuracies. Reminiscences by descendants of the colonists, written long years after the colony's dissolution, reveal the merits and the defects of such material. See an article by Mrs. Frank Liers, in *Clayton County Register* (Elkader, Iowa), August 21, 1930, and one by Kathleen M. Hempel, in Cedar Rapids *Gazette,* November 23, 1930. Other brief newspaper articles are to be found in *Clayton County Register,* March 26, 1931, and July 22, 1936.

[2] See Carl Wittke, *We Who Built America: The Saga of the Immigrant* (New York, 1939), chap. xii, on "Immigrant Utopias."

of native-American and immigrant Utopias in the ante-bellum period when the United States was a great laboratory for social experimentation of every kind. Some of these colonies were so small and short-lived that almost nothing of their history has been preserved. Others included such well-known ventures as Owen's New Harmony in Indiana and its many offshoots, such as Yellow Springs and the Kendall Community in Ohio, and the Bloomington, Indiana colony at Blue Springs. In somewhat the same category belong Frances Wright's Nashoba in Tennessee, the colony at Haverstraw in New York, Adin Ballou's Hopedale Community in Massachusetts, the Brook Farm of the New England intellectuals and transcendentalists, and John Anderson Collins' Skaneateles Community. Brisbane's type of modified Fourierism, a scheme for a planned economy which was widely publicized in Greeley's *Tribune*, produced at least thirty colonies during the years when the "plague of phalanxes" swept the country. Among the better-known colonies formed by nonreligious German groups may be mentioned the Teutonia settlement and Ginalsburg, both in Pennsylvania (the latter lost $40,000 in one year); the Germania colony of Wisconsin; and New Helvetia, Missouri, which was directly connected with Weitling's undertaking.[3]

Weitling was interested in establishing ideal communities while he was still deeply involved in the European labor movement. He contended that the teachings of Christianity logically led to such undertakings as the *Arbeiterbund* and the founding of colonies. Nevertheless, it is doubtful whether he would have had his major attention diverted to Communia in 1851 had not the accidents of history brought him into contact with the Iowa settlement. Once he had embarked on an enterprise, his imagination always outran his reason and practical judgment, and so he came to view the Iowa experiment as the first nucleus for a long succession of communist Utopias. If he could be certain of support by the *Arbeiter-*

[3] See Schlüter, *Anfänge der deutschen Arbeiterbewegung*, 110–18; and Heinrich Semmler, *Geschichte des Sozialismus und Communismus in Nord Amerika* (Leipzig, 1880), *passim.*

bund for three years, he predicted, Communia could well be developed to a point where it would be able to house all the members of the organization who might wish to live there, to take care of all its pensioners, and to draw a huge volume of German immigration into the West. In his mind's eye he pictured the building of additional city-colonies, whose raw and finished products would supply workers' co-operatives in the urban areas. With the help of the *Tauschbank,* he was confident, a large part of the financial resources of the *Arbeiterbund* could be dispatched to Communia to assure its steady expansion.

In December, 1850, *Die Republik der Arbeiter* published the constitution for the colony of "Kommunia," Iowa, with a letter from B. F. Weiss, a member, describing the settlement. According to this account, the little rural community already had a library and a musical and singing society; and the settlers were altogether satisfied with life in their new communist paradise. To be sure, differences of opinion occasionally interrupted the harmonious relations of the colonists, but these were attributed to the "quarrelsome society" from which the original members had to be recruited. Near by, a group of Mecklenburgers owned a plot of land and expected to build the following spring. In Communia itself there were several friends whom Weitling had converted to communism in Switzerland. With one of the settlers, he had shared a room in Dresden in 1832, and he had known Joseph Venus, the blacksmith, in Bern in 1841. Others of the original group undoubtedly recognized Weitling's prominence in the radical movement. He and his co-worker Franz Arnold, during their first visit to St. Louis, were invited to visit the settlement, probably in the hope that they would recommend its support by the *Arbeiterbund* as soon as that organization began to function.

The story of Communia itself begins with the career of Andreas Dietsch, a brushmaker in the canton of Aargau, Switzerland, who in 1842 published *Das tausendjährige Reich,* a little treatise which Weitling republished twelve years later in New York. In this interesting bit of Utopian literature, Dietsch, a typical son of the underprivileged with but five years' schooling and a thorough education in the sufferings of the poor, presented a moving account of the inequalities and injustices of the social order as he knew them from his own bitter experience. He decided that the "Father in heaven did not want it so; only man has made it so." He proceeded to draw a blueprint for Utopia and, having laid the theoretical basis for the new society, he was eager to put his theories into practice. In 1843, he perfected his plans for a colony in America and invited Weitling to go with him, but the latter at the moment seems to have had little faith in the success of such a scheme. As a matter of fact, Dietsch's colony of New Helvetia, Missouri, located near Westphalia about eighteen miles from Jefferson City, failed very quickly.[4] The founder died in St. Louis, probably during the winter of 1845–46, bitterly disillusioned by the selfishness of his followers. The remnants of his colony moved to the city, and today there is nothing left to remind the visitor of this early Utopia except a few graves; even the name of the colony seems to be unknown to the local historians.

Meantime, Hermann Kriege had organized communist associations in New York. Their influence spread into the interior. After contact with one of these little groups in St. Louis and with the aid of Heinrich Koch, publisher of the communist *Antipfaff*, the survivors of Dietsch's New Helvetia and several others interested in colonization formed a new organization from which the settlement in Iowa resulted in 1847. Seven years later, two of the original members of Dietsch's colony still lived in Communia.

Heinrich Koch, first leader of the Iowa colony, was a native of Bayreuth, who had come to the United States after the Revolution of 1830. He was a strange individual, sharply critical of American society, a violent opponent of the clergy, and a follower of Owen and Fourier. A fiery speaker and a fighting journalist who was called the "second Tom Paine," he had risen to leadership among the German workers of St. Louis. At the outbreak of the Mexican

[4] Andrä Dietsch, *Das tausendjährige Reich, nebst Plan und Statuten zur Gründung von "Neu Helvetia im Staate Missouri in Nordamerika"* [Aarau, 1844].

War he recruited a company of soldiers, largely from among German communists of the city, and marched off as a captain at the head of his men to join the army of General Taylor. His outfit smelled no powder and returned from the wars unscarred, but they received land warrants which could be used to found a colony.

The region around Koch's *Kommunia* was a veritable El Dorado for Utopians. An association from Cincinnati settled near Guttenberg, Iowa; Pennsylvanians located at Colesburgh, some fifteen miles away; the Mecklenburgers already referred to, including several people whom Weitling had known in Hamburg, founded near-by Liberty under the leadership of Burgomaster Wullweber. This last colony existed until 1852 when it was sold for $1,575. In the same region in Clayton County, there was the short-lived Clydesdale colony, which had been organized in Scotland under the presidency of John Craig.[5]

Communia was located on virgin prairie at the confluence of the Turkey and Volga rivers, in the southern part of Section 8 of Volga township. It was about six miles south of Elkader in Clayton County, about fifteen miles from Guttenberg, and about fifty miles from Dubuque. Elkader at the time had hardly more than a dozen houses, but it was a booming frontier town, with interest rates as high as twenty and twenty-five per cent. Guttenberg, a community of perhaps 150 dwellings had a population which was rapidly approaching a thousand. Most of the inhabitants were Germans, and many were employed in the neighboring lead mines. To reach Communia, travelers usually proceeded by steamer to Galena or Dubuque. From Galena, the trip to Clayton could be made in twelve hours by boat. A wagon road led from Clayton to Elkader and six miles beyond Elkader was Koch's colony.

Koch and his party had arrived in 1847 in this beautiful part of Iowa, noted for deer and wild turkeys, good trout fishing and

[5] See Joseph Eiboeck, *Die Deutschen in Iowa und deren Errungenschaften* (Des Moines, 1900), 95.

unique geological formations. With Koch, who was the first president, came Joseph Venus, who later succeeded to the presidency; Jakob Ponsar and Cornelius Kopp, tailors; Joseph Kremper, a farmer; Johann Enders, a locksmith; and Johann Marxer, a shoemaker. Other members of the original St. Louis group included Friedrich Meister, who returned to the city after two months to become a banker; Heinrich Babe, a carpenter; Johann Hofstaeder, a druggist; Friedrich Koenig, a dentist; and Isaac Nagel or Nage, a tailor presumably of French extraction. Venus, Enders, and Kopp were veterans of the New Helvetia colony. Though few in the group knew much about farming, they began to break the prairie sod with great enthusiasm and built a log house, twenty feet by thirty feet, several smaller log houses, a blacksmith shop, and a brickkiln. Land warrants in the possession of some of the colonists proved sufficient to acquire 160 acres; additional land was bought at $1.25 an acre.

The Koch regime was marked by much dissension and by ugly charges against the president of the colony which intimated that he had filled his pockets at the expense of the colonists and was guilty of plain embezzlement. It is a fact that he had the land registered at the land office in his own name, but Weitling believed he was a good administrator, had not violated the law, and simply had acted to protect the interests of his family.

Whatever the facts, Koch withdrew from the colony in the fall of 1849 and was paid off with $600. Title passed to Venus and Mathew Grieshaber. Shortly thereafter the latter disappeared. Koch retired to Dubuque and became a successful contractor and politician who got on well with both Whigs and Democrats.[6] The

[6] At the time of his departure, Koch produced the following poem, which may deserve preservation:

> Wie der Vogel aus dem Bauer,
> Wenn ihm seine Flucht gelingt,
> Wieder auf den grünen Zweigen
> Lustig seine Lieder singt;

troubles of the colony did not end with Koch's departure, and further divisions resulted. When Weitling's *Arbeiterbund* finally became identified with the colony there were from ten to eighteen men left in Communia (the evidence is not clear), and some worked at trades in neighboring towns during the winter months. Weitling asserted later that the whole settlement could have been bought at the time for from $1,500 to $2,000 and protested that he did not discover the true condition of the colony until several members of the *Arbeiterbund* already had invested their money in it.

Weitling set foot on "the sacred soil of brotherly association" for the first time in the fall of 1851. He found the members ready to pledge all the assets of their colony as security for whatever amounts the projected *Arbeiterbund* was prepared to invest in the enterprise, and he immediately wrote out a contract intended to consolidate the resources of the two organizations. In his initial enthusiasm, he paid out $80 of the *Arbeiterbund*'s money at once for the benefit of the colony and added another $400 within the next few months. He planned to use the colony as security for all

---

Mach'ich wieder frei und ledig
In die Welt nun meine Reis',
Sing wie sonst jetzt meine Lieder
Wieder nach der alten Weis'.

Schau mit Lächeln auf den Käfig,
Der mich so gefangen hielt.
Singe, was der freie Sänger,
Wieder in der Freiheit fühlt.

Dass er nimmermehr im Leben
In den Vogelbauer geht,
Wenn auch gleich, von Gold umflochten,
Drin das beste Futter steht.

Und nie mehr den blossen Worten
Sogenannter Brüder traut,
Bis er auch in ihre Seelen
Bis er in ihr Herz geschaut.

Reprinted in *Rep. d. Arb.*, January 1, 1854.

payments that might be made into the central treasury of the *Bund* from whatever source. When the colonists signed the agreement, Weitling commented joyfully on the unanimity that existed among "communists of the old school" who had learned the true significance of "faith and sacrifice," and he predicted a day not too far distant when all the property of the colony and all the contributions to the *Bund* would become the common property of the *Arbeiterbund*.

Colonists, like other members of the *Bund*, were expected to pay a $10 initiation fee but they were assured that such funds would be spent entirely for the development of the colony. A three months' probationary period was required for membership in Communia, and individuals were guaranteed the return of their investments if they should withdraw. Though entitled to all its rights and privileges, residents in the colony were exempted from the regular dues of the *Arbeiterbund*. The colony was guaranteed a large measure of local autonomy; its affairs were placed under the supervision of a committee chosen by the Central Commission of the *Arbeiterbund* in New York; and this body was given the right to send workers to the colony and to act as a court of appeal in case of disagreements.

A glowing description of the colony promptly was printed in *Die Republik der Arbeiter*. The 1,240 acres lying between the Turkey and Volga rivers were valued at $2,500. Three thousand acres of public land in the immediate neighborhood seemed to provide ample room for expansion. The countryside was hilly and beautiful and so healthful, according to Weitling's report, that it was free of cholera and fever or snakes, dreaded enemies of the pioneer. One of the existing houses, sixty by thirty-five feet and two stories high, containing a dining hall with a kitchen in the basement, two cellars and an attic, easily could accommodate five families. It was appraised at $1,000, and four smaller houses adaptable for lodgings and auxiliary purposes were valued at $500. Fruit and livestock were inventoried at $1,900, and the latter included 100 pigs, 30 oxen, 15 sheep, 7 horses, and many chickens, geese, and ducks. One hundred dollars was available in ready cash. The total value of the colony was estimated at $6,500 with debts amounting to only $500.

As far as the physical comforts were concerned, Weitling reported an abundance of ham at each meal and the necessary quantities of bread, butter, cheese, potatoes, pumpkins, and green vegetables. However, there was a noted shortage of milk and sugar. Coffee and buttermilk were the everyday drinks of the colonists. A keg of brandy, from Cabet's distillery at Nauvoo, was reserved for special occasions. A cellar had been set aside, and barley had been planted to make possible the brewing of *lagerbier*. Four linden trees had been planted around a well and with typical German sentimentality the spot had been named *Wirtshaus zu den vier Linden*. The colony also owned 160 acres located on both banks of the Volga, only one hour's walk from the main cluster of houses. Here it was planned to build in the following year a sawmill, a distillery, and a flour mill at a cost of $3,000 with funds provided by the *Arbeiterbund*.

Weitling's first visit to Communia was a fateful one. From that time on, he and his entire program of pensions, social insurance, banks, and co-operatives were inextricably involved in the affairs of a colony which had little chance of succeeding. The drainage of the funds of the *Arbeiterbund* into the colony began immediately and continued until more than $10,000 had been sunk in the venture. Yet neither mounting losses, internal bickering, litigation, nor personal abuse could shake Weitling's faith in an enterprise; he clung tenaciously to it until the final crash in 1855 dragged him and his movement into ruin.

As soon as *Die Republik der Arbeiter* announced the affiliation of colony and *Bund*, contributions and applications for membership began to come in from simple souls who had faith in Weitling's leadership and expected to find security and happiness in a community of equality based upon what they had read in his books. A sight draft drawn on the St. Louis *Arbeiterverein* for $500 was honored by that body and the money was spent immediately in buying coffee, yard goods, and dishes for the colony. In a communication to the "dear brethren" in New Orleans, dated January 16, 1852, Weitling requested the cash in their treasury for the colony and asked for expressions of confidence in his leadership. Minsky, the Polish barber, sent money regularly to prepare for the day when he could go in person to the Iowa Utopia. A young German communist announced his intention to invest $400 in the venture. In a letter to an ardent supporter in St. Louis, Weitling asked a friend to recruit a millwright, a brick-maker, a carpenter, two shoemakers, and two masons for the colony and reported that an architect and a fine musician who "can fiddle for our dances" already were en route to Iowa. In an out-burst of boyish enthusiasm, he announced that the leader himself would join the merrymakers in the colony, and dance "to whisky punch and buttermilk."

Before the end of the year, however, Weitling's enthusiasm had cooled somewhat, and he cautioned prospective colonists not to expect to move immediately into a "Paradise" or "Robinson Crusoe Island." The colony was still a wilderness in a wilderness he said, and could only succeed with men and women of great industry and self-denial, who were organized under an "industri-ous, temperate, truthful, honest leader" and equipped with a defi-nite plan. Weitling knew that hitherto only those colonies had succeeded whose members were bound by religious ties into a homogeneous brotherhood, and he was a little concerned whether "the rational freedom of freethinkers" would be able to set an "example of harmony" and build colonies which would flourish like those based on "superstitions and religious fanaticism."

In 1852, Weitling visited Communia for the second time. Coming up the river to Galena, he traveled on through Dubuque, Guttenberg, and Clayton and walked from there to the colony. The flora and fauna and the minerals of the region interested him greatly, and he described them in detail for the readers of *Die Republik der Arbeiter*.

In Communia he learned that the large houses were inhabited

but not entirely finished inside; that a brickyard was ready to begin operations; that the carpenter and blacksmith shops were heavily used; and that scaffolding had been erected for a barn which would house a dozen horses. Though some of the colonists still were living in three old uncomfortable blockhouses, everyone seemed to be in a good health. Breakfast was served at 6:30, the noon meal at 12, and the evening meal at 6:30; and in between, milk, cheese, whisky, and coffee were available to all who wanted them. He found the meals simple but substantial and wholesome, the beer good, and the water excellent, even on the hottest days. Meals were prepared in a common kitchen and eaten in a common dining hall, save those of mothers with small children, who were permitted to eat at home or in the kitchen. The sleeping rooms were barren and austere, but the meeting hall (*Saal*) was attractive.

Weitling made an inventory of the property and found nearly 200 head of livestock, poultry numbering 3,000, and agricultural implements valued at $600. Of the 1,240 acres of land, however, only 160 acres were under cultivation. Total assets amounted to $7,260, and he pointed out that this sum now had been added to the resources of the *Arbeiterbund*. Of the twenty-three people who constituted the colony in the spring of 1852, fourteen were men; four, women; and five, children. Weitling asked "strong, unmarried members" of the *Bund* who had the money for travel expenses and who could make the initial deposit of $100 to report at once to New York headquarters, for labor was badly needed in the fields and to build houses and a milldam; and plans already were being made for a post office and a railroad stop at Communia to enable the colony to develop into a prosperous trading center.

The inventory seemed encouraging. But when he arrived in the colony, Weitling found the colonists in an uproar. The women refused to work, except for their own families; and violent antagonisms had developed among the older members and more recent arrivals. The husbands sided with their rebellious women; there was dissatisfaction with the local president of the colony;

and opposition was rising to centralization under Weitling's leadership and to integration of the settlement with the *Arbeiterbund*. The dissension ended in a secession, the first of several still to come. The erring brethren were permitted to depart in peace and were paid off with $800 of the *Arbeiterbund*'s money. The women who remained were promised individual "hearths and homes."

Weitling in May, 1852, receipted for contributions of $1,924.34 to the treasurer of the *Bund* for purposes of the colony, but hastened to explain to his followers that he had encountered more dissatisfaction and trouble in six weeks at Communia than in any ten years of his career, and that instead of starting afresh, he had been forced to take over a colony already four years old. He commented cynically that the members of the *Bund* sigh for relief from the cares of the world, but "when they are here a little while, they remember the beer mugs of the cities. . . . They want change but they cannot be satisfied." Once again he called for a dozen recruits who were real communists and would not expect "heaven on earth," and for a half dozen strong, young girls who would be willing to do a woman's work. He wanted no more large families with children, nor "women with scolding tongues and unreasonable demands." He pointed out that Communia, unlike many other colonies, did not require its women to work in the fields but did expect them to do the housework, cooking, and laundry for all members of the colony and without masculine assistance. Weitling had discovered to his sorrow that women found it more difficult than men to adjust to communism, and he added ruefully: "if women only wouldn't get children. Children stimulate their egoism." [7]

More important, however, than these internal difficulties was the growing concern of the founder of the *Arbeiterbund* about the safety of the funds entrusted to him by the workers and now being pumped into this colonizing project. Never distinguished for practical judgment, Weitling pursued several will-o'-the-

[7] Weitling to J. Krieg. MS letter in Library of Congress.

wisps in his day, but he was honest and genuinely devoted to those who faithfully followed his leadership. On the occasion when his friend Friedrich Baumann, on whose farm in New York State he had recuperated from a long illness, wanted to invest his earnings of $1,300 in the colony, Weitling refused to accept the offer until Baumann had made a personal inspection of Communia.

In order to safeguard the *Arbeiterbund*, already deeply involved in the finances of the colony, Weitling demanded that a deed of trust, or mortgage on the property of the colony, for $5,000 for one year at ten per cent interest be made out and delivered to him as a protection for the members of his organization. Griesinger, the president of Communia, who had been elected by a majority of one, argued that a simple promissory note would be sufficient and made a personal attack on Weitling and the *Bund*. Thereupon, a new election was held amid great excitement, and Griesinger was deposed by a vote of eight to five. The defeated candidate immediately left the colony, taking with him three others and their "dissatisfied women." They were paid $750 at once and were promised an additional $50. Weitling pointed proudly to the generous conduct of the colonists toward the troublemakers, who had departed with their goods for Guttenberg in three colony wagons, and cited the incident as a convincing reply to attacks which Hassaurek continued to make in his *Hochwächter*, charging him with dishonesty, embezzlement, and collecting funds for workers' pensions under false pretenses.

Though the deed of trust remained a bone of contention between Weitling and Communia, the colony had weathered its first serious internal explosion. New members arrived, and the colony planned further expansions with *Arbeiterbund* money. Weitling was busy writing a new constitution and preparing for an official act of incorporation. He appealed for twenty-five guarantors who would be willing to make loans to the colony without interest for a ten-year period in exchange for a vote on colony matters to be exercised either directly or by proxy. Such loans, he argued, would help secure the funds already invested and win the confidence of the rank and file of the *Arbeiterbund*. Weitling proposed a plan of representation for the transaction of business and a procedure which required a unanimous vote but stipulated also that in the event unanimity could not be obtained, the president, after a reasonable interval, could make the decision on his own responsibility. His critics immediately raised the cry of dictatorship. Weitling replied that since all workers would receive equal pay and the "regent" not a penny more than the humblest worker, democracy had been adequately safeguarded. In submitting proposals to the members of the *Arbeiterbund* for comment and criticism, he reiterated that he personally had no desire to become a dictator and referred to the "freedom to scold, gossip, mistrust, slander, lie, loaf, and waste . . . as a tyranny far greater than the edicts of a simple despot."

Meantime, the colonists had gone to work, and the wheat and oats crops were promising, though the outlook for corn was not so favorable, partly because the colony lacked horses and plows and partly because the men refused to work on Sunday. Weitling bought a mowing machine in Dubuque. Materials had to be hauled to the colony over a distance requiring a full day's journey. Skilled craftsmen, including an expert gardener and a shepherd, were badly needed. In the summer of 1852, an old comrade, Simon Schmidt, the tanner, arrived from Kalamazoo. W. Caspelmann and his wife transferred their farm to the colony; an unmarried machinist from Cincinnati deposited $200; and a gardener's family of Belleville, Illinois, $600. Robert Meyer, secretary of the Central Committee in New York, paid in $190 before starting the overland journey for Iowa. Additional colonists came from Philadelphia; and J. Krieg, a close friend and regular correspondent of Weitling, and J. Först came with their families from Cincinnati. Both were cabinetmakers.

At the close of July, 1852, another inventory was taken. It listed assests of $8,680: $2,600 for the land, $1,300 for buildings, $1,380 for livestock, and $600 for agricultural implements. The harvest and existing food supplies were valued at $1,000, and the balance sheet showed receipts totaling $5,666, which included $1,408 from five members of the original colony who were still in residence, $2,600 from monthly dues of the *Arbeiterbund*, and contributions from various cities.

Six months later, Schmidt, as a more neutral person, prepared an inventory for the *Arbeiterbund* at Weitling's direction. By that time, the *Bund* had invested $7,881.62, of which $4,000 had come directly from its treasury and the rest from 17 individual members in amounts ranging from $25, contributed by Mathias Krieg, to $620 paid in by Peter Arnold. Total assets of the colony were listed at $10,958.95, and the books of the colony showed a tidy balance. The value of buildings and livestock had increased by $600 each in six months; there was $1,200 on hand in cash, and accounts receivable amounted to $339. A "library" of seventy-five books was appraised at ten dollars.

In compiling his figures Schmidt valued land under cultivation or fenced in at $6.00 an acre, and wild land at $1.50, and allowed a small depreciation for buildings. His inventory did not include personal possessions, such as clothing, bedding and tools which members had brought with them to the colony. A report on food consumption, covering the six months' period from July to the end of the year, showed an average cost per person of six and two-thirds cents a day. Based on this rather favorable statement, a new appeal for funds was promptly issued, although in September, 1852, it was necessary to announce in *Die Republik der Arbeiter* that no additional candidates could be accepted for the present because all available living quarters were occupied. Prospective colonizers were warned to check with headquarters in New York before undertaking the long journey to Iowa.

Nature proved bountiful in 1852 in Iowa, and the harvest of the colony was good. "Female caprice," gossip, and the "whims and vices" that men carry with them into every corner of the world still produced some disagreements but after six weeks in the colony Weitling could honestly say that he preferred to live there. One member of the community wrote enthusiastically, "We live here like a king, without care and without want." Robert Meyer, secretary of the *Bund,* who traveled from New York to Iowa almost wholly by rail because of the low-water mark of the rivers, was delighted to find good food, smoking tobacco, and snuff on his arrival at Communia. He reported a serious housing shortage, however, and the need for a good feather bed as well as better "general leadership"; but the colonists impressed him as honest men and women of good character, who apparently were performing their tasks well and joyously. J. Krieg wrote in October that all was peace and harmony in Communia; Karl Schock, writing to Weitling two months later, described the card and chess games in which the colonists spent their evenings, the good hunting for deer and prairie chickens on Sunday, and the delightful excursions by wagon or sleigh into the neighboring communities. Not even a big prairie fire could affect his enthusiasm. "I am working for myself and for my brothers," he concluded. Visitors were beginning to come to the colony, and to patronize its store and blacksmith shop; travelers stayed overnight occasionally, and traffic on the post road to Dubuque, which passed the houses of the colonists, increased rapidly. By December, 1852, the colony consisted of 22 men, 9 women, and 17 children. Krieg wrote, "We have more freedom here than in the cities where we are under the control of the employers."

Late in 1852, the colony acquired from a neighbor, for $1,273, a sawmill and a forty-acre plot on the Volga River. By constructing a dam, Weitling hoped to develop water power sufficient to operate a flour mill also. Six hundred dollars was paid in cash and the remainder was promised within six weeks. Confident of a steady influx of new colonists, Weitling predicted an output of 2,000 to 3,000 feet of lumber daily, depending on the water supply. In reality, the undertaking ended in disaster with a loss amounting to $4,000.

Weitling had the title to the forty acres recorded in his own name as security for the *Arbeiterbund,* which furnished the funds for the transaction. Under existing law and in view of the anomalous legal status of the colony, the land could have been bought and entered only by an individual, and under all the circumstances, it must be admitted that Weitling seemed the logical person to make the purchase. Immediately, however, a new storm broke among the colonists. It increased in violence until it spread through many of the *Gemeinde* of the *Arbeiterbund.* Griesinger, leader of the first secession, already had accused Weitling before the Cincinnati and Louisville groups of robbing honest workmen through the "swindle" of a $5,000 mortgage on the colony property and his charges, though unjustified, were sufficiently impressive to cause rifts in the organization in these two Ohio river cities. To this accusation now was added the claim that Weitling refused to transfer title to the forty-acre mill site to the colony and proposed to keep the property for himself. The colonists voted on the question and with only three dissenting votes threatened to take the issue to the courts. Weitling insisted that he would continue to hold title as security for the *Bund.* Presently the colonists expressed a readiness to issue stock certificates to every member of the *Arbeiterbund* as security for the pension and other insurance funds and to give notes for future loans, but they insisted on having the property recorded in their name. Obviously, no such proposals would satisfy the *Bund.*

The attitude of the colonists became one of distrust and increasing animosity. They wanted to free themselves of the restraints imposed by Weitling on behalf of the *Arbeiterbund* and yet retain the financial support which kept Communia alive. A recent arrival, who had studied law in Germany, worked as a sculptor in New York, and become thoroughly bored by the monotony of life in the colony, circulated the report that the *Arbeiterbund* had nothing to show for its investments in Communia except a mortgage of $5,000 and claimed that title to all the colony property still rested in the old colonists. Weitling had to agree that, legally speaking, seven persons were the owners of Communia. He suspected them of a plot to divide the colony land into private farms. Despite the fact that existing resources were inadequate to keep the project alive, the unhappy leader already was busy with plans for a new colony in which all movable property and all real estate would belong to the *Arbeiterbund* from the beginning.

No such drastic step was ever taken, however. Weitling again sought salvation in a new constitution, apparently convinced that all that was needed was a more detailed plan on paper. He carefully examined the laws governing incorporations, and in a letter to an attorney in Dubuque, seeking advice on "the triste situation in which I am envolved," he chronicled his unhappy experiences with the colony on financial matters and concluded: "Please sir! take pity with my situation and sacifice [*sic*] some of your valuable time to writ [*sic*] me a few word [*sic*] in behalf of this. It does not matter to me how these troubles end, if only they end."

By the end of March, 1853, Weitling's optimism had revived because the colony had agreed to accept a new constitution, or charter, converting Communia under the laws of Iowa into the Workingmen's League of Communia and transferring title to all property to this new organization. At the time of the transfer the stockholders and members of the *Bund* residing in the colony totaled twenty, besides Weitling. By the new agreement, the *Arbeiterbund* agreed to find workers and additional funds for the development of the colony while the members of the colony pledged their holdings as security for all funds received. Every member of the *Bund*, and each *Gemeinde* which had loaned the colony $100 or more for a ten-year period without interest, became a "guarantor" or trustee with the right to vote, directly or by proxy, on all colony matters. By this arrangement Weitling believed he had established the legal fiction that every member of the *Bund*, no matter where he resided, also was a shareholder in the colony, according to articles of incorporation. This was the main point in the constitution or charter. The other provisions dealt with the author's timeworn proposals for a bank of exchange, old-age pensions, fire insurance, sick benefits, and the like and provided practically the same detailed plan for organization and administration to be found in the *Garantieen.*

These details need not concern us here, save as the new charter's provisions indicated a retreat from pure communism. The constitution provided, among other things, that while all members should continue to receive "store bills" good for products at the central store in payment for their labor and services, rents and prices were to be fixed at cost plus ten per cent for the pension fund and another ten per cent for schools and administrative costs. Members could lease land from the colony and maintain their own households and livestock, provided they were willing to bear the total expense of such private establishments; and children henceforth would be fed and clothed at the common expense only if parents agreed to entrust their education to the directors of the colony for an eight-year period.

Every Saturday evening a "directory of the workers" met in Communia to lay out the tasks for the following week and to fix the rents charged for privately operated farms and businesses. For purposes of administration, the farms seem to have been divorced from mills and other industries and crafts. Women were required to sign quitclaim declarations before a justice of the peace, surrendering their rights to a dower and to one third of their husband's estates. A supplementary constitution for an organization resembling a building and loan association provided that anyone who contributed sufficient funds for a house could direct its construction and occupy it during his lifetime. While the widow would be permitted to live in the family home until her death, the children, if they left the colony, had no claim beyond the actual cash investment. Thus private enterprise was beginning to be recognized in the life of individual families, but stores and industries were to remain common property and be operated for equal benefits and profits for all.

On March 30, 1853, Weitling telegraphed his paper in New York that the colony was ready to accept his new charter and to surrender all deeds and mortgages to the Workingmen's League of Communia. He translated the major portions of his new constitution into English, and submitted it to a judge at the county seat of Clayton County for approval. On the latter's assurance that it conformed with the requirements of the law, it was circulated in pamphlet form in a German version; extracts were published in the *Clayton County Herald* of August 5, 1853, and later issued in an English edition printed in the plant of this newspaper. Weitling himself had copied the long document fifteen times in German and five times in English, had read it in full to the assembled colonists five times in German and once in English and had made eight trips to Garnavillo for counsel. He felt fully repaid for his labors when after full debate in five separate meetings the colonists accepted the new framework of government without a single change.

The records of Clayton County show transfers of parcels of real estate before the end of 1853 to the Communia Workingmen's League by Joseph and Christine Venus, Jakob and Eliza Ponsar, J. Enders, Cornelius Kopp, B. F. Weiss, John Taffy, and U. Pape, covering 1,440 acres in all, for a consideration of $2,449. Twenty-two members, including Weitling, signed the new constitution. "Take your money out of the banks and invest it here," the founder of the *Arbeiterbund* advised his faithful followers, and proclaimed the first of May as a day of festivities when all the *Gemeinde* throughout the land would celebrate the adoption of the new charter. Magnanimously he urged them to forget the past and to extend the hand of fellowship to all who had seceded. "We arrived in the colony on Good Friday," he wrote, lapsing into his favorite religious symbolism. "On Saturday we buried the old Judas of misunderstanding, and on Sunday, the Holy Easter of the *Arbeiterbund*, we had the resurrection to the eternal glory of our good cause." Weitling was in ecstasy, as he traveled 1,500 miles back to New York via St. Louis and Cincinnati.[8]

For a short while, his optimism seemed justified. The new ar-

[8] The constitution was printed in full in *Rep. d. Arb.*, July 16, 1853.

rivals included farmers, a physician, three women, and artisans from Baltimore, St. Louis, Cincinnati, and Philadelphia. Louis Reuther, one of the newcomers, later became a highly respected citizen of Elkader and a member of the Iowa state legislature. In August, a private of Company G, United States Army, stationed in Texas, who read *Die Republik der Arbeiter* regularly, requested copies of the new constitution for ten recruits for the colony whom he had found among his comrades. Though the colony suffered from a drouth, the wheat and peach crops were especially promising, and in July, 1853, the "Communia Association" advertised in the *Clayton County Herald* for hands to work on their milldam at "good wages." From June 1 to October 1, 1853, the *Arbeiterbund* invested $6,250, mostly in the form of sight drafts drawn by the colony on the treasurer for goods and materials. August Willich came to the *Arbeiter Halle* in St. Louis and tried to persuade Friedrich Hecker, the most famous of the revolutionists of 1848–49, to support Weitling's movement. Hecker may have made some sympathetic comments, but he refused to become involved. Later, Willich himself spent several days in the colony, but when Weitling tried to induce him to accept the post of administrator, he declined the responsibility with the realistic comment that the job would require "more courage than a charge into a cannon's mouth."

During May and June of 1853, Weitling was again in Communia. He had walked from Guttenberg to the colony on a beautiful moonlit night, and he was deeply moved by the experience. Colonists seemed more co-operative than they had been the previous year. He reported in *Die Republik der Arbeiter* that the carpenters were busy building another house on a piecework basis because it "works better that way"; that the population had grown to sixty-one souls; that the food was less abundant but the harvest promising; that the colony needed additional oxen and that the supply of whisky was exhausted; and what seemed most significant, that though there still was some dissatisfaction, no one was quarrelsome.

On the Fourth of July, forty Americans came to Communia from Elkader, in twelve wagons. They brought along plenty of whisky and a fiddler, but unfortunately the latter could play but one waltz tune, "O du lieber Augustin," and that "in wretched tempo." The Germans furnished beer, milk, butter, and delicious baked goods for the occasion, and sang German songs for their American neighbors. Dancing continued until five the next morning. Still somewhat intoxicated from this joyous interlude after many months of monotonous isolation and hard work, the colonists continued the celebration into the next day, when they all solemnly signed their new constitution.

A new inventory showed a favorable balance of nearly $3,000, but unfortunately that figure shrank to $562 by the end of the year. The pension fund of the *Arbeiterbund* was carried on the books at approximately $11,000. Weitling lauded the new constitution because it permitted "division of work by the piece" and "freedom of families to maintain their own households," and he hoped that these conditions which marked a departure from strict communism would make it easier to recruit additional farmers and craftsmen. In the course of the summer, twenty outsiders, mostly Germans from the neighborhood, were employed by the colony for wages. Weitling admonished the faithful not to become too optimistic or too "intoxicated with the ideal of a harmonious life in a colony," but he started east convinced at last that Communia now rested on a stable foundation and could face the future with assurance. On the return journey, which he made by way of Chicago and Detroit, he contracted "swamp fever" in Michigan, and was seriously ill for several weeks.

Unfortunately, trouble broke out again in Communia over the election of officials under the new charter and especially over the choice of an administrator. The colonists, still stubbornly provincial in their point of view and becoming more so, demanded the removal of *Die Republik der Arbeiter* and the headquarters of the *Arbeiterbund* with all its funds from New York to Iowa.

When Weitling vigorously opposed such a preposterous proposal, some of the colonists renewed their attacks on him personally because of his refusal to surrender title to the forty-acre mill site.

By September, a movement was under way to make the head of the *Arbeiterbund* the administrator of Communia. The demand came primarily in the form of letters from members of the *Bund*, addressed to Weitling, urging him as the "ablest" among their number to accept the "sacred duty." R. Kreter, treasurer of the *Bund*, strenuously objected to the choice of his colleague on the ground that he was far more useful as a traveling propagandist and had neither the theoretical nor practical qualifications necessary for so difficult an assignment. In due time, however, Weitling was elected administrator by the fifteen "trustees" of the colony. One voted against him, and Kreter, probably foreseeing the financial troubles ahead, promptly resigned as treasurer of the *Arbeiterbund*. J. Hagemann was chosen secretary of the Workingmen's League and Baumann, its treasurer. The directory which supervised the work of the colony consisted of Louis Arnold acting for the building division, Venus for the farmers, and Schmidt for the mills and crafts. A board of three arbitrators was selected to deal with serious differences of opinion, although under the terms of the constitution final authority in case of deadlock was specifically lodged in the administrator (*Verwalter*).

Once more, Weitling made the long, hard journey to Iowa, arriving in November. Despite protestations that he had not sought the post and had accepted it only as a solemn obligation, there is evidence to indicate that he shouldered the responsibility with keen anticipation, perhaps even with grandiose plans for a still rosier future. He frequently had expressed himself in print both in Europe and in the United States on the qualifications of a competent administrator and in regard to the necessity of complete submission to the single, higher will; he had referred on many occasions to the need for a leader who would sacrifice himself for the benefit of all and act as a "moral dam against the flood of vanity and ambition" that unfortunately characterized the human family. Now he had the opportunity, albeit under rather unfavorable conditions, to try out his own theories.

Weitling was disillusioned almost from the moment he arrived in Communia. He had no room to work in and had to carry on his heavy chores and his complicated bookkeeping in a space shared with three others. He found the dam on the Volga still uncompleted and presently admitted that the purchase of the sawmill had turned out to be "the worst speculation that could have been made with our funds." He discovered that the colony was paying its members wages at three times the prevailing rate in the neighborhood, and he learned to his great dismay that the preceding management had leased a farm near the flour mill to a member of the colony on a private, seven-year lease without adequate security and that the main farm was being worked on half-shares by six other colonists. All he could do under the circumstances was to block further leases and try to revise existing contracts and stop further private earnings at the expense of the community. "Everywhere," he wrote unhappily, "I discover a desire to protect the individual," but none to look after the interests of those who had invested their funds so generously in Communia.

Despite his commitment to the principle of a single, all-powerful leadership, the minutes of the colony show that he had endless meetings with his fellow colonists to discuss and settle almost every conceivable problem and that he was unusually patient in trying to lead his co-workers to a meeting of the minds. The records report, for example, an action by majority vote to provide additional picks and wheelbarrows for the workmen on the dam; the assignment of the men to their tasks; the allotment of five tons of hay for a prospective renter of the sawmill; and a furious altercation between the storekeeper, the builder of the mill, and the miller over a charge that the storekeeper had delivered whisky in a vinegar barrel which had not been rinsed properly. It turned out that the hay had been stored so late in the barns that the livestock of neighboring farmers had begun to eat it; that the castings for the flour mill had corroded in the open air; and that, after three months' delay, the teamsters had not yet hauled the millstones from the river front. Delays in transportation between New York and Iowa necessitated buying supplies in Dubuque at considerable loss.

It appears from the colony's records that workers were credited for board and room at a ratio of five to one between labor and the value of goods which they purchased. Wages for the various trades were fixed by majority vote and for women and children in a fashion that defied all reason. Thirty-seven workdays were charged for the construction of a temporary stable consisting of nothing but raw fence posts overlaid with straw. Carpenters were allowed $1.00 for an eight-hour day and the builders of the mill $1.25, whereas farm labor received less for a ten-hour day. Though a pound of flour cost two and one-half cents, bread was sold at less than cost and eggs at ten cents a dozen. Weitling thereupon decided to sell eggs to the highest bidder and raised the price of chickens from twelve to fifteen cents. Hats which cost $2.40 were sold for $1.00 and $1.50 at the colony store. An order to stop the free distribution of whisky led to violent protests. Though the corn and hay crops had not been leased to individual members and therefore presumably still belonged to the *Bund*, the colonists had to be paid for harvesting them. Weitling quite rightly pointed out that the colony could not expect the outside members of the *Arbeiterbund* to meet its deficits while the members living in the colony voted themselves an unreasonably advantageous scale of costs and wages.

One woman in the colony had been allowed $14 a month, and a man $22 a month, in addition to board and lodging, for operating the common kitchen, and Weitling discovered that making beds and feeding the twenty-eight unmarried members of the community was costing the colony $70 a month. Room rents for families varied from fifty cents to $1.00 a month in the ordinary dwellings and amounted to $2.25 in the brick house. According to this rate, the return was $154.80 a year instead of the $375 which the new administrator considered proper. Obviously everything was in confusion, from prices and production to rents, wages, and consumption. Weitling found not "two parties" but "dozens of interests" and ridiculous and prolonged conflicts over such minor questions as whether a cow should be slaughtered or spared to produce a calf.

It is surprising that the new administrator did not return to New York immediately. But after the shock of first impressions wore off, he became a little more hopeful. He succeeded in getting a unanimous decision to revise some of the private contracts which had replaced the principles of communal living and to cancel an increase in wages already voted. Counting the workmen who came in from the outside, there were seventy-nine persons in the colony in December, 1853. The demand for food was so heavy that the colonists had to kill some of their livestock and buy meat from the outside as well. The more confused matters became, the more the colonists held him personally responsible for rules and regulations and bylaws which made it necessary to operate with an elaborate machinery of committees. Every issue, no matter how trivial, turned out to be so explosive that Weitling's heart sank every time the bell rang to summon the colonists to a meeting. On one occasion, he was so thoroughly disgusted with "intellectual tasks" and the frailties of human nature that he went out to do heavy manual labor at the dam site, worked fourteen hours a day, and was happy again. On Saturday night the troubles of the week seemed to be forgotten. Then the colonists sang, drank whisky punch, and danced to the tunes of the flute player who was the sole member of the Communia orchestra.

Late in 1853, the erstwhile agnostic was able to thank "the Lord above for the beautiful weather" which made it possible for the delinquent colonists to save their harvests. Suddenly Weitling's hopes rose again because of the discovery on colony land of metal that "shone like silver." Providence itself seemed to provide the $10,000 which was needed for the coming year and thus made further drafts on the dwindling resources of the *Arbeiterbund* unnecessary. The New York *Tribune* of October 24, 1853, reported the discovery of a lead mine in Clayton County, said to yield 120,000 pounds a month, worth $31 a thousand pounds. But alas, Weitling's silver turned into lead, or perhaps iron or zinc, metals frequently found in that vicinity, and unfortunately the colony lacked the resources to mine even these baser metals.

By Christmas the relations between Weitling and the former treasurer of the *Arbeiterbund* had been severed; Kreter demanded a special committee to supervise the transactions between the colony and the *Bund* and insisted that Weitling make public all the orders he had drawn on the treasury since he had become administrator. To make matters worse, Simon Schmidt, stanch friend from early Swiss days, joined the opposition and proclaimed his utter disgust with the new constitution. Weitling, however, continued to advertise the colony as a "homestead for our pensioned members." The report for March, 1854, indicated expenditure of *Arbeiterbund* funds for Communia amounting to $14,447.47. An inventory made on the preceding January 1 listed the assets of the colony at nearly $20,000. The figure included $5,700 spent on the ill-fated saw and flour mills. The colony owed $818.07 to members in back pay at prevailing wage rates. "Trustees" had made loans totaling $4,483. The turnover at the colony store amounted to $3,600 a year.

The year 1854 turned out to be the most turbulent in the colony's history, and it became apparent that Communia was moving fast toward final liquidation. The colonists continued to press for the removal of the New York headquarters, the treasury of the *Bund*, and *Die Republik der Arbeiter* to Iowa, hoping no doubt that a majority vote of those actually in the colony thus would be able to legislate for the entire *Arbeiterbund*. Weitling, on the other hand, quite properly considered the colony as merely one *Gemeinde* of the *Bund* with no more rights than any other local group. He suggested calling a congress in 1855 and submitting all controversial issues to that body for settlement. At the same time, *Die Republik der Arbeiter* carried an article by

"L.A." (probably the acting editor, Leopold Alberti) which lauded the administration of the colony and reminded that Weitling had led the colonists out "of the chaos of passion and strife," even though he had been forced to observe the tedious processes of discussion and deliberation; and that it had taken Moses many years to organize the Israelites for their entry into the promised land.

The forty-acre mill site on the Volga, registered in Weitling's name, remained the center of the controversy between him and the colonists. Gradually, it dawned on the disillusioned leader that perhaps the only reason for his election as administrator was the desire to ensure a steady flow of funds from the *Arbeiterbund* to the colony. On January 6, 1854, Weitling resigned his post. He was tired of being a mere "automaton, . . . merely to let others feel how free and independent they were." He called upon the disgruntled to appeal their case to the other *Gemeinde* and he agreed to abide by the results of a referendum to be taken by mail on the controversial question: the title to the forty-acre plot. He also offered to surrender his control of *Die Republik der Arbeiter*. At the same time, however, he made it absolutely clear that under no conditions would he consent to any proposals which would make the *Bund* the milch cow of the colony. Rather than consent to such a betrayal of those who had followed his leadership and joined his organization, he would return to patching pants and abandon reform altogether.

Weitling's resignation precipitated a violent controversy. It was aired primarily in *Die Republik der Arbeiter*, which published the opposing points of view fully and without censorship. It also was aired in a voluminous correspondence between the various *Gemeinde*, in which Weitling was pictured as an incompetent administrator who had abandoned his own principles and violated the constitution of the Communia Workingmen's League by refusing to surrender title to the land in dispute. Attention was called to a written pledge by the colonists by which they promised never to ask a penny for their holdings until all outside members of the

Bund had received full security for their investments, a promise which obviously could mean no more than issuing stock certificates to cover outstanding claims.

Weitling replied from New York, and addressed his appeal to the *Gemeinde* still loyal to the *Arbeiterbund*, which at the time perhaps had not more than 500 members. Many of his followers had been offended by his frank reports on the events and personalities involved in Communia's stormy career, and so he decided that henceforth his duty would be "to quiet and heal" and to protect his organization against "danger and loss." With admirable restraint he ignored the attacks on his personal character, pleaded for unity, promised to conciliate Kreter and induce him to act as treasurer of the *Bund* again, and agreed to stop all payments to the colony for the present. He announced his readiness to transfer the title to the forty acres of mill land and proposed another new charter. His figures showed conclusively that the opposition had only $4,500 at stake in Communia, whereas the total investments of the *Arbeiterbund* were nearly $16,000. He already had delivered the earlier "deed of trust" to his friend, Heinrich Richter, with instructions to hold it as security for the *Bund* and to deliver it to the colony only when a new deed had been made out to the *Arbeiterbund* as a whole. Instead, Richter had it recorded at the County Recorder's Office.

Weitling's complete answer to "The Forty Acre Question" was published in *Die Republik der Arbeiter* on February 4, 1854. He had been directed to appear on May 22 in the Iowa courts to answer the charges pending against him. Although readily admitting his mistakes, he accepted full responsibility for his efforts to protect the *Arbeiterbund* and attributed his troubles with the colony to the fact that certain individuals still had individual property rights in Communia. He believed that a confidential letter addressed "To the Married" at the time when the women of the colony were in revolt was responsible for many of his difficulties. His frankness in reporting the actual state of affairs in *Die Republik der Arbeiter* certainly had not helped matters, but he was convinced that four or five individuals living in the colony were the ringleaders who were determined to destroy the *Arbeiterbund.* The persecution complex from which he suffered much of his life led him to the conclusion that there was a plot afoot to beat him and burn the colony, and he related a fantastic tale of crossing the river on the ice at Dubuque and proceeding on foot to Galena to escape the conspirators who wanted to prevent his return to New York. They plotted, he said, to have him arrested as an embezzler and then to report to his loyal followers that he had been killed because of "the rage of the people." He claimed to have documentary proof to substantiate these charges, but it was never presented to anyone.

Some of the larger *Gemeinde* remained steadfast in their loyalty to their leader. The Baltimore group in a public statement chided the colony for abandoning communism and advocated a new undertaking over which Weitling would have "unlimited executive power." The *Gemeinde* in Philadelphia, in a round-robin letter, supported their leader, testified to his honesty and loyalty, justified his policy with reference to the mill site, and concluded that his only fault was "too much faith in people." At the same time, an unsuccessful effort was made to launch a "Communia II," not by his friends, but by his enemies.

By the middle of February, the returns on the referendum conducted among the locals of the *Bund* were in, and the vote was favorable for Weitling. The majority approved the framing of another charter and authorized him to hold the deed for transfer to the new organization. The New York *Gemeinde* gave him full powers of attorney, and Weitling asked other groups to do likewise. Baltimore and Detroit promised $2,000 in new contributions. A few weeks later, however, opposition to Weitling broke out in Philadelphia and a "purge" of the membership in New York resulted in heavy financial loss.

Meantime, Ludwig Brandenberger, a roughhewn Bavarian who knew no English, had succeeded Weitling as administrator of the colony. He demanded additional funds from the *Arbeiterbund* to pay outstanding bills and continued to file monthly reports. Undaunted by the mounting crisis, he described in his illiterate German happy days in Communia spent by the "Bionier des fernen Westens" (pioneers of the Far West) in hunting, singing, and enjoying "Wieskei Bunsch" (whisky punch). Weitling retorted that "no colony of the *Arbeiterbund* could honorably accept a simpleton as administrator even if he had a heart of gold," and when colonists replied that they needed as administrator a man who could swing an ax, not a theoretician, he advised them to appoint an Irishman or a "Nigger." Greatly excited and deeply wounded, he made comments of an increasingly personal nature about some of his brother colonists; and his old friendship with Richter, whom he blamed for "scandalous" letters emanating from Communia, turned to bitter enmity. He advised the aged pensioners of the *Bund* to give up all hope of ending their days in such a quarrelsome community, announcing that on April 1, the colony would be formally suspended as a member of the *Arbeiterbund*.

On March 11, the Baltimore *Gemeinde* released a blistering attack on Communia, accusing the members of character assassination and demanding an end to the pending lawsuit and a public sale of the property so that the *Arbeiterbund* might have an opportunity to buy it at sheriff's sale. Weitling gladly consented to the proposal. At the instigation of the Philadelphia *Gemeinde*, a delegation was sent to the colony at a further expense of $423.29 to the *Bund* to study the situation at first hand and report directly to the membership. Weitling accompanied the group only as far as Dubuque. The delegation found no solution for the problem and could do no more than report that the colonists would leave if paid in full by June 1, that several farmers wanted to remain for the harvest, that one member insisted on being paid in gold or silver, and that none was ready to drop the lawsuit.

B. F. Weiss, a member who served as the first postmaster of Communia and who was loyal to Weitling, urged him to come in person to make a settlement, for the colonists were "fed up" with communism and had no confidence in the existing administrator. Spring floods washed away the dam and the mill wall on the Volga, and the workers refused to rebuild them unless cash wages were guaranteed. Weitling's devoted friend, J. Krieg, announced that he was through with communism and demanded his money. Brandenberger offered to complete the mill project for $6,000 and reported that he was forced to sell some of the colony's movable property to pay the seceders and provide them with travel funds and that he had been in "Dubjoch" (Dubuque) to instruct the attorney to drop the suit against Weitling.

By this time nearly all available funds of the *Arbeiterbund* had been sunk in the hapless venture. Weitling told his friends that he would rather carry a sack of meat to a pack of wolves than a bag of money to the colonists. He begged the tiny remnant of the faithful to continue to have faith in his courage. His attorney in Dubuque advised him to insist upon a chancery suit rather than a jury trial, assured him that his conduct had been perfectly legal, and approved the power of attorney which he had obtained from most of the *Gemeinde*.

Accepting this advice as a complete vindication, Weitling's spirits rose immediately. He was ready to forget the colony and begin all over again with more practical objectives. "We are not guilty of the losses which many will suffer," he insisted. "Forget that we once had brothers in Communia." He pleaded for a new propaganda purified by the fires of bitter experience, reminded his friends that virtue and things of the spirit outweigh all material things, and told them that Hannibal lost many a soldier before his army finally conquered Rome. His only practical proposal however was a plan to have all property of the *Bund* recorded hereafter in the name of "Wilhelm Weitling, trustee of the Workingmen's League," so that purified in soul and spirit the *Arbeiterbund* could move forward "into a new and more beautiful Canaan."

Die Republik der Arbeiter for June, 1854, published several letters from Communia in which settlers presented their claims and accused Weitling of defrauding the working class. Weiss, the storekeeper for the colony, advocated a public sale or a partition of colony property among the colonists. Brandenberger kept the *Gemeinde* informed of the liquidation that already was in progress under his leadership, reported that nine members had left within the last two weeks, and announced that a petition had been filed in the courts asking for a legal dissolution. Livestock was being sold rapidly, and farms, houses, and the sawmill were rented on private contracts to such members as chose to remain.

Weitling published his reply to Brandenberger on July 1, 1854. In it, he described the latter as a "fool" and compared him to a "cur barking at a bull dog." He also made comparisons between the Germans and the Yankee and Irish settlers on the frontier, to the decided advantage of the latter group. He stubbornly adhered to the notion that a dozen stalwarts from the *Arbeiterbund* still could go to Iowa and save the colony, and he hoped to raise another $3,000 to pay off all remaining claimants. Given dictatorial power, he would rally the faithful who "are the light of the world" and by means of the homestead legislation then pending in Congress, secure a new site. August Witzleben, a devoted follower who sold Weitling's books in Brazil and lent him money from time to time, advised his friend that ladies' tailors were much in demand in Rio, and suggested that he come to South America and start life all over again. Weiss, in an attack on his former leader released to a number of German papers (although not to *Die Republik der Arbeiter*), accused Weitling of claiming omniscience and being totally ignorant of all practical matters. The latter retorted that recent letters from the colony would make a good "library for a psychologist."

In November, the harassed leader again spent several days in Dubuque. He had made the journey on the request of several friends as a final effort to protect the interests of the *Arbeiterbund*. He discovered that the suit against him had been removed from the docket, but that liquidation of the colony was going on rapidly because of debts owed to outsiders. His attorney advised him to let the law take its course, and he accepted the advice because the *Bund* had nothing more to lose "except its hell." At the time, the colony actually had two administrators, Brandenberger and Venus, and each was getting injunctions and attachments against the other and calling in the sheriff to protect his rights. When Louis Weiner, who had withdrawn from the colony two years earlier but had not been fully paid, filed a suit in the district court of Garnavillo for a claim of $200, both Venus and Brandenberger were subpoenaed and ordered to bring in the account books of the Communia Workingmen's League. The court records show a settlement by consent of both parties. Weiss reported the following spring that a minority, aided by outsiders, had threatened to seize the property with knives and revolvers.[9]

Thus the colony's history ended in hopeless confusion, the details of which cannot be completely untangled. According to the court records at Elkader, three actions were filed. One was a "Criminal Information," known as "State of Iowa v. Communia Working Men's League." This case was continued from 1857 to May 16, 1859, when all records were transferred to Dubuque County and were lost. A second suit, a case in equity, entitled "Jacob Ponsar and Benjamin F. Weis [*sic*] v. Community Working Men's League" went through the same processes. In one of the notices of continuance, the defendant was identified as the "Workingmen's League of New York." The third was a replevin action brought by one Henry Barnhart. It too was continued from term to term, and there is no record of its final disposition. On May 11, 1858, an attorney of Guttenberg wrote to Weitling, then living at 195 Avenue B, New York, to press a claim by Louis Arnold in the amount of $130. F. Hofer, one of the last of the faithful who had resolved to remain on the colony site, build a house on a two-acre plot, and open a "bath house" on the Volga "because there was none in Iowa," wrote Weitling to report that the sheriff had just left the region after trying in vain to serve an attachment on behalf of Arnold.[10]

[9] The last financial report and the padded claims of some of the colonists were printed in *Rep. d. Arb.*, December 16, 1854.

[10] F. Hofer to Weitling, May 6, 1858. (Letter in possession of Terijon Weitling.)

The records of the district court of Clayton County for the September term of 1858 show suits filed against Weitling by A. Peick for $607.32, by F. Peick for $117.12, and by Louis Arnold for $187. All suits were for the recovery of loans made in 1854, except in the case of Arnold, who demanded pay for "work and labor done." When the sheriff reported that the defendant could not be found in the colony, a notice of the action was printed for four weeks, as required by law, in the Guttenberg newspaper. In the same term, another suit was filed by Jacob Ponsar and Benjamin F. Weiss against the Workingmen's League; Rudolph Kreter, treasurer; Weitling; and several others. It demanded an accounting of the colony's assets and liabilities and partition of whatever property might remain after all just claims had been met.

Dennis Quigley and John Garber were appointed receivers for the colony, and Garber filed a report with the district court of Clayton County on May 30, 1857. The court order instructed the receivers to take possession and dispose of all personal property of the colony and to rent and administer its real estate, because it "is now in the custody and control of no responsible parties and . . . is in danger of waste and damage." Garber collected a fee of $100 "for 35 days' service, expense and mileage."

His report provided a detailed inventory of the colony's property and showed real estate to the amount of 1,290 acres, of which only 174 acres were under cultivation. The real estate was temporarily leased, with the sawmill and equipment, to private persons by direction of the court, and the rental of each farm included livestock and chattel property. The latter included not only farm tools and accessories, but such things as "sythes," lye barrels, two syringes, one "night chair," a secretary's stamp, and a "Taylor table." The inventory for the store and storage room listed dry goods, groceries, one guitar, three pounds "allum," a "barrel Sour Crout," two boats on the Volga, a "large Baking Trought," a coffee burner, "47 papers chewing tobacco, 3 papers smoking Do," and a supply of ledgers and minute books. The receiver rented living quarters at 50 cents to $1.50 a month to Venus, Baumann, Weiss, the Peicks, Brandenberger, and several others who chose to remain. The receiver's inventory also included deeds and contracts, "releases," and receipts, in which Weitling's name frequently was misspelled "W. Weiching" and "W. Whiteling." The chattel property was appraised at $302.09 and the unpaid claims recorded in the colony's "Day Book" amounted to $169.55, thus leaving a balance of $132.54. "For the comfort and convenience of the Members," the receiver commented in his report, he "left the household and kitchen furniture in their possession."

The final act recorded in the Clayton County court was the conveyance of the real estate to private owners by John Garber, "Trustee of the late corporation." These conveyances were not completed until April and May, 1864. Some parcels went to old colonists, such as Ponsar, Baumann, Marxer, Meyer, and Venus. A few went to persons whose names had not appeared hitherto in the colony records. The payments ranged from $200 to $4,490, the larger figure representing the transaction with Joseph Venus on April 27, 1864. The "deed of trust" given to Weitling in 1852, the source of so much trouble, was finally released on December 4, 1897, by a commissioner appointed by a decree of the Clayton County district court. In 1880, Weitling's eldest son wrote to a judge in Dubuque to inquire what had become of the colony's land. The judge replied that he had no specific information on the subject, except that the colony had been dissolved by court order and that its property had long since passed into private hands.

Today what is left of Communia lies in the heart of a beautiful, well-cultivated farming country. The WPA *Guide* for Iowa states that its post office was finally discontinued in 1903, that the "old colony house" stands abandoned, and that a $50,000 flour mill (!) designed by John Thompson, who built many stone mills in northeastern Iowa, is in disuse.[11] As a matter of fact, regular gymnastic

[11] Federal writers' project, *Iowa, a guide to the Hawkeye state* (The American Guide Series, New York, 1938), 363; Realto E. Price, *History of Clayton County, Iowa* (Chicago, 1916), 107, 322–23; *Clayton County Register*, August 21, 1930, March 26, 1931, and July 22, 1936.

exhibitions were held on the old picnic grounds and in the Communia "hall" as late as 1910, and the hall now owned by the Communia *Turnverein* is still used occasionally for dances.

The collapse of the colony pushed the *Bund* and *Die Republik der Arbeiter* into bankruptcy. Nietzche once observed that "who falls gets kicked." Weitling's case was no exception. The New York *Demokrat* in November, 1854, intimated that the poor workers had given their money to an "evil doer." The Philadelphia *Frieie Presse* charged that before bankruptcy came "Weitling had looked out handsomely for himself." Years later, the Dubuque *Phönix* referred to the leader of the "tailor Latin" colony as a "clever fish" who, after the failure of Communia, was alleged to have sold a patent for a buttonhole machine for $30,000 and, having become a rich man, lost all interest in dividing with the poor. In the closing days of the colony fiasco, the Philadelphia *Arbeiterbund* had accused Weitling in an open letter of being an egotist, of maintaining spies and secret records, and of being an ordinary "swindler" who had robbed men of their hard-earned savings and then had driven them off their land. "To the end of time," wrote these former admirers, "Communia will make you and your deeds abhorred." Charges of muddleheadedness and dictatorship were common, as well as sarcastic jibes about Weitling's eagerness to write constitutions. The corruption of the *Arbeiterbund* was compared with the misconduct of banks, decidedly to the advantage of the latter. "You yourself destroyed your work in America as you destroyed it in Europe" was the closing line of an indictment by another group of erstwhile comrades. A letter, signed by the "founders" of Communia, charged Weitling with exploiting his fellowmen in the name of communism and brotherly love and concluded: "If there is a hell for liars, you are ripe for it."

Weitling lashed back in one of the last issues of his paper with countercharges of "libeler," "defamer," and "slanderer." Then he became silent and apparently never referred to colony matters again, even in the intimate circle of his family. During his remaining years he lived in straitened circumstances if not actual poverty, and when he died he had nothing to leave to his family. These facts are sufficient evidence that he did not make money out of either the colony or the *Arbeiterbund*.

No man can be expected to diagnose his own shortcomings with complete objectivity. From Weitling's own pen comes an analysis of his failures which he excused in part by claiming that he had never had adequate authority, either in the *Bund* or in the colony, and had yielded too often to "the folly of majority rule." He was forced to admit that most men are egotistical, that many lack courage and virtue and confidence in their fellows. He believed also that existing laws, drafted by "lawyers, priests and capitalists," were unfair to labor organizations.

In one of the later issues of *Die Republik der Arbeiter* he compared the theories and principles which he had advocated in the *Garantieen* with his actual experience in Europe and America. In self defense, he pointed out that the plans outlined in his magnum opus were intended for a whole state—indeed, for the whole of human society—and that at least fifty years of cleansing and purification by revolution and possibly war were needed before they could be put into practice successfully. He maintained also that a socialist state isolated in a capitalist world would encounter great obstacles in trading with its capitalist neighbors and would need a huge military establishment to defend itself.

The principles of the *Garantieen*, when applied to a little colony in pioneer Iowa, simply would not work. The colonists had to deal constantly with outsiders, had to seek credit and pay interest, had to sell at a profit, and had to meet the prices and wages of outside competitors. Moreover, Weitling was forced to admit that workers in Communia could not be dismissed or ordered to their jobs, and on that account the productive capacity of a society based on free enterprise and competition was bound to be greater. The disillusioned Utopian had discovered that every little difference of opinion in the colony was likely to turn into a scene and a scandal. With rare candor and the virtual repudiation of all he had advocated earlier he concluded, "I regard a communism without wages, and without the liberty to refrain from working if one wants to, and common food and equal work hours, an impossibility in our present society, and not even appealing for the future, and therefore, impractical."

Chapter XIV

FAREWELL TO REFORM

After nearly thirty years of agitation for the causes in which he had believed and sacrificed, Weitling returned to New York to eke out an existence by taking up the needle and shears of the tailor again. His remaining years were spent in efforts to satisfy interests which his restless spirit had been forced to neglect during the years devoted to reform.

Relatively little is known about the personal life of Wilhelm Weitling. Most of his time and energy, until he was nearly fifty, were devoted to the cause of the workers and to his theories of social reconstruction. He had been a wanderer in six countries and not until he was forty-six years of age, long after most men experience the stabilizing and sobering effects of family responsibilities, was Weitling ready to abandon the life of a roving propagandist and settle down in New York to lead the life of an ordinary German craftsman and rear a family. In the city which had welcomed him as a refugee and had served as the headquarters of the organization he expected would control the American labor movement, he lived inconspicuously for the rest of his days as a simple citizen. He withdrew almost entirely from all public activity, and was quickly forgotten by most of the German craftsmen whose champion he had been.

Among the manuscripts which Weitling preserved, there are a number of poems, evidently written in the early 1840's, which do not appear in his published collection of *Kerkerpoesien.* They include several sentimental lyrics which may have been inspired by a romantic relationship between the young journeyman and some forgotten maid whom he met during his Continental *Wanderjahre*. One is a love poem about a rose which is picked by the beautiful hands of the beloved only to fade upon her lovely bosom, while the banished lover yearns for a similar fate. Another, entitled "Life's Dream," is a farewell to a loved one forever lost. Still another, in script that has so faded from the old yellow paper that it is almost indecipherable, is a passionate declaration of devotion. Several stanzas, dated August 24, 1844, purport to be a lover's song of gratitude to a bride with whom he soon will share all the joys of matrimony. A week later, the poet wrote of a forgotten "Anna" who, like an angel, had led him to heaven and taught him all the blissful suffering of love. Though the lover vowed his undying devotion, the poet had produced another poem before a month had passed about a "little sister" whose love had cooled and the "other sisters" whom God had sent to comfort him.

These poetic fragments are written in a lyric style that has elements of grace and charm, yet they may have been only the literary fancies of a youth whose spirit soared into the world of romance primarily for relief from the routine cares of the day. It is not known by whom these stanzas were inspired, nor whether they were addressed to any particular woman among the scores whom an attractive and jovial young journeyman was likely to meet as he wandered from village to village and town to town through the romantic German and Austrian countryside.

In 1854, Weitling married the young German girl who shared the joys and sorrows of the rest of his years. Her life with the man whose mind never found peace at the tailor's bench was marked by complete devotion to her husband and to their children and a willingness to make every sacrifice for their welfare. Dorothea Caroline Louise Toedt, twenty-two years old, married a man more than twice her age. She had come to the United States from Wittenberg in Mecklenburg-Schwerin in 1852 with her parents, a sister, and two half-brothers.

In the church records of the pastor of her native town, the

family name was spelled Tödt. Caroline, as she was known to her family, was the daughter and eldest child of Christian Friedrich Toedt, an honest, hard-working locksmith whose shop was in the rear of the building in which he lived with his family. Caroline was born June 19, 1832, and baptized six days later in the Lutheran faith. The family lived in a substantial, middle-class home, probably in moderate circumstances. A huge two-foot key hung over the front door as a symbol of the father's craft.

When Caroline was twenty years old the head of the house decided to go to the United States. On the *Southerner*, a converted, cotton-carrying, sailing vessel, the family made the difficult voyage from Hamburg to New York in sixty-four days as part of the huge German immigration of the 1850's. They proceeded at once into upstate New York, where the father bought a small farm in Herkimer County, near Utica, a region in which the newcomers found several friends and neighbors from their old home in Mecklenburg. The twenty-year old daughter, already a skillful seamstress, went to work in Utica for a milliner at fifty cents a week plus board and room.

Before long, Caroline Toedt was summoned to New York City by an uncle, John Toedt, to help care for his sick wife, Mathilda. John Toedt, a skilled worker in leather, did fine bookbinding and leather gilding and belonged to one of the early German craft organizations of the 1850's. In this connection he became acquainted with Wilhelm Weitling, and the latter frequently visited him in his home on the Bowery. There he met the niece who was nursing her aunt back to health, and it may be assumed that not all of the tailor's visits to the Toedt home had to do strictly with the business of the labor movement. In due time Weitling journeyed to Herkimer County to ask the father for the hand of Caroline in marriage.

The young couple were married in upstate New York, probably in Utica, but they moved at once to New York City. Some time after they had established their new home there, they were joined by Caroline's sister, Johanna, who was eight years her junior. "Aunt Johanna" developed into an expert tailoress and eventually began a small business in the Weitling home for the manufacture of fancy vests, an activity in which the Weitlings joined. The head of the house probably worked for other custom tailors in the early years of his married life, but before long the sole source of income for the family was the fancy-vest business carried on at home. "Aunt Johanna" was a faithful, hard-working, kindly soul, who became a second mother to Weitling's children. Her relationship with her sister and brother-in-law seems to have been remarkably harmonious and close. After the death of the elder Weitlings, the aunt was revered as the head of the family by all the children and lived to enjoy the devotion and gratitude of her niece and nephews until her death in New York in 1929.

For a short time after their marriage the Weitlings lived among the Germans on the East Side on Allen Street and later on Avenue B, Norfolk Street, and Stanton Street. Weitling's account book shows that when they moved in April, 1856, at a cost of $11.50, they had "four loads" and that the usual rent paid in the various residences was $25 a month. These stray items may throw some light on the family's circumstances, at least at the beginning of their marriage. Life in the modest homes of the tailor-philosopher and the two hard-working women seems to have been fairly placid and unusually harmonious. Perhaps this demonstrates the ability of the women to appreciate the solid virtues and kindly heart of the head of the family, to overlook some of his childish vagaries, and to indulge him in the activities which resulted from his irrepressible search for new truths, however impractical they might be. The many hours spent in study and experimentation were hardly helpful in replenishing an always precarious family income, and there were periods when the question of where the next week's food or the next month's rent would come from was far more important than the possible results of the quest by the head of the house for a new cosmogony or a universal language.

On November 7, 1855, Caroline Weitling gave birth to her first son, who was born at 126 Allen Street and was promptly named by the father, William Wangansky. The elder Weitling had recently read an article on Chinese socialism in *Chamber's Journal.* His interest in Chinese revolutionary currents had always been great, and he gave due credit to the Christian missionaries for raising the level of civilization in China. Weitling believed that the Chinese Wanganski had advocated reforms more like his own system than any other reformer he knew. Determined that his first-born son should not forget his father's doctrines nor those of the Chinese leader whom he admired, he gave the boy this curious and cumbersome Oriental name. At home the lad was known as "Wangan," but as he grew to manhood he solved his problem simply by reducing the name to the initial W.

The boy grew to be a man of whom the family could well be proud. He went to work at fourteen as office boy for Poppenhausen and Koenig, after the father had secured the job for him by answering a newspaper advertisement. He remained with the firm for the rest of his life, becoming its vice-president and chairman of the American Hard Rubber Company, the name of the larger firm into which it developed. In addition, he was president of a bank, vice-president of the Pequanco Rubber Company, and president of the Poppenhausen Institute of Learning, a school for adult education to whose endowment he contributed. Like his father, he had little formal education and a great interest in astronomy, although he could not accept his father's astronomical theories. He published several articles in this field and one on the atom in 1921. As the son prospered, he contributed faithfully and generously to the support of his widowed mother and Aunt Johanna.

At the time of the birth of his first child, Weitling started the notebook which fortunately was preserved and which throws light on many phases of his later career. He wanted first of all to record for his son an interesting account of significant happenings, but before long he recorded a miscellany of items, trivial details from his daily experiences and some which "may be of great interest to others." In this little book he recorded the exact time of arrival of a second son, born June 18, 1858, and named Gracchus Babeuf Robert—Gracchus for the champion of the plebs and advocate of free lands for the poor in ancient Rome and Babeuf for the noted radical of the French Revolution. Both men, according to Weitling, had exposed the illusions of democracy and both had paid for their convictions with their lives. The second son also managed to extricate himself in later life from the inconvenience of these revolutionary names and became known as Bob.

A third son, born in 1862, was named Tycho Brahe Edward, after the famous Danish scientist of the late sixteenth century whose distinguished work at his observatory at Uraniborg made his little country the center of European astronomy in his day. As the boy grew up, he was known only by the last of the three names which his father had given him. Two years later, in 1864, a fourth son, Charles Frederick, was born in the family home at 107 Avenue A. The fifth son, born in 1866, was named Terijon after his French grandfather. Apparently he inherited some of his father's ability in the field of invention, and he manifested a special interest in architecture. For years he was an export manager for a New York firm which exported steel structures in sections to Brazil. The last of the children, a daughter named Caroline Johanna after the mother and the aunt, was born at 126 Norfolk Street, received a college education at Hunter College and served for many years as a teacher in the New York schools. All of her brothers had gone directly from public school or evening school to jobs, although surprisingly enough the family had found it possible to pay for some private tutoring for the two older boys before they entered the public schools.

On Weitling's fiftieth birthday, his wife gave him a daguerreotype of herself and her first two children. He was a devoted and responsible parent and was genuinely interested in what today would be called child psychology. The Weitling home believed in discipline for growing children but apparently had to apply serious measures very rarely. The parents seem to have been in perfect agreement on the problems of child education.

The father in view of his long record as an enemy of organized religion was particularly concerned about what to do in the matter of religious instruction for the children. As a lad, he had been reared in the Catholic faith by his maternal grandmother. His wife was born and reared a Lutheran and occasionally attended services of that denomination, though she was never a member of any church in this country. Weitling apparently never went to church. Yet, as he pondered his responsibility to his growing family, he readily acknowledged that his strict, Catholic upbringing to his twelfth year had strengthened his character and enabled him to withstand many temptations, including those of sex. "I know of nothing that has had a better or stronger influence on the development of my emotions and my intellect than the religious instruction I received in my youth," he wrote in the late 1860's. "This conviction has remained with me through the years, though I cannot accept what is in the religious books, nor the miracles and fables that have grown up around them. . . . But of one thing I am sure," he added, "and that is that whatever schools or churches the boys may attend, and whatever religion may be chosen for them as their support in life, my wife and I will be in agreement. I am afraid—or I hope—I am still uncertain—that the result will stir up surprise and enmity among my friends." At the close of 1869, when his first-born was thirteen, he recorded the statement: "Wangansky has become a good boy without religion. He neither lies nor steals because he regards that as unprincipled." The children attended Protestant Sunday schools, and Terijon became a Presbyterian.

Weitling believed that no child should be taught a religion that conflicted with his reason and powers of understanding. He would have welcomed a new book which reconciled and combined the teachings of Jesus and the best of the Bible with the progress made in the sciences; disposed of the old myths and miracles, but "without mockery"; and inspired the reader with a sense of humility before the higher mystery which he could not comprehend. In an editorial entitled "Comfort in Sorrow," one of his most beautiful

Daguerreotype Presented by Mrs. Weitling to Her Husband on His Fiftieth Birthday, Showing Her with Their First Two Children

pieces of prose writing written for *Die Republik der Arbeiter* in 1853, Weitling spoke of the "faith and power to do good" which is the holiest of all men's possessions and of the ability to gather new strength by mobilizing the resources of faith, hope, and love which are part of the universe and of every person's inner self. This was the essence of his religion, and this he tried to convey to his children. He grew weary in his mature years of what he called "the eternal chatter about God, Bible and priests" in which so many radical freethinkers among the German immigrants indulged. He was never sure whether what man called God does or does not exist; yet he faced the uncertain future with about as much confidence as most other men. He was not concerned with immortality and was wont to say with Faust: "*Nach drüben ist die Aussicht uns verrannt.*"

As soon as he had a home Weitling spent most of his time there with his family. There is no evidence that he ever belonged to a singing society, or a skat club, or to any of the other social organizations which were so popular with the German-Americans. He needed little recreation and had little money to spend for it. He found whatever happiness and peace of mind he had in working on inventions and puzzling over the mysteries of the stars. Occasionally he attended a German play in the *Stadttheater* of New York or a concert of one of the German musical societies. On Sundays and holidays he would spend hours on a boat ride or walking with his wife and sister-in-law and the children in the city parks. As far as we know, he did not bowl or fish or spend time at cards or chess. He was temperate in his habits and did not smoke. Occasionally, he took his family for Sunday dinner to the Shakespeare Hotel, the scene of so many German-American activities, or for a ride on the horsecars, or on the ferry to the New Jersey side to stroll about in Jersey Heights and Hoboken. Many Sunday afternoons were spent in Tompkins Square Park in the German neighborhood on Avenue A between Seventh and Tenth Streets known as *Der Weisse Garten.* The only membership Weitling held was in the Custom Tailors' Union, whose annual picnic in

Jones Wood on the East River between Sixtieth and Seventieth Streets he attended whenever possible. Occasionally, he called on an "old communist" friend and active organizer and propagandist of his earlier days.

German was spoken in the Weitling home among the adults and with the children, though the women as well as the head of the family could speak and read English. Weitling read English, German, and French newspapers. In 1854, he read four papers daily. Judging from his collection of clippings, the New York *Tribune* must have been his favorite. Among the German-language papers which he read regularly, he especially enjoyed the *New Yorker Kriminal Zeitung und Belletristisches Journal*, and *Die Neue Zeit*, a radical paper started in New York near the end of his life. Some of the entries in his notebook were made in excellent French. When Mrs. Weitling and her sister received calls from their relatives, the conversation usually lapsed into the "Low German" of the Mecklenburg area.

One of Weitling's hobbies was collecting pennies, and he tried to get a complete set dated from 1798 to 1855. His household pets were cats and canaries. On one occasion, he saved a dog from the abuse of a group of children, who sold him the animal for a dime; he took him home, gave him the name Filou, and made a family pet of the mongrel with the roguish French name.

Among Weitling's friends of these later years was a fairly well-to-do tobacco merchant, Charles F. Tag, who gave him some financial help to enable him to complete his inventions; and Toaspern, a builder of pianos and organizer of a piano makers' co-operative in Brooklyn who tried to sell Weitling a piano. Years later, the eldest son bought one of the instruments which his father could never afford. Other friends included Heinrich Ahrends, an enthusiastic laborite whose photograph Weitling possessed; F. A. Sorge, the leading Socialist of the period, and a friend of the early days in Switzerland; Hermann Schlüter, once editor of the *New Yorker Volkszeitung*, who was allowed to use some of Weitling's papers when he wrote his monograph on the

German labor movement in the United States; and John Toedt, the uncle, at whose home he had met his bride.

The library in the Weitling home was small, but it contained some volumes that must have exercised considerable influence on the development of many of their owner's views. Among the books were the volumes of Josiah Warren, and a book published in London in 1839, entitled *The Revolt of the Bees.* This curious allegory on communism described a revolt among the bees against communal living in favor of free enterprise and private profit; the consequent exploitation of the many by the few; the chaos into which the empire of the bees degenerated because the "Apiarian Economists" could not agree on any plan; the flight of one of the bees, à la Owen, to found a colony of its own; and the greed and wars from which they suffered until they at last accepted a "science of Social Union" and realized that rapid advancement in mere scientific power without the application of the principles of Christianity would not solve social problems. Another little volume, printed in Germany in 1814 and entitled *Selected Tales and Parables,* emphasized much the same themes, offered good advice for the rearing of children, and recounted little tales intended to inculcate morality and the Christian virtues. Since this book obviously was intended as literature for the young, it may be that Weitling read these tales to his children. His library also contained books on the structure and use of the French and Italian languages and, like many Germans, he knew his Goethe and Schiller thoroughly.

By far the largest section of his small collection, however, was devoted to books on astronomy. They included Franz Arazo's *Astronomic;* Humboldt's *Kosmos;* Moritz A. Stern's *Himmelkunde;* Carl Schoepfer's *Uranus;* Jean Baptiste Biot's *Astronome physique;* W. A. Norton's *Elementary Treatise on Astronomy,* which was heavily used if one may judge by the marginal notes and calculations; and Denison Olmsted's *A Compendium of Astronomy.*

In addition to such items, Weitling preserved quantities of

clippings from German, English, and French newspapers dealing with astronomy, linguistics, science, politics, China, the American Civil War, labor items, the northern lights, eclipses, comets, meteors and planets, meteorology, mathematics and physics, spiritualism, telepathy, and phrenology. The last-named, which intrigued so many of his generation, he disposed of with the terse comment, "I know just enough about this skull business to know it is a colossal error."

Among his papers he also preserved a tracing made by his own hand of a cartoon referring to him and his reforms, which had appeared in the *Fliegende Blätter* of Munich in 1851.[1] He was jealous of his reputation and almost pathologically concerned with what impression he may have made on the world at large. When an acquaintance in 1869 called his attention to a brief account of his career in a German *Conversations-Lexicon*, Weitling became furious because of what he considered unfair references to his published works and attributed authorship of the unsatisfactory article to a Jew. It should be added, however, that he preserved both favorable and unfavorable comments about himself in his collection of clippings. Late in life, during a serious illness, he unfortunately destroyed many of his manuscript letters and other papers.[2]

Though forced to rely for a livelihood primarily on his work as a tailor and on the help which the two women members of his family could give him, Weitling once held a political appointment for a short time. He apparently got the appointment as registrar of immigrants at Castle Garden through friends in the Democratic party, i.e., Tammany Hall. The duties of the post involved preparing annual reports and registering the passengers who arrived on immigrant ships from the British Isles and Germany. Looking after the German immigrants soon became his chief re-

[1] *Fliegende Blätter* (Munich), XII (1851), 152.

[2] For another reference to Weitling, see Fritz Ens, Carl Schaeffer, and Franz Zinkernagel (eds.), *Hebbels Werke* (Leipzig, 1913), I. In "Mutter und Kind," Canto 7, line 1903, written in 1858, Hebbel mistakenly referred to Weitling as though he had died.

sponsibility. In his own account of his troubles Weitling related that his chief, a "general agent" named Murray, was absent frequently from work because of illness and political activity but received a salary of $4,500, ten times the amount paid his subordinate.

Part of Weitling's duties proved to be very disagreeable, for he was expected to persuade the newcomers to volunteer for the Union army in the early days of the Civil War, and this he refused to do. He became quite discouraged with his job and saw little chance to change the system under which he had to work. In a letter in which he applied for another job he pointed out that "I write English and French easily and correctly, if not elegantly." His chief, according to his account, could not write a hundred words of his mother tongue correctly.

In his Account Book for June 11, 1862, Weitling recorded his version of the facts which led to his dismissal. Apparently he had been swamped by the practically simultaneous arrival of four ships, by the flood of questions addressed to him by Irish immigrants, and by the request of a German passenger to write a letter for him immediately. Rushing around excitedly in an effort to discharge all these responsibilities, he became involved in an argument with a superior about the importance of a particular request, and the dispute ended by Weitling losing his temper and telling his chief that he was neither his "fool" nor his "servant." Thereupon, he packed his effects and was dismissed for insubordination. Several years later, his distress was so acute that he swallowed his pride and applied for reinstatement, but to no avail. Another unfinished and undated letter preserved among his manuscripts was addressed to a municipal judge applying for the post of court interpreter in Essex Market Court in New York City. On October 15, 1867, at the age of fifty-nine, Weitling was admitted to American citizenship in a New York court of common pleas.

Although the appointment as registrar at Castle Garden could not have been without its political implications, Weitling definitely had decided to abandon all forms of public agitation. The labor movement took on new life among the Germans in New York in the 1860's; there were German labor papers in Chicago, New York, San Francisco, and other leading cities, and the German radical groups kept in close touch with events abroad and celebrated the anniversaries of the European revolutions in the United States; but Weitling remained out of the public eye. His friend Sorge, a Forty-eighter who became general secretary of the First International, an organization whose headquarters Marx eventually moved to New York in order to escape the influence of Bakunin and his followers, belonged to the *New Yorker Kommunisten Klub*, founded in 1857 by freethinking communists. Though it repudiated all religious faith, it included a number of non-Marxians in its membership. Weitling refused to take any part in its propaganda, though he seems to have attended an occasional meeting probably more for the sake of sociability with old friends than for reasons of politics. In the many reports of the great hunger parade in New York in 1857, when several thousand destitute workers marched past the offices of the leading newspapers and into Wall Street carrying banners bearing the inscription "Work–Arbeit," there is no reference to Weitling, either as one of the demonstrators or as one of the "several fierce Dutch and Irish orators" who addressed the crowd from the steps of the City Hall.

Weitling continued, however, to receive letters from former coworkers here and abroad. In 1855, for example, a tailor who had returned to Germany after two years' residence in Baltimore wrote from Hanover to say that he had shipped a box of printed matter containing revolutionary plays "too radical" for publication in Germany. One of the plays was dedicated to a settler residing in Communia, and Weitling was asked to arrange for the publication of his fellow tailor's manuscripts. His reply was that he had seen this fellow but once in Hamburg, that he was greatly irked by his request for a loan of twenty-five dollars, and that he resented having to pay sixty-two cents postage due to get the material out of the New York post office.

On February 27, 1861, the New York *Tribune* reported that because of an "act of royal grace" by His Majesty, the King of Prussia, German refugees now could become repatriated. Weitling still was sufficiently well known in New York that his name appeared among a list of those who might take advantage of this opportunity to return to their European fatherland. Though he was not then naturalized, Weitling had no intention of giving up his residence in the United States.

In 1868, desperately in need of help for his publication projects and his inventions, he carried on a strange correspondence with a curious individual known as Otto von Rudgisch, a former supporter in Hamburg who now lived in Jasper County, Illinois, and with a Freiherr von Schleunitz, a captain in the German navy, who was also an acquaintance from the old days in Hamburg. Such letters indicate Weitling's desperate plight and the extremes to which he was willing to go to find funds for his inventions. Von Rudgisch replied with several peculiar letters, reaffirming his faith in the author of the *Garantieen*, pleading for his return to the political arena to lead a new revolution in Germany, and insisting that no reform was possible until all the Rothschilds had been buried. He promised financial aid but never did anything for his friend in New York except write him long and incoherent letters.

In 1868, a *Soziale Partei* (Social Party), was founded in New York as an outgrowth of the German Communist Club of 1857. The little party has significance in the history of the modern socialist movement in the United States, though it had little practical success in the arena of American politics. As a labor party, it appealed to all the organized tradesmen of the city. Weitling was selected as a member of its executive committee of fifteen, "because his name still had a good reputation among the workers of New York." The committee included Sorge, who had known Weitling's *Arbeitervereine* in Switzerland and had been an employee at the headquarters of his *Arbeiterbund* in New York, and other prominent Germans, like Siegfried Meyer, Adolf S. Weyler, and the brothers Lücke, who were tailors. But the old communist leader refused to permit the use of his name, even by such a group of friends and fellow propagandists. In a letter dated February 12, 1868, addressed to the gentlemen of the committee, he wrote: "My circumstances do not make it possible for me to attend your deliberations, so please fill my place with another choice. In any case, my thirty years' activity have proved to me that means and ends of a good cause are never achieved by parliamentary procedures, but are actually injured thereby."

The party polled several thousand votes in New York but of course made little impression on the state of the nation. Yet it addressed eloquent appeals to sympathizers in Chicago, Vienna, Brussels, and Geneva, and gratefully acknowledged the receipt from abroad of replies equally eloquent, addressed to the "brethren in the West." [3]

[3] Weitling's letter of declination is reprinted in F. A. Sorge *et al.*, *Briefe und Auszüge aus Briefen*, 5. See also Franz Mehring, "Der Sorgesche Briefwechsel," *Die Neue Zeit*, I (1907), 15.

Chapter XV

NEW FRONTIERS

The quest for a universal language has not been a specialty limited to experts on linguistics and phonetics; it also has been a major objective of many reformers. The literature of the subject is extensive. Weitling was neither the first nor the last to work on plans to unify mankind into "one world" by the simple device of inventing a new common tongue.

The *Promethean* (London) of February, 1842, reprinted a letter from Lewis Masquerrier of New York to Goodwyn Barmby, its editor, in which the writer expressed his desire to join the London communist society and offered to send "my universal alphabet, improved orthography, etc." and "get you to become its godfather." In an earlier number Barmby had published his own "Essay Towards Philanthropic Philology, or Ideas on Language in reference to the future, or transition and community." The author maintained that "we must no longer have only learned philology; we must have philanthropic philology. The benevolent reformers of society, with prophetic hope, call out with a voice of high and harmonious cadence, for a universal language." Barmby was convinced that what the world needed was "a general tongue" and a "grammar of humanity" for hitherto the "various idioms and tongues of languages" had been a barrier to the "greatest designs of humanity." He referred to other pioneers in this field, including Benjamin Franklin, and suggested that English, "a decomposition of Greek, Latin, French, German" and other languages, might well serve as the transitional tongue until a universal language was available.[1] In America the editors of the controversial *Woodhull and Claflin's Weekly* worked assiduously for a "universal language," a reform less shocking to some of their contemporaries than their ultra-radical proposals about sex, woman's rights and government by "pantarchy."

Weitling's interest in a universal language (*Allgemeine Denk und Sprachlehre, nebst Grundzügen einer Universalsprache der Menschheit*) dates from the early 1840's. In his conversations with Fröbel in Zurich while he was taking English lessons, Weitling after the fashion of modern students of semantics became greatly interested in philosophical discussions about the use of words. He was shocked to discover that so many different shades of meaning existed for the same word even among those who thought they were in substantial agreement. A reference to a book by Proudhon aroused his interest in the prevalence of metaphysical concepts instead of "a system of pure reason"; and it may have been then that he conceived the idea of classifying all things that were perceptible to the senses and all concepts on the basis of symbols which would clearly and accurately express men's inner reactions to all outward stimuli. He could not begin his ambitious undertaking until after his release from prison, though he had plenty of time to plan it during his confinement. Apparently he believed that he had come upon the philosopher's stone which men had been seeking for ages to give them the perfect "criterion of truth." Comparing himself with Newton and Copernicus, he reflected solemnly on what the world would lose if he should die in prison.

The new researcher into the realm of philology was amazed to discover that the German language alone used 80,000 words to express what he had in mind; that the majority of the German people did not know more than 10,000 of these terms and could get along well with only 5,000. Weitling claimed to have worked a whole year "without interruption" on his classifications of concepts and words and to have revised his lists at least five times. Before long he came to the conclusion that the task was too great for

[1] London *Promethean*, January, 1842, No. 1, p. 18.

any one individual and that he needed the help of the specialists. Perhaps this discouraging discovery explains the long interval between the conception of his project in Switzerland and the time when it was partially completed and ready, to that extent, for publication.

Weitling stated that he completed the major portion of the treatise, as finally published, in 1844. It is certain that he worked hard on the first draft in London, to the neglect of the propaganda for social reform, much to the disgust of the cosmopolitan radicals assembled in the English metropolis. Georg Schirges reported that "Weitling has thrown himself into the arms of learning and, among other things, is studying Latin." [2] A redraft of the London manuscript was made in Brussels in 1846, and Marx's refusal to interest himself in its publication and Engels' sarcastic comments may have affected the final break with Marx and Engels at the Brussels conference. The manuscript of Weitling's *Gerechtigkeit*, which saw the light of day fifty years after his death, contained a glossary to explain the author's use of words and concepts. After another revision of his philological studies made in Hamburg in 1848–49 and a final recast in the United States about 1855, part of the material dealing with his universal language was set in type and printed, but it was never bound in book form. The author's account books for 1854, 1855, and 1856 show occasional entries for expenditures from the treasury of the *Arbeiterbund* totaling $70.88 to pay for setting type. Weitling regarded his efforts to produce a universal language as his most important work. Whatever other material may have been on hand to complete the manuscript was either lost or destroyed in 1869.

The 196-page unbound treatise, with a prospectus issued years earlier in Europe, and several other fragments are all that exist of this curious exercise in semantics. Weitling's theories of language may be stated in rather simple terms, and much that he said on this subject was sensible and clear, but the classifications and symbols for the new artificial world tongue defy all attempts at

[2] Barnikol, *Weitling der Gefangene*, 31.

analysis and comprehension. Yet the author was sure that his fantastic creation would have value far into the "distant future."

Weitling believed that all words or languages developed by accident, then became a habit, and finally were improved and recorded by intellectuals and professors. He later supported his thesis by using the experience of his own children, whose speech he observed carefully. He attributed additional alterations in the structure and form of a language to the work of such "speech-matadores" as the brothers Grimm and to mere printers' errors. English, as far as its "logic" was concerned, impressed him as one of the best of all languages, but he regarded its pronunciation as "one of the most difficult" and positively ugly. He could find in no existing language the precise imagery, or the tonal and written form, which would justify its universal acceptance. The confusion of genders in English, French, and German, the three languages he knew well, irritated him. In the German language, he found heavy borrowings from other tongues and too few terms which referred to the better and lovelier concepts of human intercourse. He wanted both a logical and a beautiful language, and he hoped to break down the prejudices based on language differences which divided peoples and nations.

In addition to objectives which were related to his notions about a race united by language into one world, Weitling wanted to produce a new form of expression that would be easy to learn, "shorter, richer and better sounding," without the false and complicated rules which characterized all existing tongues. He expected his new invention in the field of linguistics to do for language what a new machine does for industry, namely, to shorten the time of production from a thousand to ten thousand times. He was convinced that the study of language must begin with physiology, for before one could study the causes and effects of language, one must learn how its concepts originated. Only then would it be possible to formulate rules which had no exceptions, to get rid of such useless impedimenta as regular and irregular verbs, and to enable the learner to discern at once from the form and spelling of the word whether the object to which it referred was a plant, a mineral, a tool, a machine, or to what other category it might belong.

Weitling's psychology of language was based on the simple theory that impressions as they reach the brain from the outside are sound and accurate and true, but what reissues from the mind in words, writing, or gestures may be something quite different, even false. In part, he traced this difficulty to a wrong kind of training in morals, with inadequate emphasis on the obligation always to speak the truth but, in large measure, he accounted for the problem by the lack of accurate language tools. To prove the confusion that resulted from a lack of precise expressions, he cited the conflict of philosophers, like Descartes and Hegel, over such concepts as *Geist* (spirit), and blamed the whole field of "speculative philosophy" for much of the existing confusion. He contended that no truth ever was finally established until no other word or phrase or sentence could be found to express it more precisely, and he advised disputants in every argument or controversy to insist on a definition of terms before proceeding with their discussion. Existing dictionaries, he believed, contained both too much and too little; in any case, none was satisfactory. He would rebuild language on the basis of the best possible classification of all the phenomena of the universe as recorded by the senses, and thus he believed he was dealing with a process that was fundamentally physiological.

When one tries to fathom the meaning of Weitling's "physiological observations," one becomes lost in hopeless confusion. Weitling's discussion of man begins with the assertion that he is first of all a chemical compound which is affected by the reaction of other bodies and substances from the outside, and which develops and deteriorates according to fixed chemical laws of "attraction" and "repulsion." These "attractive" and "repulsive" chemical reactions center in the nervous system and finally in the brain, and it is from the reflection on the impressions caused by these impulses that perception and consciousness result. Without this "capacity for conception," which Weitling defined as essentially a matter of chemistry, there could be no world, no reality, no body, no truth, and no God. By referring to the analogy of making daguerreotypes, a process with which he seems to have been familiar, he discussed the transformation of impressions into memory. Thereupon he expounded a theory of "organic electromagnetic force" which activated the body. He maintained that the senses constitute the electric part of this force or power and that these electric impulses are conducted to the brain by means of the nervous system. It was his contention that the electric impulses that reached the brain both attracted and repelled, depending on "earlier impressions and acquired characteristics." Memory he defined as the "organically stimulated picture gallery of our perceptions."

By his theories of electromagnetic currents, Weitling explained such phenomena as sleep, exhaustion, dreams ("thinking without will" while the senses are closed by sleep to outside stimuli), and "magnetic sleep," under which he included somnambulism, fainting, and death. Emotion and feeling thus were reduced to a simple matter of stimuli and nerve tension. As a result Weitling was forced to conclude that there really is no free will, though man thinks there is, and that everything is a matter of stimuli, impressions, and reactions, a type of psychology not too different from the theories of some modern behaviorists.

It is when one reaches the pages and pages of classifications of concepts, which follow these fairly plausible introductory discussions of the processes of perception, that one encounters a completely impractical and incomprehensible system. The classifications cover such subjects as natural causes and results; inorganic and organic substances; the artificial, utilitarian and ideal; earth forms, minerals, plants, forms, sounds, theory and practice; the arts and the sciences; fantasies and facts; and scores of others. It is useless to try to give many examples of the new language, for it was far more artificial than any it was expected to supersede. The following sentences may serve as illustrations of the fantastic proposals with which Weitling hoped to revolutionize man's existing means of communication:

GERMAN	ENGLISH	NEW LANGUAGE
Du wirst das Mädchen haben	You will have the girl	Pi Papai li sas
Ich werde das Mädchen gehabt haben	I will have had the girl	Pi Papai sas
Ich werde Mann werden	I will become a man	Pi wavivi fif
Ich war gesund geworden	I became well	bi sanoe
Wir werden gesund geworden sein	We will have become well	by sanoa
Du warst gesund	You were well	ba sanou

Weitling ended this flight into linguistics and phonetics with additional speculations on the nature of the universe and the unity of all life and concluded that no matter how much their learning might increase men would never be able to comprehend "eternity" or "reach the boundaries of the Universe"; for everything was part of a "single, unified, endless, indivisible whole," a "great, organic unity." Scientific observation alone would never solve the riddle of the universe, and Weitling believed that man's concepts extended far beyond his senses and his nervous system and that man possessed a spirit which sharply differentiated him from the animals, enabling him to function in the realm of fantasy, working hypotheses, and ideals.

Weitling realized that his theories of language would be scorned and ridiculed by professors living in their "scholar's nimbus," but he contended that time would prove that his universal language was as much superior to existing languages as the "railroad to the medieval cart" and the "telegraph to the postrider." His old communist comrade Becker had maintained long ago that unity among the nations was possible without a universal language, and that the quest for a common tongue was all nonsense and doomed to failure from the outset; [3] but to Weitling, this new system of thought and language, incomplete as it was, was the key with which man could open the door to a new life based on pure reason and "trampel the monster of national hatreds underfoot."

[3] Becker, *Was Wollen die Kommunisten?*, 45.

With this observation, we may leave the discussion of Weitling's curious interest in a universal language. It is easy to dismiss his artificially constructed samples of a new universal tongue as utter nonsense, for they were far more confused and difficult to understand than the national languages which he wanted to dethrone. The result of his efforts was a philological hodgepodge. Yet this little treatise revealed that the author had done an incredible amount of desultory reading in science, language, history, and the arts. Parts of his argument were well written, with much of the reformer's earlier eloquence and fire, and the amount of scientific terminology with which the author was familiar is astounding. Much of it is correctly used. From many sources, he had picked up considerable information in natural history, and especially in botany, zoology and mineralogy, and he was thoroughly familiar with Linnaeus' classifications of the species and natural phenomena. The information is unorganized and spotty, but life had given him little opportunity to drink deeper of the wells of knowledge. His curiosity and his passion to know equaled that of many of the "professors and doctors" whom he thoroughly disliked and secretly envied.

The beginning of his interest in astronomy cannot be so clearly dated as the origin of his study of a universal language. Perhaps it was not strange that a nature with such a strong ingredient of romanticism should be awed by the grandeur of the starry heavens at night and should turn to a study of the "Queen of the Sciences." Furthermore, for a man of Weitling's temperament, it was as easy to challenge the theories of Newton and Copernicus as it was to challenge all the existing theories of social organization. Perhaps the comet of 1843 to which he referred in the *Gerechtigkeit* first aroused his interest in astronomy, though in his pamphlet *Der bewegende Urstoff* he reported that his attention was turned to a study of the heavens in 1854, when he reached the word astronomy in preparing the classifications for his universal language. He could not find an adequate bridge between chemistry, physics, and astronomy, and that fact disturbed him. It may also be true that he sought "escape from this disgraceful earth" because he became disillusioned by his experiences as a social reformer. His former European colleague, Moses Hess, went through the same development in his later years when he wrote *The Sun and Its Light* and *The History and Physical Composition of Our Planetary System*,[4] and it will be remembered that Fourier too had his peculiar theory of the nature of the universe.

At any rate, six months after he left his job at Castle Garden, Weitling wrote a sixteen-page document, entitled "The Mysteries of Astronomy, solved by Wilhelm Weitling," and sent a copy for safekeeping to a friend, James Purdy. The paper, written in English, announced the discovery of a "great Idea" that revealed "the symmetry of the mechanics of heaven." The new mechanics contradicted the prevailing notions about the distances of sun and planets from the earth and from each other but did not challenge the location of the moon; referred to "an electrical polar power which affected the rotations and revolutions of the heavenly bodies by electro-magnetical streams passing through their axes and forming a kind of elastic and transparent shell around them." It was obvious that Weitling had become involved beyond his depth in questions of the aberration of light and parallax, phenomena that had long been known to astronomers and physicists. He was so stirred by his discovery that he regarded it as providential, sacrificed everything "not absolutely essential to the welfare of my family" to his new interest, and spent the two weeks' vacation from his duties as registrar of immigrants at home, checking and rechecking mathematical calculations which fill pages and pages of his papers. He deeply regretted that he would probably have to write his definitive work in German because of an inadequate command of English, and he fully expected scientists and academicians to be skeptical, but he was sure that he, a layman, had solved "what had appeared to them an everlasting unsolvable

[4] Zlocisti, *Moses Hess,* 266.

mystery." To add a further touch of the dramatic, he made a notation in his notebook that the world-shaking idea came to him on the day when his first child was born.

These are the words of a fanatic, with a somewhat unbalanced, one-track mind. Small wonder that he spent the rest of his life bombarding the scientists and the academies with his theories, convinced that there was a conspiracy against him, and that he would die without the opportunity to proclaim these new truths to the world. Weitling's correspondence of the next dozen years was with men of scientific reputation in all parts of the western world.

In February, 1856, he wrote a letter to his friend Petersen, in which he likened his joy at his discovery with Newton's when the latter came upon the law of gravitation. Yet Newton had enjoyed certain advantages. He was a mathematician, probably rich, and could count on support in high places, for his name had never been anathema to the wealthy and he had never been a propagandist for communism.[5] From October, 1858, to December, 1860, there is not a single entry in Weitling's notebook. During that period he was employed at Castle Garden and devoted all his spare time to his astronomical studies and his patents. Presently, Weitling was in correspondence with Humboldt, Michel Chevalier, l'Institut de France, the Royal Institute in London, an astronomer in Greenwich, the director of the observatory in Berlin, Sir John Herschel, Agassiz in Boston, academies in Berlin, Vienna, Munich, Leipzig, and St. Petersburg, and the Smithsonian Institution in Washington. In all these letters he explained in detail his new system which restored the earth to the center of the planetary system which it had occupied under the Ptolemaic astronomy.

A number of his correspondents, including Humboldt, were courteous enough to reply, but none offered to help publish his "Mechanic of the Heavens." Weitling had employed a typesetter who set up a section of his larger work in 1856 and indicated that the material would constitute pages 195 to 214 of his complete

[5] Quoted in Schlüter, *Anfänge der deutschen Arbeiterbewegung*, 122.

manuscript. The fragment was entitled "The moving element (*Urstoff*) in its cosmo-electro-magnetic effects—a picture of the Universe respectfully submitted to the academies of science for examination, by Wilhelm Weitling"—and he enclosed copies of the publication with many of the letters which he later addressed to the scientists.

In the old account book which was no longer needed for the *Arbeiterbund* or Communia, one finds pages and pages of incomprehensible figures, angles like the demonstrations used to prove geometrical theorems, computations about the orbit of the sun and the moon and the passing of the seasons, and angles of inclination for the earth, and figures about its volume and circumference. It is clear from the material that has been preserved that the calculator had examined a number of texts on physics and astronomy, and he specifically referred to some of the experiments described therein dealing with light waves and the spectrum. The calculations run into fifteen digits and more. The account book also reveals that it cost $23 to have the fragment of his book on astronomy published, and itemizes the expenditures on postage for the many letters addressed to the learned in America and Europe.

Weitling's most extensive correspondence was with Joseph Henry, director of the Smithsonian Institution in Washington. The latter revealed unusual patience and tact in dealing with this ardent and irrepressible novice in the field of astronomy. In March, 1856, Henry acknowledged the receipt of a letter and a pamphlet, "relative to the motion of the heavenly bodies," and commented that it "evinces much originality of thought and fertility of invention," but also pointed out that it was still in such an "unverified condition" and so loosely constructed "in regard to established facts" that he would not be warranted in recommending it to the special attention of the Institution. Eighteen months later, Henry acknowledged receipt of another communication on "zodiacal light" and agreed to forward it to the academy in Vienna at Weitling's risk. In 1859, the latter wrote again to Henry, taking exception to the report of an expert referee to whom Weitling's claims had been referred. The former had completely rejected his major contention that phenomena heretofore explained by the motion of light were due to parallax. This time the director tactfully suggested that the amateur astronomer direct his talents "to some less cultivated field of science" in which his labors might produce "more valuable results." Weitling remained unconvinced, however, and the correspondence with the Smithsonian Institution continued until 1866. Two of Weitling's papers are preserved in the archives of the Institution. One of the letters referred to the invention of an instrument "for indicating the mean changes of different astronomical elements," which the Institution tactfully declared to be outside its proper sphere of interest.

In Weitling's files there were copies of letters dated 1859 and later, to Professor Anton Schrötter, secretary of the academy in Vienna; to Professor O. G. Ehrenberg of Berlin, who courteously acknowledged the material but would not risk a judgment on it; to the secretary of the institution in Paris, to whom Weitling had explained his theories on twelve large sheets and in lucid French; and to the director of the United States Naval Observatory. An undated letter from a French correspondent referred to Weitling's reputation abroad as a well-known communist and urged a return of the "veteran of the economic war of liberation" to the scenes of his earlier triumphs but declined to find financial help or a publisher for his astronomical papers. In 1867, Otto Wigand, a publisher in Leipzig, suggested that Weitling's demands for royalties from his scientific works were too high to warrant undertaking such an uncertain proposition.

Rebuffed on all sides, Weitling nevertheless continued his work with a persistence that is amazing. In 1864, he was in especially high spirits because an article in the *Scientific American* on electric waves had taught him the new terms, cathode and anode. Two years later, he was engaged in building what he called a "mechanical Celeste" to illustrate the true motions of sun and earth. Despite constant discouragements from those he thought should help him to make his discoveries known to the world, despite the total lack of financial resources, Weitling nevertheless derived extreme pleasure from his astronomical labors. Near the close of 1861, he sent a copy of his work to Dr. Karl Gutzkow, an old acquaintance of Paris days now living in Weimar, with the request that he preserve it so that some day the world might know that he and no one else was the "discoverer of the correct mechanics of the heavens."

Only an expert astronomer could deal adequately with Weitling's alleged discoveries and point out the errors and the truths in his calculations and deductions. For purposes of this biography, the man's passion for investigation, the tremendous amount of reading which he did in the astronomical field, and the sacrifice which he was ready to make to satisfy his craving for knowledge are more important than his mathematics.

By way of summary, however, it may be added that Weitling's main contentions were that the sun rotates from west to east around the earth, which in turn moves both from east to west and swings from north to south between the poles in the form of an ellipse, on electromagnetic streams which hold all heavenly bodies in their axes and envelop their atmospheres in a kind of shell. He held that the earth carried the moon, the sun, Mercury, and Venus with it in the orbit over which it traveled from east to west, and he rejected the theory of parallax and concluded that all astronomical distances, except the distance from the earth to the moon, were based on false calculations and assumptions. In his seventy-five-page manuscript, entitled "The Mechanic of the Heavens," he developed these theories and reviewed in detail the claims of other astronomers. In another manuscript, written in 1865 and entitled "The Size of the Earth," he calculated laboriously that the diameter of the earth at the equator was 7,920 "English miles" and its circumference, 24,881 miles; he contended that the sun was nearer the earth by one sixtieth than all other astronomers had figured; and he accused the professionals of inventing "aberration of light" to save their honor and cover their mistakes, "with foreign and artificial terms."

According to Weitling, his efforts to invent a buttonhole accessory and other improvements for sewing machines dated from the day when he was working by the side of his wife, discoursing on the problems of the world in general and on his lack of funds for astronomical researches in particular. According to his own story, at that point in the conversation his wife suggested that he turn to something more practical and work on inventions more directly related to improving their precarious financial status. As one pictures her at work in the humble Weitling home making buttonholes by hand, one easily can imagine what prompted the hard-working, hard-pressed wife and mother to make so pointed a suggestion, and understand her efforts to shake her husband out of his intellectual labors and bring him back from flights of fancy into stellar space to something more remunerative for the family exchequer.

It probably took little persuasion to turn Weitling's mind in the direction of mechanical inventions, for he always was deeply interested in such things. He had published many scientific articles in *Die Republik der Arbeiter* and as editor had been especially interested in such problems as the use of carbon dioxide instead of steam to propel engines, perpetual motion, color daguerreotypes, smoke consumers, the origin of Bock beer, man's conquest of the air, and the eradication of disease.

The New York *Tribune* of January 18, 1854, called attention to the "soulless seamstress, the Sewing Machine" on display in a show window on Broadway "in the midst of a glory of gaslight." The battle between the inventors of this revolutionary machine was violent and long. It was frequently aired in paid advertisements in the newspapers in which Howe and Singer, two of the rival inventors, charged each other with wholesale patent infringements and frauds. Howe once sued Greeley for libel because he had published an advertisement paid for by Singer in the *Tribune*. Elias Howe, Jr., J. M. Singer, A. B. Wilson, Otis Avery, and several others in the United States and in France who claimed credit for the invention carried on their legal battle for many years.

Weitling went to work at once on the assignment which his wife had given him and in a few weeks he had completed the plans for a buttonhole machine and employed a machinist to make a working model. The patent for his invention was issued as No. 33,619 on October 29, 1861, and, in due course, the inventor filed no less than eight applications for patents for improvements on the sewing machine, five of which were allowed by the United States Patent Office.

The resourceful tailor made all of his drawings without outside assistance and had them attested by old friends, such as Heinrich Ahrends, Friedrich Eilenberg, Louis Kämmerer, Philipp Eckstein, R. Reichel and L. Kullmann, Josef Fickler, and Augustus Merkle. Tag loaned him $2,000 to carry on his experiments, and J. Keller loaned him $200 in 1866 for materials. Louis Schade, an attorney of Washington, D.C., gave him legal advice, and in 1863 Carl Schurz, writing from his camp near Stafford Courthouse, gave Weitling a letter to the Secretary of the Interior introducing him as "a gentleman of high character among the Germans and an old supporter of our cause" and requesting the secretary to show him special attention in his patent affairs. Weitling's patents included improved devices for stitching edging and buttonholes, crimping ribbons and cloth in fancy lines, and regulating the tension of the thread in sewing machines.

Always the philosophical tailor who needed to reduce his ideas to a system, Weitling produced a "Treatise" "on sewing machines generally and on the arrangements for sewing by it buttonholes and embroidering especially." In this document, he described and illustrated all the known methods of sewing by machine, including the different ways of making buttonholes, and explained in detail how his device was superior to and different from the three already on the market and from a fourth which was attached to Wheeler and Wilson's sewing machine. His discussion of these machines reveals the expert tailor thoroughly familiar with his trade who had made a sound analysis of the Singer patent of 1855 and of the claims of other inventors. Weitling claimed that by his invention any machine could be equipped with an attachment for embroidering, and sewing and embroidering could be done on the same machine.

With his inventions, as with his astronomy, Weitling encountered the usual handicap of lack of funds. Before long he was involved in controversies about infringements on his patent rights and felt that he was being victimized by powerful exploiters. His notebook contains the names and addresses of men to whom he did or might appeal for aid. Among them were Wilhelm Farr, whom he had known in Lausanne; Eduard Degener, a Forty-eighter who had gone to Texas; Ezra Cornell; Horace Greeley; Commodore Vanderbilt; Charles A. Dana; and "*Mr. John Jay, petits fils, de l'un des signataires du traite de Paris.*" Dana, then with the Chicago *Republican*, replied that all his friends who would be willing to invest in such a project had no money, and that "those who are rich take little interest in scientific inventions." Weitling also approached some of his more prosperous German friends in New York and was ready to join forces with several other inventors of devices similar to his.

By 1862, Weitling suspected that others were trying to cheat him of the fruits of his inventive genius. In 1864, utterly without cause, he accused a clerk in the patent office of trying to deprive him of one of his patents and he made a trip to Washington on $100 of borrowed money only to learn that his claims were being processed in the regular way. He inspected every machine on display in New York which was in any way related to the sewing machine, including a "chain stitching" device for sewing threads of several colors, and occasionally he took his wife along on these tours of inspection as an expert witness.

By 1867, Weitling was sure that the American Buttonhole Company and the Singer and Aetna Companies were infringing on his embroidery attachment. A friend reported having seen Singer machines all over Germany equipped with his buttonhole device. At once Weitling calculated that at five dollars' royalty per machine, the Singer Company and the American Buttonhole Com-

Sample of Work Done by Weitling's Embroidering Device

pany now owed him $280,000. He consulted an attorney about filing a criminal suit, received some encouragement, and instructed him to see the lawyers of the "sewing machine combination" about a possible amicable settlement. In 1869, however, he wrote his old friend Schilling, who was living in straitened circumstances in Leipzig among a faithful group of socialists: "I am still being cheated out of my patents. Whoever is without funds in this country has no chance against those that have. Heaven save humanity from such republics of the money bags." [6]

Needless to say, the inventor never realized a penny from his five patents. A story made the rounds of the German-language press in 1863 to the effect that Weitling had sold his buttonhole machine patent to Singer for $30,000 plus a royalty for each machine, and the St. Louis *Westliche Post* rejoiced over the good fortune of the man who for years had worked so "unselfishly and under the greatest handicaps and sacrifices" in the cause of labor, but the tale was utterly without foundation.[7] There is a family legend to the effect that just before his death, the Singer Company offered Weitling $500 in settlement of his claim that the company had infringed his embroidery and buttonhole patents. The inventor refused to take less than ten times that amount and pledged his wife never to accept less than $5,000. A letter from the Singer Manufacturing Company reports no evidence in its files pertaining to any patent controversy between Weitling and Singer.[8]

In 1907, when the Singer estate was involved in litigation, the socialist *New Yorker Volkszeitung* recounted the story of Weitling's invention and alleged that both Howe and Singer, accompanied by expert mechanics, had called on the old communist to copy and steal his patent and then had marketed his improvements as part of their own machines. The story referred to the inventor's demand for $5,000 and recounted that because of the lack of funds his widow had been unable to press her suit and therefore had re-

[6] Quoted in *Die Zukunft* (1878), I, 585.
[7] Quoted in Cleveland *Wächter am Erie*, April 8, 1863.
[8] A. G. Osborne to writer, June 25, 1946.

ceived nothing in settlement of her husband's claims. The editor ended his story with the observation, "the Communists wanted to divide. . . . Singer took it all." [9]

[9] *New Yorker Volkszeitung*, March 28, 1907. See also *Official Gazette of the U.S. Patent Office*, II, No. 9 (August 13, 1872), 223–24, for a commissioner's decision favorable to a claim by Weitling concerning interference with an improvement for a fluting machine.

CHAPTER XVI

CLOSING YEARS

THE closing years of Weitling's life were for the most part years of frustration and defeat. His efforts to weld the working masses into a great labor movement for the realization of his pretentious program of social reconstruction along new lines of communal partnership had ended in failure and disaster. The theories which he had expounded so eloquently in workers' halls and in printer's ink have had little effect upon the world to this day, although their author rooted them firmly in the principles of religion and social justice. Weitling believed that some day they would be remembered and revived.

Disillusioned and disappointed with the world and with many of his co-workers, blind to his own shortcomings, and defeated here and abroad in all his attempts to impress the existing economic classes, he had turned to exploring the mathematics of the heavenly bodies and to the need for a universal language, only to experience frustration again in these new areas of investigation. He could see no reason for his failures except the lack of financial resources to bring his ideas properly to the attention of the world. Like most men, he did not realize how much of his disappointment could be traced to his own shortcomings and to the inadequate knowledge and training with which he attacked fields of investigation that required the most rigorous mental discipline and long years of preparation.

Harassed by financial worries, using hard-earned money that might better have been spent for other things to promote his experimentation in fields that yielded no return, and tortured by the thought that he had a hungry family to feed and might die before he had completed the work that he regarded so important for humanity, he was condemned to struggle on, his restless spirit chained to the tailor's table, his hands occupied with shears, needle and thread, but his mind lost in fancy and churning with ideas about new inventions and discoveries. Unable to break the economic fetters that held him in bondage, he was forced to labor day in and day out at the mundane task of producing food and shelter and clothing for a sizable family to whom he was deeply devoted.

With the two women of his household and with the occasional help of a servant girl who did some of the housework and the sewing, Weitling manufactured fancy white vests and did custom tailoring for well-known New Yorkers such as the Astors, Fisks, and Vanderbilts, who often attended the social functions of their class in neatly starched vests from a home which is remembered today only because its senior member occupies a prominent place in the history of Utopian communism. Weitling's own specialty was ladies' tailoring. For a "dress costume," he received the standard pay of ten dollars. With his wife he belonged to the Journeyman Tailors' Protective and Benevolent Union, founded in 1863, and the records show that his widow continued to pay her dues at least until 1879, eight years after her husband's death. After her family began to prosper, however, she and her sister stopped working and enjoyed comfortable homes with the children to the end of their lives.

Thanks to the careful entries in Weitling's notebooks, we can obtain a fairly accurate picture of the family income and of his financial status during the half-dozen years preceding his death. In 1866, the Weitlings were living on an income derived entirely from the manufacture of vests by the three adult members of the household. The pay for a man's vest was a dollar, for boys' vests seventy-five cents, and for vests of a somewhat inferior grade, sixty-two cents. The total income of the three producers amounted to approximately $100 a month. Six men's vests, or eight boys' vests, could be completed in one day by the two women, working together, but unfortunately, orders came in quite sporadically. Weitling generally made the buttonholes himself. At the time, the Weitlings were paying twenty-five dollars a month rent for two rooms, three "chambers," and two attic rooms. They sublet their attic for $10.50 a month. Whenever there was a servant girl in the house (and such an arrangement must be regarded as a necessity rather than a luxury because of the occupation of the women with their sewing), her wages were $5.00 a month. The family paid $1.87 for "school money" and $2.20 for laundry.

It requires little calculation to demonstrate that a family with such a limited budget was bound to run frequently into serious difficulties. As a matter of fact, Weitling actually was bankrupt during the last years of his life. His debts in 1866 amounted to nearly $3,400, including a debt of $200 to patent attorneys in Washington, and $2,000 borrowed from Tag for the completion of certain inventions. A loan of $100, owed to Joseph Fickler, a fellow refugee who had died in the meantime, was marked "paid." Though the ledger showed payments of $419 on old debts, it also revealed new borrowings in 1867 and later in amounts ranging from $20 to $100. Appeals for additional financial help proved unsuccessful. It may be concluded from these figures that Weitling spent considerable sums for purposes other than family expenses. Late in 1868, he wrote that his situation was becoming steadily worse. His rent had been increased to $28, earnings had fallen to $21 a week, and the business of making vests had entered upon a period of sharp decline. He predicted a deficit of at least $20 a month because of rising costs and declining earnings and frankly admitted that the only hope for improvement in his financial situation depended on forcing a cash settlement from the sewing-machine companies or finding a partner who would produce and market his inventions.

Two years before his death, Weitling himself used the ugly word "bankrupt" to describe his condition. He had been forced to turn to making "shop vests" because custom tailoring no longer yielded sufficient income. He and his family moved to what he called the "New Jerusalem," an area which he disliked, and he expected to be evicted momentarily even from this new location because of his inability to pay the monthly rent of $26. Completely discouraged, he listed the names and addresses of a half-dozen persons who were to be notified in the event of his death. The list included old friends like Toaspern, the piano maker, Ahrends, and the tailoring firm, Müller and Brother. Apparently his relations with his father-in-law were strained also, for just before Christmas, 1869, Weitling made special note of the fact that for "the first time again in 4 years" the family had received a gift of meat from the upstate farmer. He was inclined to blame his mother-in-law as much as his wife's father for the strained relations and he claimed that once he had loaned the latter $600 and had been repaid in depreciated greenbacks. Yet the next year the mercurial temperament of the bankrupt tailor had rebounded sufficiently from its depression that he could write to a friend that several sewing-machine companies were seriously interested in his inventions and that another group was ready to prosecute his patent suit for him. When he wrote these lines during the winter of 1870, his earnings actually were about one sixth of what they had been six months earlier, there was no coal, flour, or potatoes in the house, and the tailors' union had found it necessary to excuse him temporarily from paying his dues. Some allowance always must be made for Weitling's flair for the dramatic, but such evidence clearly shows how near the brink of disaster he and his family were. That the group held together so valiantly must be credited largely to the character of the wife and the aunt, and to the sterling qualities of the children and the training which they had received from their parents.

Meantime, Weitling's health was beginning to fail. He had driven himself hard all his life, he had felt the pangs of hunger and deprivation in his earlier years, and now, at the close of a turbulent career, he was bedeviled with financial worries and depressed with

Mrs. Wilhelm Weitling (about 1910)

frustrations. We know little about his health during the first few years of his residence in the United States, except that he suffered from a long and serious illness during his propaganda tour in 1852 and had to spend many weeks recuperating at the home of his friend Baumann on a farm in New York State. Apparently, the illness was typhoid fever, though Weitling also referred to what might have been symptoms of gall-bladder trouble and to the "aigue" which was the common malady of the American frontier. In 1852 he embraced homeopathy, which one of his friends described as "good only for rich, elegant people who are sick from ennui."

In 1868 Weitling fell on the ice in the yard of his home and so severely stubbed his toe that it became badly infected. When a second doctor was called in for consultation, it was decided to operate, and the injured member was amputated at home. Thereafter, the patient's health seems to have declined, and there are reasons to believe that he was suffering from diabetes.

With his usual desire to reduce his observations to writing, Weitling devoted pages of his diary to keeping a clinical chart of his own afflictions and carefully noted the multiplying evidences of his physical decline. The "Pathological Items" begin with March, 1869, and include notations about urine, chest pains, the pulse rate, frequent headaches and spells of dizziness, night sweats, swollen feet, and pressures on stomach and liver. One day when the patient considered his appetite particularly poor he "ate butter, bread, cheese, and chocolate." At other times he reported using massage treatments, mustard plasters, sulphur and cream of tartar. His eyesight became worse, though it was not until he was sixty-one years old that he recorded that he could no longer read without glasses. He slept well, apparently, and could not quite decide whether a decrease in headaches and spells of dizziness was the result of his use of sulphur or of giving up coffee. Thus, even as he watched the mounting symptoms of his own approaching old age, Weitling remained the avid observer and investigator and kept a record of the mysteries of his own physiology with as keen an interest as that with which he had calculated the distances of the stars.

On January 24, 1871, the veteran agitator for social justice attended his last public meeting, a fraternal feast and festival of the German, French, Czech, and English sections of the Workers' International of New York. The occasion provided a fitting climax for the career of the pioneer communist and that touch of the dramatic which Weitling always appreciated. The next morning he suffered a stroke and fourteen hours later he was dead. He died at 178 Stanton Street in a modest two-story house, with a little grocery store in the basement. The Weitlings occupied the rooms on the second floor.

An advertisement in one of the German-language papers of New York, signed "several friends," requested the "comrades" of the deceased to meet at the home for funeral services and to assemble later at the hall of the tailors' union. The funeral, held on Sunday, was largely attended by friends, fellow-craftsmen, and members of some of the old co-operatives which Weitling had helped to found. We know nothing about the nature of the services, but we may assume that the ceremonies probably were directed by kindred spirits from the tailors' organization and were appropriate for the burial of a man who had never been on friendly terms with the clergy. Weitling was buried in a "humble location" in Greenwood Cemetery in Brooklyn. Later the body was removed for reburial in the family plot. On the day of the funeral the tailors presented the widow with a purse of $100, and fellow employees of her eldest son collected a like amount.[1] A committee of seven, including Sorge, was designated to receive contributions to provide additional financial relief to the needy family.

Most of the New York papers took little or no notice of the passing of a man whose name once had been well known in the ranks of radicals and labor leaders on two continents. The New York *Times*, however,[2] published a fairly long obituary, headed

[1] *New Yorker Staatszeitung*, January 27, 1871.
[2] New York *Times*, January 27, 1871.

"William Weitling—An Inventor of Prominence—A Remarkable Career." In it, the writer reviewed the main events in Weitling's career, but the account was marked by many errors and was embellished with dramatic touches quite at variance with the facts. The obituary notice pointed out that the deceased had "never received any benefit" from his inventions and had left an unfinished treatise on astronomy, "the fruit of 14 years of mental toil" which had been "pronounced by competent critics as interesting and worthy of commendation."

For some years after his death, Weitling's widow continued to hear from old friends of her husband who had known him here and in Europe. They wrote to ask for a photograph of their old comrade or to inquire where they might procure copies of his writings. Several people were interested in issuing a new and definitive edition of his works but that objective was never realized.

Karl Heinzen, in his Boston *Pionier* [3] paid tribute to his old opponent as a man of talent, honesty and courage who had proved far more respectable than Marx, and announced his readiness to accept contributions for the bereaved family. The New York *Tages Nachrichten* [4] commented mainly on Weitling's inventions and referred to his "highly inventive and keen brain." In far-off Hamburg, where the deceased had tarried several times during the European phase of his career, the *Reform* published an obituary notice and retold the story of his life.

The tribute by the *New Yorker Belletristisches Journal*, one of Weitling's favorite papers, probably was the most accurate and significant and may well be quoted in closing this biography of the Utopian tailor. "Wilhelm Weitling," wrote the editor, "is the name of a forgotten man, one of the many who, after a stormy career abroad, became lost and were forgotten and found their last resting place in America, confused by their own theories. . . . Germany had forgotten him long ago, until Heinrich Heine recently directed attention for a fleeting moment to the philosophi-

[3] Boston *Pionier*, February 1, 1871.
[4] New York *Tages Nachrichten*, January 27, 1871.

cal tailor, the gifted thinker, the founder of German communism." The writer of the obituary thought the *Evangelium* deserved republishing, though he knew that Weitling had lost his following completely after the fiasco of the *Arbeiterbund* and the colony. "Men ceased to believe in him," the article continued, "and the waves tossed him upon the beach. The last words we heard him utter many years ago were—'why talk to men about liberty? I recognize no liberty, only order.' " Disillusioned by his ventures in social revolution and labor reforms, and unable to attract or hold any appreciable number of disciples in an America of relatively equal opportunity and rugged individualism, the tailor had returned to his old trade, become an inventor, and sought "the harmony which he could not find among his fellows, under the stars." "Throw no stone at him," the obituary notice concluded, "for he proved to be a man amidst the storms of life, and his driving motive was something higher than ambition and selfishness."

BIBLIOGRAPHICAL NOTE

The main sources for this biography are Weitling's own published works, and the files of the journals which he published in Europe and the United States. Of these journals, *Die Republik der Arbeiter*, published in New York from 1850 to 1855, is the most important.

Though Weitling destroyed many of his papers two years before his death, a mass of material survived and was made available to the author by his last surviving son, Terijon Weitling of New York. These manuscripts include correspondence with co-workers in Europe and America, account books of the *Arbeiterbund*, two notebooks with a miscellany of personal items, and a great many items dealing with the colony of Communia, Iowa, and with Weitling's interest in astronomy, a universal language, and inventions. The Library of Congress also has a few Weitling items.

There are several earlier monographs, of varying excellence but of great value, which deal almost entirely with the European phase of Weitling's career. The best are Wolfgang Joho, *Wilhelm Weitling: Der Ideengehalt seiner Schriften, entwickelt aus den geschichtlichen Zusammenhängen* (Heidelberg, 1932) and Emil Kaler, *Wilhelm Weitling: Seine Agitation und Lehre im geschichtlichen Zusammenhange dargestellt* (Zurich, 1887). F. Caille, *Wilhelm Weitling: Theoricien du Communisme, 1808–1870* (Paris, 1905) is less detailed.

Because of Weitling's great importance in what the Germans call *Frühsozialismus*, there are many widely scattered references to him and his work in primary and secondary sources. The number of citations have been reduced to a minimum, but reference has been made at least once in the footnotes to the most significant publications which deal with Weitling's career before he came to the United States.

In developing the story of Weitling's career in America, the phase of his life to which an attempt has been made to give new emphasis, the author has used, besides the Weitling manuscripts and the file of *Die Republik der Arbeiter*, the following papers for the period from 1850 to 1855: the New York *Tribune*, the Columbus (Ohio) *Westbote*, the *Belleviller Zeitung* of Illinois, the Cincinnati *Volksfreund*, the Cleveland *Wächter am Erie*, and the various papers edited during these years by Karl Heinzen. In addition, for shorter periods, available newspaper material from other German-language papers has been cited in the footnotes. Hermann Schlüter's *Die Anfänge der deutschen Arbeiterbewegung in Amerika* (Stuttgart, 1907) is the only important monograph dealing with the American phase of Weitling's career. Though that author had the advantage of interviews with Wilhelm Weitling's widow and eldest son, his work is superficial and disappointing.

INDEX